CONTENTS

PREFACE TO STUDENT

Dear Student:

Essentials of College English was written to assist college students in reviewing English grammar, punctuation, style, and usage. It contains comprehensive information and numerous reinforcement exercises designed to lead college students to mastery of the concepts. This is a compact version of *Essentials of College English* that has been edited by Dr. Elizabeth T. Tice, Dean of General Studies, University of Phoenix. It covers the same material as the full version, but it has been reconfigured to meet the needs of accelerated, nontraditional programs and returning adult students who need only a refresher. This version of *Essentials of College English* has been condensed in the following ways:

- It assumes a basic knowledge of English grammar and does not devote large sections to the basics.
- It contains fewer exercises on the topics that are covered.

Depending on your current skills, you can spend as much or as little time in each chapter as is necessary. The following features from the original version of *Essentials of College English* have been retained:

- Hotline Queries
- Marginal Annotations
- Self-Checked Learning Exercises
- Reinforcement Exercises

When you finish reading and studying this book, we personally guarantee that your language skills will be much better than when you started. However, your mind is not a computer and can't record everything for instant recall. Like most professionals, you will occasionally need reference books to find answers. That's why you'll probably want to keep this book, along with a good dictionary and a reference manual, for review and use after you leave this class.

If you have any comments about this book or suggestions for improvement, please write to us. We wish you well in your studies.

Dr. Mary Ellen Guffey
Professor of Business
P.O. Box 6011
Malibu, CA 90264
meguffey@west.net

Carolyn M. Seefer
Professor of Business
Diablo Valley College
321 Golf Club Road
Pleasant Hill, CA 94523
cseefer@dvc.edu

UNIT

1

Knowing the Namers

1 Nouns

OBJECTIVES When you have completed the materials in this chapter, you will be able to do the following:

- Spell troublesome plural nouns ending in *y*, *o*, and *f*.
- Form the plurals of compound nouns, numerals, letters, degrees, and abbreviations.
- Recognize and use correctly foreign plural nouns and selected special nouns.
- Use plural personal titles appropriately.

Nouns *name* persons, places, things, qualities, and concepts. The principal emphasis of this chapter will be on forming and spelling plural nouns, an area of confusion for many business writers.

TROUBLESOME NOUN PLURALS

Your ability to spell certain troublesome nouns can be improved greatly by studying the following rules and examples.

STUDY TIP

In making surnames plural, never change the original spellings. Adding *s* or *es* is acceptable, but changing *Kennedy* to *Kennedies* changes the original spelling.

- ***Common nouns ending in* y** form the plural in two ways.

  a. When the *y* is preceded by a vowel (*a, e, i, o, u*), the plural is formed with the addition of *s* only.

attorney, attorneys	essay, essays	play, plays
survey, surveys	valley, valleys	Murray, Murrays

  b. When the *y* is preceded by a consonant (all letters other than vowels), the plural is formed by changing the *y* to *ies.*

baby, babies	company, companies	copy, copies
laboratory, laboratories	policy, policies	specialty, specialties

  Note: This rule does *not* apply to the plural forms of proper nouns: Sally, Sallys; January, Januarys; Billy, Billys; Henry, Henrys.

- ***Nouns ending in* f *or* fe** follow no standard rules in the formation of plurals. Study the examples shown here, and use a dictionary when in doubt. When two forms are shown, the preferred appears first.

ADD *S*	CHANGE TO *VES*	BOTH FORMS RECOGNIZED
brief, briefs	half, halves	calves, calfs
proof, proofs	knife, knives	dwarfs, dwarves

ADD *S*	CHANGE TO *VES*	BOTH FORMS RECOGNIZED
safe, safes	leaf, leaves	wharves, wharfs
staff, staffs	shelf, shelves	scarves, scarfs
sheriff, sheriffs	wife, wives	
wolf, wolfs	wolf, wolves	

■ ***Nouns ending in o*** may be made plural by adding *s* or *es.*

a. When the *o* is preceded by a vowel, the plural is formed by adding *s* only.

studio, studios curio, curios radio, radios

b. When the *o* is preceded by a consonant, the plural is formed by adding *s* or *es.* Study the following examples, and again use your dictionary whenever in doubt. When two forms are shown, the preferred one appears first.

SPOT THE BLOOPER

In an advertisement for Accelerated Schools in Colorado's *Rocky Mountain News*: "STUDENT'S DON'T HAVE TO FAIL."

ADD *S*	ADD *ES*	BOTH FORMS RECOGNIZED
photo, photos	echo, echoes	cargoes, cargos
typo, typos	embargo, embargoes	commandos, commandoes
logo, logos	hero, heroes	mosquitoes, mosquitos
patio, patios	potato, potatoes	tornadoes, tornados
ratio, ratios	tomato, tomatoes	volcanoes, volcanos
Angelo, Angelos	veto, vetoes	zeros, zeroes

■ ***Compound nouns*** may be written as single words, may be hyphenated, or may appear as two words.

a. When written as single words, compound nouns form the plural by appropriate changes in the final element.

bookshelf, bookshelves	classmate, classmates	letterhead, letterheads
stockholder, stockholders	photocopy, photocopies	payroll, payrolls

b. When written in hyphenated or open form, compound nouns form the plural by appropriate changes in the principal noun.

accounts payable	bills of lading	boards of directors
editors in chief	leaves of absence	hangers-on
mayors-elect	brothers-in-law	runners-up

c. If the compound noun has no principal noun at all, the final element is made plural.

cure-alls	get-togethers	go-betweens
hang-ups	has-beens	know-it-alls
so-and-sos	trade-offs	walk-throughs

d. Some compound noun plurals have two recognized forms. In the following list, the preferred form is shown first.

attorneys general, attorney generals

cupfuls, cupsful; teaspoonfuls, teaspoonsful

courts-martial, court-martials; notaries public, notary publics

■ ***Numerals, alphabet letters, isolated words, and degrees*** are made plural by adding *s, es,* or *'s.* The trend is to use the *'s* only when necessary for clarity.

a. Numerals and uppercase letters (with the exception of *A, I, M,* and *U*) require only *s* in plural formation.

1990s	all Cs and Ds	the three Rs
401Ks	W-2s and 1040s	7s and 8s

b. Isolated words used as nouns are made plural with the addition of *s* or *es*, as needed for pronunciation.

ands, ifs, or buts	dos and don'ts	pros and cons
yeses and noes (*or* yeses and nos)	ups and downs	whys and wherefores

c. Degrees are made plural with the addition of *s.*

A.A.s	B.S.s	Ph.D.s
R.N.s	M.B.A.s	M.D.s

NOTABLE QUOTABLE

"The English language has far more lives than a cat. People have been murdering it for years."
—*Farmers' Almanac*

d. Isolated lowercase letters and the capital letters *A, I, M,* and *U* require *'s* for clarity.

M&M's p's and q's A's

- ***Abbreviations*** are usually made plural by adding *s* to the singular form.

bldg., bldgs.	CEO, CEOs	RSVP, RSVPs
IOU, IOUs	mgr., mgrs.	No., Nos.
wk., wks.	yr., yrs.	VCR, VCRs

The singular and plural forms of abbreviations for units of measurement are, however, often identical.

deg. (degree or degrees)	in. (inch or inches)
ft. (foot or feet)	oz. (ounce or ounces)

Some units of measurement have two plural forms.

lb. or lbs. yd. or yds. qt. or qts.

SPECIAL PLURAL FORMS

STUDY TIP

Language purists contend that the word *data* can only be plural (*the data are*). However, see the Hotline Queries for another view.

- ***Nouns borrowed from foreign languages*** may retain a foreign plural. A few, however, have an Americanized plural form, shown in parentheses below. Check your dictionary for the preferred form.

Singular	Plural
alumna (*feminine*)	alumnae (pronounced a-LUM-nee)
alumnus (*masculine*)	alumni (pronounced a-LUM-ni)
analysis	analyses
bacterium	bacteria
basis	bases
cactus	cacti (or cactuses)
criterion	criteria (or criterions)
curriculum	curricula (or curriculums)
datum	data*
diagnosis	diagnoses
erratum	errata
formula	formulae (or formulas)
larva	larvae

*See discussion in the Hotline Queries.

Singular	Plural
memorandum	memoranda (or memorandums)
millennium	millennia (or millenniums)
parenthesis	parentheses
phenomenon	phenomena

■ ***Personal titles*** may have both formal and informal plural forms.

Singular	Formal Plurals	Informal Plurals
Miss	the Misses Kelly	the Miss Kellys
Mr.	Messrs.* Sanchez and Larson	Mr. Sanchez and Mr. Larson
Mrs.	Mmes.† Stokes and Aboud	Mrs. Stokes and Mrs. Aboud
Ms.	Mses.‡ Freeman and Moya	Ms. Freeman and Ms. Moya

*Pronounced MES-erz (abbreviation of Messieurs).

†Pronounced May-DAHM (abbreviation of Mesdames).

‡Pronounced MIZ-ez (Ms. is probably a blend of Miss and Mrs.).

■ ***Special nouns,*** many of which end in *s*, may normally be *only* singular *or* plural in meaning. Other special nouns may be considered *either* singular *or* plural in meaning.

STUDY TIP

You can practice these special nouns by using them with the singular verb *is* or the plural verb *are*. For example, *Aeronautics is fascinating* (sing.); *scissors are useful* (plural).

Usually Singular	Usually Plural	May be Singular or Plural
aeronautics	belongings	species
mathematics	clothes	deer
mumps	earnings	Chinese
economics	scissors	salmon
news	premises	headquarters

■ ***Single-letter abbreviations*** may be made plural by doubling the letter.

pp. (pages)	See pp. 18–21. (pages 18 through 21)
ff. (and following)	See pp. 18 ff. (page 18 and following pages)

HOTLINE QUERIES

Business people are very concerned about appropriate English usage, grammar, and style. This concern is evident in the number and kinds of questions called in to grammar hotline services across the country. Among the callers are business supervisors, managers, executives, clerks, administrative assistants, and word processing specialists. Writers, teachers, librarians, students, and other community members also seek answers to language questions.

Selected questions and appropriate answers to them will be presented in the following chapters. In this way you, as a student of the language, will understand the kinds of everyday communication problems encountered in the work world. The original questions in our Hotline Queries came from the Los Angeles Pierce College Business English Hotline, which is no longer in service. More recently, questions have come from grammar hotline services across the country. To receive a list of these Hotline services, send a self-addressed, stamped envelope to **Grammar Hotline Director, Writing Center, Humanities Division, Tidewater Community College, Virginia Beach, VA 23456**. For immediate access, this list of currently operating hotlines is also maintained at a Web site **<http://www.tc.cc.va.us/writcent/gh/hotlinol.htm>**. If this URL (address) is not operative, use a search tool and look for "grammar hotline directory."

QUESTION We're having a big argument in our office. What's correct? *E-mail, e-mail, email,* or *Email*? And is it *on-line* or *online*?

ANSWER Initially, most people capitalized *E-mail* and hyphenated *on-line.* With increased use, however, both of these forms have been simplified: *e-mail* and *online,* which we recommend. Although the *Merriam-Webster College Dictionary,* Tenth edition (our standard reference) clings to *E-mail* when used as a noun, it does recognize the lowercase form for the verb form (*I will e-mail my response to you*). In our observation most publications today are moving toward *e-mail* for both noun and verb forms and *online* for both adjective and adverb functions. You might want to check with your company's in-house style manual for its preferred style for these words.

QUESTION Could you help me spell the plurals of *do* and *don't*?

ANSWER In forming the plurals of isolated words, the trend today is to add s and no apostrophe. Thus, we have *dos* and *don'ts.* Formerly, apostrophes were used to make isolated words plural. However, if no confusion results, make plurals by adding s only. Most readers will not confuse the lowercase *dos* for the acronym *DOS,* which stands for "disk operating system."

QUESTION One member of our staff consistently corrects our use of the word *data.* He says the word is plural. Is it never singular?

ANSWER The word *data* is indeed plural; the singular form is *datum.* Through frequent usage, however, data has recently become a collective noun. Collective nouns may be singular or plural depending on whether they are considered as one unit or as separate units. For example, *These data are much different from those findings.* Or, *This data is conclusive.*

QUESTION I don't have a dictionary handy. Can you tell me which word I should use in this sentence? *A [stationary/stationery] circuit board will be installed.*

ANSWER In your sentence use *stationary,* which means "not moving" or "permanent" (*she exercises on a stationary bicycle*). *Stationery* means "writing paper" (*his stationery has his address printed on it*). You might be able to remember the word *stationery* by associating *envelopes* with the *e* in *stationery.*

QUESTION My mother is always correcting me when I say, *I hate when that happens.* What's wrong with this? I hear it on TV all the time.

ANSWER Your mother wants you to speak standard English, the written and spoken language of educated people. Hearing an expression on TV is no assurance that it's acceptable. The problem with an expression like *I hate when that happens* is that an adverbial phrase (*when that happens*) is used as the object of a verb (*hate*). Only nouns, noun clauses, or pronouns may act as objects of verbs. Correction: *I hate it when that happens,* or *I hate this to happen.*

QUESTION As a sportswriter, I need to know the plural of *hole-in-one.*

ANSWER Make the principal word plural, *holes-in-one.*

NAME ____________________

1 REINFORCEMENT EXERCISES

A. (Self-check) Provide the correct plural form of the words shown in parentheses.

1. The project (chief) could not agree on a solution. chiefs
2. Our two (attorney) have advised us not to speak to you. attorneys
3. Because of the (company) involved, the press was interested in the event. companies
4. Learning the (do and don't) of negotiation will help in an interview. dos and don'ts
5. How many (stockholder) are expected to attend the meeting on Friday? stockholders
6. Make sure your (account payable) are up-to-date. accounts payable
7. Weigh the (trade-off) carefully before making your decision. trade-offs
8. The vice president's (memorandum) were read with interest. memoranda
9. The joint ventures of (Mr.) Jobs and Wozniak revolutionized the personal computer industry. ~~Mrs~~ Messrs,
10. Accuracy is one of the (criterion) for a good evaluation. criteria

Check your answers below.

B. Write plural forms for the nouns listed. Use a dictionary if you are unsure of the spelling.

1. liability liabilities
2. portfolio portfolios
3. tax taxes
4. scenario scenarios
5. mayor-elect mayors-elect
6. M M's
7. bill of lading bills of lading
8. toothbrush toothbrushes
9. RSVP RSVP's
10. Murray Murrays
11. run-in run-ins
12. attorney attorneys
13. valley valleys
14. in and out ins and outs
15. contralto contraltos
16. company companies
17. 10 10s
18. July Julys
19. IOU IOU's
20. leave of absence leaves of absence
21. chef chefs
22. disc jockey disc jockeys
23. mother-in-law mothers-in-law
24. write-up write-ups
25. No. No's
26. memo memos
27. 1990 1990's
28. CPA CPA's
29. port of entry ports of entry
30. yr. yrs

1. chiefs, 2. attorneys, 3. companies, 4. dos and don'ts, 5. stockholders, 6. accounts payable, 7. trade-offs, 8. memoranda or memorandums, 9. Messrs., 10. criteria

C. Write the correct plural form of the words shown in parentheses.

1. A meeting was set up between the two (attorney general). attorneys general

2. Our president holds (Ph.D.) from two universities. PH.Ds

3. Adding (notary public) to the staff will save time in our department. notaries public

4. We are required to make (photocopy) of all letters we send. photocopies

5. How many (leave of absence) are you allowed in one year? leaves of absence

6. What percentage of (CEO) are women? CEOs

7. Both of our publications managers were former (editor in chief). editors in chief

8. The (datum) we collected were used to support a new theory. data

9. Galileo's (hypothesis) about the solar system were rejected by his peers. hypotheses

10. The paralegals had to write three (brief) by the end of the week. briefs

11. Many varieties of (cactus) can be found in the Mojave Desert. cactuses/cacti

12. The (curriculum) offered by the two schools are quite similar. curricula

13. The (crisis) within higher education will only be worsened by budget cuts. crises

14. Doctors offered several (diagnosis) to explain her symptoms. diagnoses

15. The Human Resources Department mailed all the (W-2) on time. W-2s

D. Complete the following sentences, selecting the proper singular or plural verb to agree with the nouns.

1. Aeronautics (is, are) an exciting career to pursue. ______________

2. Our belongings (was, were) left behind by mistake. ______________

3. Kenneth found that the scissors (was, were) not sharp enough. ______________

4. Criteria for judging (is, are) listed on the coupon. ______________

5. (Was, Were) proper thanks given you for your efforts? ______________

2 Possessive Nouns

OBJECTIVES When you have completed the materials in this chapter, you will be able to do the following:

- Distinguish between possessive nouns and noun plurals.
- Follow five steps in using the apostrophe to show ownership.
- Use apostrophe construction for animate nouns.
- Distinguish between descriptive nouns and possessive nouns.
- Pluralize compound nouns, combined ownership nouns, organization names, and abbreviations.
- Understand incomplete possessives.
- Avoid awkward possessives.
- Determine whether an extra syllable can be pronounced in forming a possessive.
- Make proper nouns possessive

CAREER TIP

"Everything comes to those who hustle while they wait."
—Will Rogers

In this chapter you will review how to use the apostrophe in making nouns possessive.

SHOWING POSSESSION WITH APOSTROPHES

Notice in the following phrases how possessive nouns show ownership, origin, authorship, or measurement:

the carpenter's hammer (ownership)
Mexico's currency (origin)
Clancy's novels (authorship)
two months' time (measurement)

In expressing possession, speakers and writers have a choice. They may show possession with an apostrophe construction, or they may use a prepositional phrase with no apostrophe:

the hammer of the carpenter
the currency of Mexico
the novels of Clancy
the time of two months

SPOT THE BLOOPER

From Lois and Selma DeBakey's collection of bad medical writing: "The receptionist called the patients names." (How does the omitted apostrophe alter the meaning?)

The use of a prepositional phrase to show ownership is more formal and tends to emphasize the ownership word. The use of the apostrophe construction to show ownership is more efficient and more natural, especially in conversation. In writing, however, placing the apostrophe can be perplexing. Here are five simple but effective steps that will help you write possessives correctly.

Five Steps in Using the Apostrophe Correctly

■ ***Look for possessive construction.*** Usually two nouns appear together. The first noun shows ownership of (or a special relationship to) the second noun.

the woman['s] briefcase
the children['s] toys
a month['s] wages
several printers['] quotes
the singers['] voices

STUDY TIP

Whenever you have any doubt about using an apostrophe, always put the expression into an "of" phrase. You'll immediately recognize the ownership word and see whether it ends in an *s*.

■ ***Reverse the nouns.*** Use the second noun to begin a prepositional phrase. The object of the preposition is the ownership word.

briefcase of the *woman*
toys of the *children*
wages of a *month*
quotes of several *printers*
voices of the *singers*

■ ***Examine the ownership word.*** To determine the correct placement of the apostrophe, you must know whether the ownership word ends in an *s* sound (such as *s*, *x*, or *z*).

- If the ownership word does not end in an *s* sound, add an apostrophe and *s*.

SPOT THE BLOOPER

Headline in the *Examiner* [Bellefontaine, OH]: "TWINS FATHER FACE'S BATTERY CHARGES."

the woman's briefcase
the children's toys
a month's wages

- If the ownership word does end in an *s* sound, usually add only an apostrophe.

several printers' quotes
the singers' voices

A word of caution: Once writers begin to study apostrophes, they tend to use a shotgun approach on passages with words ending in *s*, indiscriminately peppering them with apostrophes. Do *not* use apostrophes for nouns that simply show more than one of something. In the sentence *These companies are opening new branches in the West*, no apostrophes are required. The words *companies* and *branches* are plural; they are not possessive. In addition, be careful to avoid changing the spelling of singular nouns when making them possessive. For example, the *secretary's* desk (meaning one secretary) is *not* spelled *secretaries'*.

Pay particular attention to the following possessive constructions. Perhaps the explanations and hints in parentheses will help you understand and remember these expressions.

a year's experience (the experience of one year)
ten years' experience (the experience of ten years)
a dollar's worth (the worth of one single dollar)
your money's worth (the worth of your money)
today's newspaper (there can be only one today)
tomorrow's appointments (there can be only one tomorrow)
the stockholders' meeting (we usually assume that a meeting involves more than one person)

NOTABLE QUOTABLE

"Even if you're on the right track, you'll get run over if you just sit there."
—Thomas Edison

The guides for possessive construction presented thus far cover the majority of possessives found in business writing.

PROBLEM POSSESSIVE CONSTRUCTIONS

■ ***Animate versus inanimate nouns.*** As a matter of style, some careful writers prefer to reserve the apostrophe construction for people and animals. For other nouns use prepositional phrases or simple adjectives.

wing of the airplane, or airplane wing (better than *airplane's wing*)
style of the suit, or the suit style (better than *suit's style*)
terms of the contract, or contract terms (better than *contract's terms*)

STUDY TIP

To identify descriptive nouns, ask whether ownership is involved. Does *Department* belong to *Sales*? Is *industry* possessed by *electronics*? When the answer is no, omit the apostrophe.

■ ***Descriptive versus possessive nouns.*** When nouns provide description or identification only, the possessive form is *not* used. Writers have the most problems with descriptive nouns ending in *s*, such as *Claims* Department. No apostrophe is needed, just as none is necessary in *Personnel* Department.

Sales Department (not *Sales' Department*)
electronics industry (not *electronic's industry*)
Arkansas Razorbacks (not *Arkansas' Razorbacks*)

■ ***Compound nouns.*** Make compound nouns possessive by adding an apostrophe or an *'s* to the final element of the compound.

editor in chief's desk
board of directors' decision
stockholders' portfolios

■ ***Incomplete possessives.*** When the second noun in a possessive noun construction is unstated, the first noun is nevertheless treated as possessive.

I left my umbrella at Colleen's [house].
They are meeting at the lawyer's [office] to discuss the testimony.
His score beat the champion's [score] by 20 points.

STUDY TIP

Look at the object owned (*agreement, home*). If that object is singular, ownership is usually combined.

■ ***Separate or combined ownership.*** When two names express separate ownership, make both names possessive. When two names express combined ownership, make only the *second* name possessive.

SEPARATE OWNERSHIP	COMBINED OWNERSHIP
nurses' and doctors' orders	actor and agent's agreement
Nadine's and Katie's birthdays	my father and mother's home

■ ***Names of organizations.*** Organizations with possessives in their names may or may not use apostrophes. Follow the style used by the individual organization. (Consult the organization's stationery or a directory listing.)

Farmers Insurance Group	McDonald's
U.S. Department of Veterans Affairs	Macy's

■ ***Abbreviations.*** Make abbreviations possessive by following the same guidelines as for animate nouns.

AMA's annual convention	both CEOs' signatures
MTV's fall schedule	Marketing Dept.'s memo

STUDY TIP

To avoid an awkward possessive, use an *of* phrase starting with the object owned, such as *prizes.*

■ ***Awkward possessives.*** When the addition of an apostrophe results in an awkward construction, show ownership by using a prepositional phrase.

AWKWARD: runners-up's prizes
IMPROVED: prizes of the runners-ups

AWKWARD:	my company's conference room's equipment
IMPROVED:	the equipment of my company's conference room
AWKWARD:	her boss, Mr. Wilde's, office
IMPROVED:	office of her boss, Mr. Wilde

SPOT THE BLOOPER

Announcement pasted on top of each Domino's pizza box: "We accept all competitors coupons."

You have learned to follow five steps in identifying possessive constructions and in placing the apostrophe correctly. The guides presented thus far cover most possessive constructions. The possessive form of a few nouns, however, requires a refinement of the final step.

ADDITIONAL GUIDELINE

Let us briefly review the five-step plan for placing the apostrophe in noun possessives. Having done so, we will then add a refinement to the fifth step.

1. Look for possessive construction. (Usually, but not always, two nouns appear together.)
2. Reverse the nouns.
3. Examine the ownership word.
4. If the ownership word does *not* end in an *s* sound, add an apostrophe and *s*.
5. If the ownership word does end in an *s* sound, usually add just an apostrophe. *However, if an extra syllable can be easily pronounced in the possessive form, most writers will add an apostrophe and an s to singular nouns.*

SINGULAR NOUN ENDING IN AN *S* SOUND; EXTRA SYLLABLE CAN BE EASILY PRONOUNCED	ADD APOSTROPHE AND *S*
role of the actress	actress's role
request of the boss	boss's request
yoke of the ox	ox's yoke

MAKING DIFFICULT PROPER NOUNS POSSESSIVE

Of all possessive forms, individuals' names—especially those ending in *s* sounds—are the most puzzling to business communicators, and understandably so. Even experts don't always agree on the possessive form for singular proper nouns.

Traditionalists, as represented in *The Chicago Manual of Style* and *The Modern Language Association Style Manual,* prefer adding an apostrophe and an *s* to troublesome *singular proper* nouns that end in *s* sounds. On the other hand, writers of more popular literature, as represented in *The Associated Press Stylebook and Libel Manual,* prefer the simpler style of adding just an apostrophe to singular proper nouns. You may apply either style, but be consistent. Please note in the following examples that the style choice applies *only* to singular names ending in *s* sounds. Plural names are always made possessive with the addition of an apostrophe only. Study the examples shown.

STUDY TIP

The word *the* preceding a name is a clue that the name is being used in a plural sense. For example, *the Harrises* means the entire *Harris* family.

SINGULAR NAME	SINGULAR POSSESSIVE—TRADITIONAL	SINGULAR POSSESSIVE—POPULAR	PLURAL POSSESSIVE
Mr. Harris	Mr. Harris's	Mr. Harris'	the Harrises'
Mrs. Sanchez	Mrs. Sanchez's	Mrs. Sanchez'	the Sanchezes'
Mr. Lewis	Mr. Lewis's	Mr. Lewis'	the Lewises'
Ms. Horowitz	Ms. Horowitz's	Ms. Horowitz'	the Horowitzes'

Here's a summary of the possessive rule that should be easy to remember: If an ownership word does not end in an *s*, add an apostrophe and *s*. If the ownership word does end in an *s*, add just an apostrophe—unless you can easily pronounce an extra syllable. If you can pronounce that extra syllable, add an apostrophe and *s*.

HOTLINE QUERIES

QUESTION Where should the apostrophe go in *employee's handbook*?

ANSWER This is tricky because the writer of that phrase must decide whether he or she considers the handbook from one employee's point of view or from all employees' points of view. Depending on the point of view, the apostrophe could be justified for either position. The trend today seems to favor the singular construction (*employee's handbook, driver's license, user's manual*).

QUESTION I'm addressing a letter to the American Nurses Association. What salutation shall I use? One person in our office suggested *Gentlewomen*. Is this being used?

ANSWER We recommend that you use *Greetings*. Another possibility is *Ladies and Gentlemen;* however, this salutation is seldom seen in business messages. We would not use *Gentlewomen* because it sounds artificial. Businesses and individuals can avoid sexism in language without using stilted constructions. The best solution is to write to an individual in an organization and use that person's name.

QUESTION Should *undercapitalized* be hyphenated? I can't find it in my dictionary.

ANSWER The prefixes *under* and *over* are not followed by hyphens.

QUESTION Is there an apostrophe in *Veterans Day*, and if so, where does it go?

ANSWER *Veterans Day* has no apostrophe, but *New Year's Day* does have one.

QUESTION My boss's report says, *I respectfully call <u>you</u> and your client's attention to . . .* What's wrong with this? How can I make *you* possessive?

ANSWER The best way to handle this awkward wording is to avoid using the possessive form. Instead, use a prepositional phrase (*I respectfully call to your attention and to your client's attention . . .*).

QUESTION Here at the Cancer Society we have a bureau of speakers. Where should the apostrophe go when we use the possessive form of the word *speakers*?

ANSWER *Speakers' bureau.*

NAME ______________________________

2 REINFORCEMENT EXERCISES

A. (Self-check) Rewrite the following phrases avoiding the use of the apostrophe. Use a prepositional phrase. Does the ownership word end in an *s* sound?

	Revision	End in *s* Sound?
EXAMPLE: the officer's orders	orders of the officer	No
1. the men's chorus	____________	______
2. our children's futures	____________	______
3. all players' uniforms	____________	______
4. the defendant's plea	____________	______
5. two years' research	____________	______

Select an acceptable possessive form.

6. Bill (a) Gates' or Gates's, (b) Gates, (c) Gates' wealth makes him America's richest citizen ______

7. Have you seen Annie (a) Leibovitz' or Leibovitz's, (b) Leibovitzes' photographs? ______

8. Our (a) waitress', (b) waitress's service was outstanding. ______

9. All (a) customer's, (b) customers' complaints have been addressed. ______

10. The (a) Harris' or Harris's, (b) Harrises' home has been on the market for months. ______

Check your answers below.

B. Using apostrophes, change the following prepositional phrases into possessive constructions. Ownership words are italicized.

EXAMPLE: treatment of *prisoners* — prisoners' treatment

1. qualifications of the *engineer* ____________

2. salary of a *year* ____________

3. policies of the *company* ____________

4. benefits of *employees* ____________

5. meeting of *managers* ____________

C. Study the italicized words in the following sentences. If they should be made possessive, write the correct form. If the sentence is correct as it stands, write *C*.

1. Confused by the two *agencies* policies, Jan gave up on the project. ____________

2. Only two *years* have passed since our last reunion. ____________

3. An *inventors* patent protects his invention for seventeen years. ____________

4. We received quotes for the brochures from several *printers*. ____________

5. Marietta always wants to put her two *cents* worth in. ____________

1. No, 2. No, 3. Yes, 4. No, 5. Yes, 6. a, 7. a, 8. b, 9. a, 10. b.

NAME ____________________

D. Underline the errors in the following sentences. Write the correct form at the right. If the sentence is correct as it stands, write *C*.

EXAMPLE: She designed many <u>ladies</u> purses. ladies'

1. He has ten year's experience in the software industry. ________
2. I always get my moneys worth from L. L. Bean. ________
3. The sports section is missing from todays' newspaper. ________
4. A companys customer service department is critical to its success. ________
5. All of our customer's complaints are addressed promptly. ________
6. How many classes are required for a contractors license? ________
7. She accepted the job without a moments' hesitation. ________
8. The six secretaries demands were not met. ________
9. Were all the investors reports sent out this week? ________
10. The Horowitzes' car has been in the shop for a week. ________

E. For each of the following sentences, underline any possessive construction that could be improved. Write an improved form in the space provided. If the sentence is acceptable as it stands, write *C*.

1. Edison tried many substances for the light bulb's filament before choosing tungsten. ________
2. Where can I find the editor in chiefs office? ________
3. One of the CEOs children works in the mail room. ________
4. We need all the stockholders votes before we can change the policy. ________
5. Send your application to the Human Resource's Department. ________
6. Two of the table's legs were damaged in transit. ________
7. They took their complaint to small claim's court. ________
8. Attorneys salaries have increased significantly in the last decade. ________
9. The Fenmore Co.'s sales declined when discount department stores entered the market. ________
10. She opened a small business with two of her brother's-in law. ________

F. **Review.** Each of the following sentences has one error in the use of a possessive. Write the corrected form in the space provided.

1. César Chavezs organization was the United Farm Workers. ________
2. Many of Dickens books are considered classics. ________
3. To live in this complex, you must join the homeowners association. ________
4. The painting *An Arrangement in Gray and Black* is better known as *Whistlers Mother*. ________
5. Elvis home, Graceland, is located in Memphis, Tennessee. ________
6. May we have the agenda for tomorrows' meeting? ________

7. We were surprised when Kim married her boss son. ____________

8. Twenty dollars worth of groceries will barely fill one bag. ____________

9. Today's weather is much rainier than yesterday. ____________

10. Despite a weeks delay the package finally arrived. ____________

3 Personal Pronouns

OBJECTIVES When you have completed the materials in this chapter, you will be able to do the following:

- Use personal pronouns correctly as subjects and objects.
- Distinguish between personal possessive pronouns (such as *its*) and contractions (such as *it's*).
- Choose the correct pronoun in compound constructions, comparatives, and appositives.
- Use reflexive pronouns correctly.
- Use nominative case pronouns with subject complements.
- Select the correct pronouns for use with the infinitive *to be.*

Pronouns are words that substitute for nouns and other pronouns. They enable us to speak and write without awkward repetition. Grammatically, pronouns may be divided into seven types (personal, relative, interrogative, demonstrative, indefinite, reflexive, and reciprocal). Rather than consider all seven pronoun types, this textbook will be concerned only with those pronouns that cause difficulty in use.

GUIDELINES FOR USING PERSONAL PRONOUNS

Personal pronouns indicate the person speaking, the person spoken to, or the person or object spoken of. Notice in the following table that personal pronouns change their form (or *case*) depending on who is speaking (called the *person*), how many are speaking (the *number*), and the sex (or *gender*) of the speaker. For example, the third person feminine objective singular case is *her.* Most personal pronoun errors by speakers and writers involve faulty usage of case forms. Study this table to avoid errors in personal pronoun use.

	Nominative Case*		Objective Case		Possessive Case	
	Sing.	Plural	Sing.	Plural	Sing.	Plural
FIRST PERSON (person speaking)	I	we	me	us	my, mine	our, ours
SECOND PERSON (person spoken to)	you	you	you	you	your, yours	your, yours
THIRD PERSON (person or things spoken of)	he, she, it	they	him, her, it	them	his, her, hers, its	their, theirs

*Some authorities prefer the term *subjective case.*

STUDY TIP

This list is so important that you must memorize it. You must also know how these pronouns function in sentences.

SPOT THE BLOOPER

***Vanity Fair* interview with famous Hollywood** action hero: "If I got married, it would be a unique situation where me and the woman would have a certain kind of format . . ."

SPOT THE BLOOPER

On KNCB-TV, Los Angeles, a reporter twice said, "The gunman shot at she and her fellow officers."

SPOT THE BLOOPER

From Marilyn Monroe in *Seven-Year Itch:* "A girl like I hardly ever gets to meet interesting men."

STUDY TIP

Never use *it's* unless you can substitute *it is*. Because they'd rather be safe than sorry, many writers mentally say *it is* every time they use *it's*.

SPOT THE BLOOPER

From the side of a box of General Mills' Cinnamon Toast Crunch cereal: "What gives Cinnamon Crunch it's totally intense taste?"

Basic Use of the Nominative Case

Nominative case pronouns are used primarily as the subjects of verbs. Every verb or verb phrase, regardless of its position in a sentence, has a subject. If that subject is a pronoun, it must be in the nominative case.

I thought *she* would pay me back.
We wondered whether *they* would ever arrive.

Basic Use of the Objective Case

Objective case pronouns most commonly are used in two ways.

■ ***Object of a verb.*** When pronouns act as direct or indirect objects of verbs, they must be in the objective case.

Offer *her* the job.
Ellen took *him* to the doctor.

■ ***Object of a preposition.*** The objective case is used for pronouns that are objects of prepositions.

Brandon bought the ring for *her.*
The instructions were given to *us.*
Just between *you* and *me,* the negotiations have stalled.

When the words *between, but, like,* and *except* are used as prepositions, errors in pronoun case are likely to occur. To avoid such errors, isolate the prepositional phrase, and then use an objective case pronoun as the object of the preposition. (*Every employee [but Tom and him] completed the form.*)

Basic Use of the Possessive Case

Possessive pronouns show ownership. Unlike possessive nouns, possessive pronouns require no apostrophes. Study these five possessive pronouns: *hers, yours, ours, theirs, its.* Notice the absence of apostrophes. Do not confuse possessive pronouns with contractions. Contractions are shortened (contracted) forms of subjects and verbs, such as *it's* (for *it is*), *there's* (for *there is*), *they're* (for *they are*), and *you're* (for *you are*). In these examples the apostrophes indicate omitted letters.

Possessive Pronouns	Contractions
Those seats are *theirs.*	*There's* not a seat left in the theater.
My iguana has escaped from *its* cage.	*It's* an unusual pet.

PROBLEMS IN USING PERSONAL PRONOUNS

Compound Subjects and Objects

When a pronoun appears in combination with a noun or another pronoun, special attention must be given to case selection. Use this technique to help you choose the correct pronoun case: Ignore the extra noun or pronoun and its related conjunction, and consider separately the pronoun in question to determine what the case should be.

Mindy asked [you and] *me* for help. (Ignore *you and.*)
[Allison and] *he* registered for the seminar. (Ignore *Allison and.*)
Will you allow [Tony and] *them* to join you? (Ignore *Tony and.*)

Notice in the first sentence, for example, that when *you and* is removed, the pronoun *me* must be selected because it functions as the object of the verb.

SPOT THE BLOOPER

Television commercial for Continental Insurance Co.: "Nobody does it better than us."

Comparatives

In statements of comparison, words are often implied but not actually stated. To determine pronoun case in only partially complete comparative statements introduced by *than* or *as*, always mentally finish the comparative by adding the implied missing words.

> Shelley earns as much as *he*. (Shelley earns as much as *he* [not *him*] earns.)
> Nader Sharkes is a better cook than *she*. (. . . better cook than *she* [not *her*] is.)
> Does her attitude annoy you as much as *me*. (. . . as much as it annoys *me* [not *I*].)

Appositives

SPOT THE BLOOPER

From the KOB-TV [Albuquerque, NM] weather reporter: "Good news for we skiers!"

Appositives explain or rename previously mentioned nouns or pronouns. A pronoun in apposition takes the same case as that of the noun or pronoun with which it is in apposition. In order to determine more easily what pronoun case to use for a pronoun in combination with an appositive, temporarily ignore the appositive.

> *We* [consumers] must protest these rate hikes. (Ignore *consumers*.)
> The responsibility belongs to *us* [citizens]. (Ignore *citizens*.)

Reflexive (or Compound Personal) Pronouns

Reflexive pronouns that end in *-self* emphasize or reflect on their antecedents (the nouns or pronouns previously mentioned).

> I will take care of this problem *myself*. (Reflects on *I*.)
> The president *himself* presented the award. (Reflects on *president*.)

SPOT THE BLOOPER

Advice from a Canadian telephone company booklet: "Hang up if the caller doesn't say anything, at the first obscene word, or if the caller doesn't identify themself to your satisfaction."

Errors result when reflexive pronouns are used instead of personal pronouns. If no previously mentioned noun or pronoun is stated in the sentence, use a personal pronoun instead of a reflexive pronoun.

> Address your questions to your manager or *me*. (Not *myself*.)
> Brenda and *I* wrote the proposal. (Not *myself*.)

Please note that *hisself* is substandard and should always be avoided.

ADVANCED USES OF NOMINATIVE CASE PRONOUNS

Subject Complement

As we saw earlier in this chapter, nominative case pronouns usually function as subjects of verbs. Less frequently, nominative case pronouns also perform as subject complements. A pronoun that follows a linking verb and renames the subject must be in the nominative case. Be especially alert to the linking verbs *am, is, are, was, were, be, being,* and *been*.

STUDY TIP

Whenever a pronoun follows a linking verb, that pronoun will be in the nominative case.

> It *was I* who called the meeting.
> Is it *he* who has the key?
> If you *were I*, would you go?

When a verb of several words appears in a phrase, look at the final word of the verb. If it is a linking verb, use a nominative pronoun.

> It *might have been they* who asked the question.
> The culprit *could have been he*.
> If the owner *had been I*, your money would have been refunded.

In conversation it is common to say, *It is me*, or more likely, *It's me*. Careful speakers and writers, though, normally use nominative case pronouns after linking verbs. If the resulting constructions sound too "formal," revise your sentences appropriately. For example, instead of *It is I who placed the order,* use *I placed the order.*

Infinitive *To Be* Without a Subject

Infinitives are the present forms of verbs preceded by *to*—for example, *to sit, to run,* and *to walk.* Nominative pronouns are used following the infinitive *to be* when the infinitive has no subject. In this instance the infinitive joins a complement (not an object) to the subject.

STUDY TIP

This memory device may help you remember the correct pronoun to use with the infinitive *to be*: No subject, then nominative. That is, if the infinitive *to be* has no subject, supply a nominative pronoun. For example, *I was thought to be she.*

Her twin sister was often taken to be *she.* (The infinitive *to be* has no subject; *she* is the complement of the subject *sister.*)

Mikhail was mistakenly thought to be *I.* (The infinitive *to be* has no subject; *I* is the complement of the subject *Mikhail.*)

Why would Lien want to be *she*? (The infinitive *to be* has no subject; *she* is the complement of the subject *Lien.*)

ADVANCED APPLICATIONS OF PERSONAL CASE PRONOUNS

When the infinitive *to be* has a subject, any pronoun following it will function as an object. Therefore, the pronoun following the infinitive will function as its object and take the objective case.

The plant manager believed Jennifer to be *her.* (The subject of the infinitive *to be* is *Jennifer*; therefore, the pronoun functions as an object. Try it another way: *The plant manager believed her to be Jennifer.* You would not say, *The plant manager believed she to be Jennifer.*)

John expected the callers to be *us.* (The subject of the infinitive *to be* is *callers*; therefore, the pronoun functions as an object.)

Colonel Dunn judged the winner to be *him.* (The subject of the infinitive *to be* is *winner*; therefore, use the objective case pronoun *him.*)

Whenever you have selected a pronoun for the infinitive *to be* and you want to test its correctness, try reversing the pronoun and its antecedent. For example, *We thought the winner to be her (We thought her [not she] to be the winner)* or *Cheryl was often taken to be she (She [not her] was often taken to be Cheryl).*

SUMMARY OF PRONOUN CASES

The following table summarizes the uses of nominative and objective case pronouns.

SPOT THE BLOOPER

Sign at Bob's Big Boy restaurant in Monrovia (CA): One side says, "There back!" The other side says, "Their back!" [Which side is correct?]

Nominative Case	
Subject of the verb	*They* are sky divers.
Subject complement	That is *he.*
Infinitive *to be* without a subject	Josh pretended to be *he.*

Objective Case	
Direct or indirect object of the verb	Give *him* another chance.
Object of a preposition	Send the order to *him.*
Object of an infinitive	Ann hoped to call *us.*
Infinitive *to be* with subject	We thought the guests to be *them.*

HOTLINE QUERIES

QUESTION On the radio I recently heard a talk-show host say, *My producer and myself . . . .* A little later that same host said, *Send any inquiries to the station or myself at this address.* This sounded half right and half wrong, but I would have trouble explaining the problem. Can you help?

ANSWER The problem is a common one: use of a reflexive pronoun (*myself*) when it has no preceding noun on which to reflect. Correction: *My producer and I* and *Send inquiries to the station or me.* Reflexive pronouns like *myself* should be used only with obvious antecedents, such as *I, myself, will take the calls.* Individuals in the media often misuse reflexive pronouns, perhaps to avoid sounding egocentric with overuse of *I* and *me.*

QUESTION I have a question about the use of *etc.* in this sentence: *We are installing better lighting, acoustical tile, sound barriers, and etc.* Should I use two periods at the end of the sentence, and does a comma precede *etc.*?

ANSWER Although the use of *etc.* (meaning "and so forth") is generally avoided, do not, if it is to be used, include the redundant word *and.* When *etc.* is found at the end of a sentence, one comma should precede it. When *etc.* appears in the middle of a sentence, two commas should set it off. For example, *Better lighting, acoustical tile, and sound barriers, etc., are being installed. Never* use two periods at the end of a sentence, even if the sentence ends with an abbreviation such as *etc.*

QUESTION We're having a disagreement in our office about the word *healthy.* Is it correct to write *Exercise is healthy?*

ANSWER Strictly speaking, *healthy* means "to have or possess good health." For example, *The rosy-cheeked schoolchildren look healthy.* The word *healthful* means "to promote or be conducive to good health." Your sentence should read: *Exercise is healthful.*

QUESTION Should a hyphen be used in the word *dissimilar?*

ANSWER No. Prefixes such as *dis, pre, non,* and *un* do not require hyphens. Even when the final letter of the prefix is repeated in the initial letter of the root word, no hyphens are used: *disspirited, preenroll, nonnutritive.*

QUESTION I thought I knew the difference between *to* and *too,* but could you provide me with a quick review?

ANSWER *To* may serve as a preposition (*I'm going to the store*), and it may also serve as part of an infinitive construction (*to sign his name*). The adverb *too* may be used to mean "also" (*Andrea will attend too*). In addition, the word *too* may be used to indicate "to an excessive extent" (*the letter is too long*).

QUESTION I have a lot of trouble with the word *extension,* as in the expressions *extension cord* and *telephone extension.* Is the word ever spelled *extention?*

ANSWER You are not alone in having trouble with *extension.* No, it is never spelled with the familiar suffix *tion.* Perhaps you could remember it better if you associate the word *tension* with *extension.*

3 REINFORCEMENT EXERCISES

A. (Self-check) Select the correct form.

1. Everyone except (he, him) went on the ski trip. ____________
2. (She, Her), in addition to the president, will speak at the meeting. ____________
3. Consult our lawyer and (he, him) before you respond to the letter. ____________
4. (There's, Theirs) no room left in our carpool. ____________
5. No one but (she, her) can convince Allen to stay. ____________
6. Interviews for (we, us) applicants will be held on Friday. ____________
7. His bank and (he, him) worked out a payment schedule. ____________
8. Both Nancy and (she, her) are working toward advanced degrees. ____________
9. Performance reviews were conducted by the manager and (me, myself). ____________
10. The expense reports submitted by (her and me, she and I) were accepted. ____________
11. Bonnie is often taken to be (she, her). ____________
12. The president asked the agency and (I, me) to plan the campaign. ____________
13. If I were (he, him), I would accept the offer. ____________
14. It might have been (he, him) who called this morning. ____________
15. Ms. McCorkle asked me to contact you and (they, them). ____________

Check your answers below.

B. In this set of sentences, all the omitted pronouns serve as subjects of verbs. Write the correct pronoun for each sentence.

1. Bruce and (he, him) worked on the project together. ____________
2. Do you know when Scott and (she, her) are planning their wedding? ____________
3. Because the seminar is so popular, other employees and (they, them) could not register. ____________

In the next set of sentences, all the omitted pronouns serve as objects of verbs or prepositions. Selected prepositions have been italicized to help you recognize them. Write the correct pronoun for each sentence.

4. Music for the movie was composed *by* (she, her). ____________
5. Nobody *but* (they, them) objected to the terms of the conference. ____________
6. Send Minh Ngo and (I, me) your latest prices for Model T-S40. ____________

C. Select the correct pronoun and write it in the space provided.

1. The winning log was (there's, theirs, their's). ____________
2. Just between you and (I, me), the board meeting did not go well. ____________

1. him, 2. She, 3. him, 4. There's, 5. her, 6. us, 7. he, 8. she, 9. me, 10. her and me, 11. she, 12. me, 13. he, 14. he, 15. them.

3. (It's, Its) already the third quarter, and we have not met our sales quota. ____________
4. When Janice and (he, him) work on projects together, the results are predictable. ____________
5. No one but (I, me) received a raise this year. ____________
6. He has no one but (hisself, himself) to blame. ____________
7. The presenters, Ms. McCollum and (he, him), asked us to share our notes. ____________
8. The argument between Nicki and (she, her) caused problems in the office. ____________
9. Melanie and (I, me, myself) wrote the proposal. ____________
10. No one knows that problem better than (I, me). ____________
11. Did the article in today's paper upset you as much as (I, me)? ____________
12. Everyone but Sandy and (I, me) attended the meeting. ____________
13. Can you finish the project more quickly than (he, him)? ____________
14. Pins were given to (we, us) volunteers after one year of service. ____________
15. Contracts were sent to the authors, Mrs. Richards and (she, her). ____________
16. If you were (I, me), what would you do? ____________
17. We tried to call (he, him) and her at the convention. ____________
18. Terry thinks it was (she, her) who wrote the memo. ____________
19. Raphael believed it was not (they, them) who caused the problem. ____________
20. After Joe made the announcement, he expected to hear from you and (he, him). ____________

D. Underline any pronoun errors in the following sentences. Write the correct form in the space provided. Write C if a sentence is correct.

1. It must have been them who took the reports from my printer. ____________
2. We hope you and he will be in town for our next meeting. ____________
3. If that is her at the door, please let her in. ____________
4. Our administrative assistants hoped their new supervisor would be she. ____________
5. Are you certain it was him who left this message? ____________
6. We asked Jenny and she to speak at the awards banquet. ____________
7. This problem is between you and I. ____________
8. Are you sure that Mark and him have the right directions? ____________
9. Send your application to the human resources department or myself. ____________
10. Were the proposals submitted by Ms. Douglas and she accepted? ____________

4 Pronouns and Antecedents

OBJECTIVES When you have studied the materials in this chapter, you will be able to do the following:

- Make personal pronouns agree with their antecedents in number and gender.
- Understand the traditional use of common gender and be able to use its alternatives with sensitivity.
- Make personal pronouns agree with subjects joined by *or* or *nor.*
- Make personal pronouns agree with indefinite pronouns, collective nouns, and organization names.
- Understand the functions of *who* and *whom.*
- Follow a three-step plan in selecting *who* or *whom.*

Pronouns enable us to communicate efficiently. They provide short forms that save us from the boredom of repetitious nouns. But they can also get us in trouble if the nouns to which they refer—their *antecedents*—are unclear. This chapter shows you how to avoid pronoun–antecedent problems. It also presents solutions to a major problem for sensitive communicators today—how to handle the *his/her* dilemma.

FUNDAMENTALS OF PRONOUN–ANTECEDENT AGREEMENT

When pronouns substitute for nouns, the pronouns must agree with their antecedents in number (either singular or plural) and gender (either masculine, feminine, or neuter). Here are suggestions for using pronouns effectively.

Making Pronoun References Clear

Do not use a pronoun if your listener or reader might not be able to identify the noun it represents.

UNCLEAR: Roger's manager said that his report was incomplete.
CLEAR: Roger's manager said that Roger's report was incomplete.
UNCLEAR: In the computer lab they do not allow you to eat.
CLEAR: The management does not allow anyone to eat in the computer lab. *Or:* Eating is not allowed in the computer lab.
UNCLEAR: When Dave Evola followed Brad Eckhardt as president, many of his policies were reversed.
CLEAR: When Dave Evola followed Brad Eckhardt as president, many of Eckhardt's policies were reversed.

SPOT THE BLOOPER

From a letter to members of the National Council of Teachers of English: "It takes a special person to choose teaching as their life goal."

Making Pronouns Agree with Their Antecedents in Number

Pronouns must agree in number with the nouns they represent. For example, if a pronoun replaces a singular noun, that pronoun must be singular.

> *Columbus* thought that *he* had reached India. (Singular antecedent and pronoun.)
> Many *explorers* believed *they* could find a faster route. (Plural antecedent and pronoun.)

If a pronoun refers to two nouns joined by *and*, the pronoun must be plural.

> The *president* and the *stockholders* discussed *their* differences. (Plural antecedent and pronoun.)
> *Mitchell* and *Nancy* asked that questions be directed to *them*. (Plural antecedent and pronoun.)

Pronoun–antecedent agreement can be complicated when words or phrases come between the pronoun and the word to which it refers. Disregard phrases such as those introduced by *as well as*, *in addition to*, and *together with*. Find the true antecedent and make the pronoun agree with it.

> The *CEO*, together with her executive committee, is considering *her* strategy carefully. (Singular antecedent and pronoun.)
> The *chiefs* of staff, along with the general, have submitted *their* plans. (Plural antecedent and pronoun.)
> A female *member* of the group of protesting hospital workers demanded that *she* be treated equally. (Singular antecedent and pronoun.)

Making Pronouns Agree with Their Antecedents in Gender

Pronouns exhibit one of three *genders*: masculine (male), feminine (female), or neuter (neither masculine nor feminine). Pronouns must agree with their antecedents in gender.

> Natalie ate *her* lunch. (Feminine gender.)
> Jeremy brought *his* printouts. (Masculine gender.)
> The plan had *its* advantages. (Neuter gender.)

DID YOU KNOW

Despite efforts for the past 140 years, no one has yet come up with an acceptable multipurpose, unisex pronoun. Suggested replacements: *ne* (1850), *le* (1884), *se*, (1938), *ve* (1970), *e* (1977), and *ala* (1988). What would you suggest to fill the void in our language?

Choosing Alternatives to Common-Gender Antecedents

Occasionally, writers and speakers face a problem in choosing pronouns of appropriate gender. English has no all-purpose singular pronoun to represent indefinite nouns (such as *a student* or *an employee*). For this reason writers and speakers have, over the years, used masculine, or common-gender, pronouns to refer to nouns that might be either masculine or feminine. For example, in the sentence *An employee has his rights*, the pronoun *his* referred to its antecedent *employee*, which might name either a feminine or masculine person.

Communicators today, however, avoid masculine pronouns (*he*, *his*) when referring to indefinite nouns that could be masculine or feminine. Critics call these pronouns "sexist" because they exclude women. To solve the problem, sensitive communicators rewrite those sentences requiring such pronouns. Although many alternatives exist, here are three common options:

COMMON GENDER:	A passenger must show *his* ticket before boarding.
ALTERNATIVE NO. 1:	Passengers must show *their* tickets before boarding.
ALTERNATIVE NO. 2:	A passenger must show *a* ticket before boarding.
ALTERNATIVE NO. 3:	A passenger must show *his or her* ticket before boarding.
WRONG:	A passenger must show *their* ticket before boarding.

SPOT THE BLOOPER

Television commercial for *Encyclopedia Britannica:* "Every parent has a wish list for their child."

In Alternative No. 1 the subject has been made plural to avoid the need for a singular common-gender pronoun. In Alternative No. 2 the pronoun is omitted, and an article is substituted, although at the cost of making the original meaning less emphatic. In Alternative No. 3 both masculine and feminine references (*his or her*) are used. Because the latter construction is wordy and clumsy, frequent use of it should be avoided. Substituting the plural pronoun *their* is incorrect since it does not agree with its singular antecedent, *employee.*

PROBLEMS WITH PRONOUN–ANTECEDENT AGREEMENT

Antecedents Joined by *or* or *nor*

When antecedents are joined by *or* or *nor*, the pronoun should agree with the antecedent closer to it.

> Either Sondra or *Janine* left *her* briefcase in the conference room.
> Neither the manager nor the *employees* objected to *their* salary cuts.

You may be wondering why antecedents joined by *and* are treated differently from antecedents joined by *or/nor.* The conjunction *and* joins one plus one to make two antecedents; hence, a plural pronoun is used. The conjunctions *or/nor* require a choice between two antecedents. Always match the pronoun to the closer antecedent.

Indefinite Pronouns as Antecedents

Pronouns such as *anyone, something,* and *anybody* are called *indefinite* because they refer to no specific person or object. Some indefinite pronouns are always singular; others are always plural.

Always Singular		Always Plural
anybody	everything	both
anyone	neither	few
anything	nobody	many
each	no one	several
either	nothing	
everybody	somebody	
everyone	someone	

When indefinite pronouns function as antecedents of pronouns, make certain that the pronoun agrees with its antecedent. Do not let prepositional phrases obscure the true antecedent.

> *Someone* on the men's volleyball team left *his* sneakers on the court.
> *Each* of the corporations had *its* own home office.
> *Few* of the vendors missed the show to demonstrate *their* equipment.
> *Several* of the lawyers filed *their* papers after the deadline.

STUDY TIP

When *either* or *neither* is followed by an "of" phrase, it's functioning as a singular pronoun. For example, *Either of the books is available.*

The words *either* and *neither* can be confusing. When these words stand alone and function as pronoun subjects, they are always considered singular. When they are joined with *or* or *nor* to form conjunctions, however, they may connect plural subjects. These plural subjects, then, may act as antecedents to plural pronouns.

> Has *either* of the boys joined his little league team? (*Either* is a singular pronoun and functions as the subject of the sentence.)

Either the professor *or* her colleagues expressed their support for the project. (*Either/or* is used as a conjunction to join the two subjects, *professor* and *colleagues.* The pronoun *their* agrees with its plural antecedent, *colleagues.*)

Collective Nouns as Antecedents

Words such as *jury, faculty, committee, union, team,* and *group* are called *collective* nouns because they refer to a collection of people, animals, or objects. Such words may be either singular or plural depending on the mode of operation of the collection to which they refer. When a collective noun operates as a unit, it is singular. When the elements of a collective noun operate separately, the collective noun is plural.

No action can be taken until the *committee* announces *its* decision. (*Committee* operating as one unit.)
The *jury* delivered *its* verdict. (*Jury* operating as one unit.)
The *jury* took *their* seats in the courtroom. (*Jury* operating as individuals.)

However, if a collective noun is to be used in a plural sense, the sentence can often be made to sound less awkward by the addition of a plural noun (*The jury members took their seats in the courtroom*).

Company and Organization Names as Antecedents

DID YOU KNOW

English is the first language in history in which the majority of speakers are nonnative. Of the 750 million people who use English regularly, only 300 million are native speakers. It is the universal language of scholarship, science, and trade.

Company and organization names are generally considered singular. Unless the actions of the organization are attributed to individual representatives of that organization, pronouns referring to organizations should be singular.

Abercrombie & Fitch is having *its* annual half-price sale.
The United Nations, in addition to other organizations, is expanding *its* campaign to fight hunger.
Smith, Felker & Torres, Inc., plans to open *its* new branch in Chicago this year.

The Antecedents *each, every,* and *many a*

If the limiting adjectives *each, every,* and *many a* describe either noun or both nouns in a compound antecedent, that antecedent is considered singular.

Each player and coach on the women's team has *her* assigned duties.
Many a son and father will receive *his* award at the banquet.

ADVANCED PRONOUN USE

The Problem of *who* and *whom*

SPOT THE BLOOPER

Famous singer on NBC's "Today" show: "I began to recognize whom I am, and I wasn't afraid of whom I was."

The use of *who* and *whom* presents a continuing dilemma for speakers and writers. In conversation the correct choice of *who* or *whom* is especially difficult because of the mental gymnastics necessary to locate subjects and objects. In writing, however, an author has ample time to analyze a sentence carefully and make a correct choice—if the author understands the traditional functions of *who* and *whom.* *Who* is the nominative case form. Like other nominative case pronouns, *who* may function as the subject of a verb or as the subject complement of a noun following the linking verb. *Whom* is the objective case form. It may function as the object of a verb or as the object of a preposition.*

**Whom* may also function as the subject or object of an infinitive. Since little confusion results from these constructions, they will not be discussed.

Who do you think will be elected? (*Who* is the subject of *will be elected.*)
Susan wondered *who* my boss is. (*Who* is the complement of *boss.*)
Whom should we choose? (*Whom* is the object of *should choose.*)
Edmund is the one to *whom* I wrote. (*Whom* is the object of *to.*)

How to Choose Between *who* and *whom*

The choice between *who* and *whom* becomes easier if the sentence in question is approached according to the following procedure:

SPOT THE BLOOPER

From *Newsweek*: "Why did Clinton nominate someone whom advisers knew would be a lightening rod?"

1. Isolate the *who/whom* clause.
2. Invert the clause, if necessary, to restore normal subject–verb–object order.
3. Substitute the nominative pronoun *he* (*she* or *they*) for *who*. Substitute the objective pronoun *him* (*her* or *them*) for *whom*. If the sentence sounds correct with *him*, replace *him* with *whom*. If the sentence sounds correct with *he*, replace *he* with *who*.

Study the following sentences and notice how the choice of *who* or *whom* is made:

Here are the addresses of those (who/whom) we are inviting.

ISOLATE:	________ we are inviting
INVERT:	we are inviting ________
SUBSTITUTE:	we are inviting __him__
EQUATE:	we are inviting __whom__
COMPLETE:	Here are the addresses of those *whom* we are inviting.

Do you know (who/whom) his doctor is?

ISOLATE:	________ his doctor is
INVERT:	his doctor is ________ (*or* ________ is his doctor)
SUBSTITUTE:	his doctor is __he__ (*or* __he__ is his doctor)
EQUATE:	his doctor is __who__ (*or* __who__ is his doctor)
COMPLETE:	Do you know *who* his doctor is?

In choosing *who* or *whom*, ignore parenthetical expressions such as *I hope*, *we think*, *I believe*, and *you know*.

Manuel is the applicant (who/whom) we believe is best qualified.

ISOLATE:	________ we believe is best qualified
IGNORE:	we believe ________ is best qualified
SUBSTITUTE:	we believe __he__ is best qualified
EQUATE:	we believe __who__ is best qualified
COMPLETE:	Manuel is the applicant *who* we believe is best qualified.

EXAMPLES:

Whom do you think we should call? (Invert: you do think we should call him/*whom.*)
The person to *whom* we gave our evaluation was Allison. (Invert: we gave our evaluation to her/*whom.*)
Do you know *who* the plaintiff is? (Invert: the plaintiff is he/*who.*)
Whom would you like to include in the acknowledgments? (Invert: you would like to include him/*whom.*)

NOTABLE QUOTABLE

"What is written without effort is, in general, read without pleasure."
—Samuel Johnson

The Use of *whoever* and *whomever*

Whoever, of course, is nominative and *whomever* is objective. The selection of the correct form is sometimes complicated when *whoever* or *whomever* appears in clauses. These clauses may act as objects of prepositions, objects of verbs, or subjects of verbs. Within the clauses, however, you must determine how *whoever* or *whomever* is functioning in order to choose the correct form. Study the following examples and explanations.

> Offer the clothes to *whoever* needs them. (The clause *whoever needs them* is the object of the preposition *to.* Within the clause itself, *whoever* acts as the subject of *needs* and is therefore in the nominative case.)
>
> A scholarship will be given to *whoever* has the qualifications. (The clause *whoever has the qualifications* is the object of the preposition *to.* Within the clause, *whoever* acts as the subject of *has* and is therefore in the nominative case.)
>
> The baker will add to the cake the names of *whomever* you wish. (The clause *you wish* is the object of the preposition *of.* Within the clause, *whomever* is the object of *you wish* and is therefore in the objective case.)

HOTLINE QUERIES

QUESTION My friend insists that the combination *all right* is shown in her dictionary as one word. I say that it's two words. Who's right?

ANSWER *All right* is the only acceptable spelling. The listing *alright* is shown in many dictionaries to guide readers to the acceptable spelling, *all right.* Do not use *alright.* By the way, some individuals can better remember that *all right* is two words by associating it with *all wrong.*

QUESTION I don't seem to be able to hear the difference between *than* and *then.* Can you explain it to me?

ANSWER The conjunction *than* is used to make comparisons (*your watch is more accurate than mine*). The adverb *then* means "at that time" (*we must complete this task; then we will take our break*) or "as a consequence" (*if all the angles of the triangle are equal, then it must be equilateral as well*).

QUESTION What is the order of college degrees, and which ones are capitalized?

ANSWER Two kinds of undergraduate degrees are commonly awarded: the associate's degree, a two-year degree; and the bachelor's degree, a four-year degree. A variety of graduate degrees exist. The most frequently awarded are the master's degree and the doctorate. Merriam-Webster dictionaries do not capitalize the names of degrees: associate of arts degree, bachelor of science, master of arts, doctor of philosophy. However, when used with an individual's name, the abbreviations for degrees are capitalized: Bruce Gourlay, M.A.; Rhianna Landini, Ph.D.

QUESTION Why does the sign above my grocery market's quick-check stand say *Ten or less items*? Shouldn't it read *Ten or fewer items*?

ANSWER Right you are! *Fewer* refers to numbers, as in *fewer items. Less* refers to amounts or quantities, as in *less food.* Perhaps markets prefer *less* because it has fewer letters.

QUESTION If I have no interest in something, am I *disinterested*?

ANSWER No. If you lack interest, you are *uninterested.* The word *disinterested* means "unbiased" or "impartial" (*the judge was disinterested in the cases before him*).

QUESTION Everyone says "consensus of opinion." Yet, I understand that there is some objection to this expression.

ANSWER Yes, the expression is widely used. However, since *consensus* means "collective opinion," the addition of the word *opinion* results in a redundancy.

QUESTION I'm disgusted and infuriated at a New York University advertisement I just saw in our newspaper. It says, *It's not just <u>who</u> you know . . . ,* Why would a leading institution of learning use such poor grammar?

ANSWER Because it sounds familiar. But familiarity doesn't make it correct. You're right in recognizing that the proper form is *whom* (isolate the clause *you know him* or *whom*). The complete adage—or more appropriately, cliché—correctly stated is: *It's not what you know but <u>whom</u> you know.*

QUESTION Should an e-mail message begin with a salutation or some kind of greeting?

ANSWER When e-mail messages are sent to company insiders, a salutation may be omitted. However, when e-mail messages travel to outsiders, omitting a salutation seems curt and unfriendly. Because the message is more like a letter, a salutation is appropriate (such as *Dear Courtney, Hi Courtney, Greetings,* or just *Courtney*). Including a salutation is also a visual cue to where the message begins. Some writers prefer to incorporate the name of the recipient in the first sentence (*Thanks, Courtney, for responding so quickly.*)

QUESTION At the end of a letter I wrote: *Thank you for attending to this matter immediately.* Should I hyphenate *thank you*?

ANSWER Do not hyphenate *thank you* when using it as a verb (*thank you for writing*). Do use hyphens when using it as an adjective (*I sent a thank-you note*) or as a noun (*I sent four thank-yous*). Since *thank you* is used as a verb in your sentence, do not hyphenate it. Notice that *thank you* is never written as a single word.

QUESTION A fellow worker insists on saying, *I could care less.* Seems to me that it should be *I couldn't care less.* Who is right?

ANSWER You are right. The phrase *I couldn't care less* has been in the language a long time. It means, of course, "I have little concern about this matter." Recently, though, people have begun to use *I could care less* with the same meaning. Most careful listeners realize that the latter phrase says just the opposite of its intent. Although both phrases are clichés, stick with *I couldn't care less* if you want to be clear.

NAME ______________________________

4 REINFORCEMENT EXERCISES

A. (Self-check) Select the correct word(s) to complete the following sentences.

1. Someone has left (his, her, his or her, their) keys on the counter. ____________
2. Crate & Barrel changed (its, their) merchandise mix to include more furniture. ____________
3. Either Tanya or Melissa will bring (her, their) cooler to the picnic. ____________
4. Nobody wanted to drive (his, her, his or her, their) own car on the steep, winding road. ____________
5. Although the judge hoped for a speedy verdict, he cautioned the jury to take (its, their) time. ____________
6. Are you the person (who, whom) wants to buy a car? ____________
7. First prize will go to (whoever, whomever) submits the winning essay. ____________
8. (Who, Whom) do you want to invite to your party? ____________
9. (Who, Whom) may I say is calling? ____________
10. Never recommend anyone (who, whom) you haven't worked with personally. ____________

Check your answers below.

B. Select the correct pronoun(s) to complete the following sentences.

1. A coach, along with all the members of the team, must do whatever (he, she, he or she, they) can to maintain the team's morale. ____________
2. The Supreme Court will announce (their, its) decision sometime next week. ____________
3. Sometimes an attorney must review (his, her, his or her) notes before a cross-examination. ____________
4. Both Mr. Ferguson and Ms. Dewar have stated (his or her, their) opposition to the plan. ____________
5. Mary Anne, one of our mentors, has given us (her, their) evaluation. ____________
6. An employee does not always know all the factors on which (his, her, his or her, their) evaluation is based. ____________
7. Shelby's mother, along with others in the neighborhood, made (her, their) contribution to the community. ____________
8. Tennis players are sometimes afflicted with inflammation of the tissue surrounding (his or her, their) elbows. ____________
9. Dun and Bradstreet bases (their, its) financial ratings on business accounting reports. ____________
10. Once the contributions were all collected, the fund-raising committee submitted (their, its) report. ____________
11. Carmen, (who, whom) left last week, was the most experienced paralegal in our office. ____________

1. his or her, 2. its, 3. her, 4. his or her, 5. its, 6. who, 7. whoever, 8. Whom, 9. Who, 10. whom.

12. Jake will help (whoever, whomever) is next in line. ____________

13. Do you know (who, whom) Ms. Knapp is talking about? ____________

14. Marina wondered (who, whom) she could ask to speak at next week's meeting. ____________

15. Can you put the call through to (whoever, whomever) is in charge of the project? ____________

C. Rewrite the following sentences to avoid the use of common-gender pronouns. Show three versions of each sentence. Although the *his or her* alternative will be one of the options for this exercise, strive to avoid using it in your writing—unless no other alternative works.

1. Every driver must have *his* car certified before January 1.

(a) ____________________

(b) ____________________

(c) ____________________

2. Be sure that each new employee has received *his* orientation packet.

(a) ____________________

(b) ____________________

(c) ____________________

3. When is a supervisor required to submit *his* performance evaluations?

(a) ____________________

(b) ____________________

(c) ____________________

D. Underline any errors and write a correction in the space provided. Write *C* if the sentence is correct.

1. The staff adjourned their meeting an hour early. ____________

2. To whom do we owe this money? ____________

3. Neither the plaintiff nor the defendant changed their minds. ____________

4. Please tell us the name of whoever you recommend for this position. ____________

5. Any customer may ask for their money back. ____________

NAME ______________________________

4 UNIT 1 REVIEW ■ Chapters 1–4 (Self-Check)

Begin your review by rereading Chapters 1–4. Then test your comprehension of these chapters by filling in the blanks in the exercises that follow. Compare your responses with those at the end of the review.

1. Do you think the (a) Schwartzes, (b) Schwartz, (c) Schwartz's have been asked to attend? _____

2. Each summer I search the farmers' market for the best (a) peachs, (b) peaches. _____

3. We dropped the (a) childs, (b) children, (c) childrens off at the playground on our way over. _____

4. With only two (a) years', (b) years, (c) year's experience, she received a 10 percent salary increase. _____

5. My (a) companies', (b) company's benefits get better every year. _____

6. How did the (a) sales, (b) sale's, (c) sales' department manage to avoid layoffs? _____

7. Many of our (a) employees', (b) employees, (c) employee's have difficulty with possessive constructions. _____

8. Can you turn the table on (a) its, (b) it's side? _____

9. That blue Mustang convertible is (a) theirs, (b) there's, (c) their's. _____

10. I think we should offer (a) her, (b) she the position of product manager. _____

11. Evelyn gave the checks to (a) we, (b) us to deposit after work. _____

12. Just between you and (a) me, (b) I, what should I do? _____

13. Everyone except Mitch and (a) he, (b) him received one-year pins. _____

14. Tell both of the champions that (a) he, (b) he or she, (c) they should prepare for the next round. _____

15. For an employee to be fired, (a) he or she, (b) they must have received warnings. _____

16. Several of the (a) attorneys, (b) attornies were on the mediation panel. _____

17. Regina and Kim asked their (a) mother-in-laws, (b) mothers-in-law to join them. _____

18. In her five years with the company, she had learned the (a) do's and don't's, (b) dos and don'ts of dealing with the board. _____

19. (a) Wendy's and Greg's, (b) Wendy and Greg's children hoped for reconciliation. _____

20. I certainly hope that today's weather is better than (a) yesterday's, (b) yesterdays. _____

21. Sarah was studying for a degree in (a) economic's, (b) economics. _____

22. Brad and (a) I, (b) me will be there by 4:30. _____

23. Can you give the schedule to Anna and (a) he, (b) him? _____

24. Ernesto earns almost as much as (a) he, (b) him. _____

25. Beverly ordered the books for you and (a) he, (b) him. _____

26. Either Captain Picard or (a) I, (b) me, (c) myself will lead the mission. _____

27. (a) We, (b) Us senior employees must set a good example. _____

28. It was (a) he, (b) him who asked us to be here early for the meeting. _____

29. Neither the father nor his sons wanted (a) his, (b) their salaries to be revealed. _____

NAME ____________

30. Every doctor and every nurse planned to cast (a) his or her, (b) their vote for the new information system. ______

31. Several (a) analysises, (b) analyses, (c) analysis were offered to explain the problem. ______

32. The (a) curriculum, (b) curricula offered by the two schools are quite similar. ______

33. Because of its excellent work, thanks (a) is, (b) are in order for our organizing committee. ______

34. Is it the (a) Morrises, (b) Morrises', (c) Morris's home that won the landscaping award? ______

35. I am certain that my (a) bosses, (b) boss's, (c) bosses' signature will be forthcoming. ______

36. The IRS is checking Mr. (a) Gross's, (b) Grosses' return. ______

37. The composer who wrote the score was believed to be (a) him, (b) he. ______

38. Laura was often taken to be (a) her, (b) she. ______

39. If you were (a) I, (b) me, would you attend the conference? ______

40. To (a) who, (b) whom have you decided to offer the position? ______

41. (a) Who, (b) Whom has been chosen for the award? ______

42. Distribute the supplies to (a) whoever, (b) whomever needs them. ______

43. (a) Who, (b) Whom would you prefer to conduct the audit? ______

44. Can you believe (a) who, (b) whom I saw at the trade show? ______

45. It may have been she (a) who, (b) whom wrote the memo. ______

Hotline Review

46. (a) To, (b) Too many cooks spoil the stew. ______

47. Check your (a) owner's, (b) owners' warranty carefully. ______

48. A diet rich in beta-carotene is (a) healthful, (b) healthy. ______

49. This frozen yogurt has (a) less, (b) fewer calories than your ice cream. ______

50. It's (a) alright, (b) all right, (c) allright with me if you borrow my camera. ______

1. a, 2. b, 3. b, 4. a, 5. b, 6. a, 7. b, 8. a, 9. a, 10. a, 11. b, 12. a, 13. b, 14. c, 15. a, 16. a, 17. b, 18. b, 19. b, 20. a, 21. b, 22. a, 23. b, 24. a, 25. b, 26. a, 27. a, 28. a, 29. b, 30. a, 31. b, 32. b, 33. b, 34. b, 35. b, 36. b, 37. b, 38. b, 39. a, 40. b, 41. a, 42. a, 43. b, 44. b, 45. a, 46. b, 47. a, 48. a, 49. b, 50. b.

UNIT

2

Showing the Action

5 Verb Tenses, Parts, and Voices

OBJECTIVES When you have completed the materials in this chapter, you will be able to do the following:

- Write verbs in the present, past, and future tenses correctly.
- Use the emphatic tense correctly.
- Recognize and use present and past participles.
- Write the correct forms of 60 irregular verbs.
- Supply correct verb forms in the progressive and perfect tenses.

English verbs change form to indicate number (singular or plural), person (first, second, or third), voice (active or passive), and tense (time).

To indicate precise time, English employs four rather complex sets of tenses: primary tenses, emphatic tenses, progressive tenses, and perfect tenses.

PRIMARY TENSES

Present Tense

Verbs in the present tense express current or habitual action. Present tense verbs may also be used in constructions showing future action.

> We *order* office supplies every month. (Current or habitual action.)
> He *flies* to Washington tomorrow. (Future action.)

Past Tense

Verbs in the past tense show action that has been completed. Regular verbs form the past tense with the addition of *d* or *ed.*

> Mr. Pasternak *needed* the forms yesterday.
> Our vendor *provided* toner cartridges.
> The report *focused* on changes in our department.

Future Tense

Verbs in the future tense show actions that are expected to occur at a later time. Traditionally, the helper verbs *shall* and *will* have been joined with principal verbs to express future tense. In business writing today, however, the verb *will* is generally used as the helper to express future tense.

> Daniel *will need* help with his next assignment.
> You *will receive* your order on Thursday.

EMPHATIC TENSES

To express emphasis, place *do*, *does*, or *did* before the present tense form of a verb.

> She *does have* the qualifications for the job. (Present emphatic tense.)
> I *do believe* the statistics presented in the report. (Present emphatic tense.)
> He stated that he *did help* you with the project. (Past emphatic tense.)
> You *did say* you had enough supplies. (Past emphatic tense.)

PRESENT AND PAST PARTICIPLES

Present Participle

NOTABLE QUOTABLE

"For good or ill, your conversation is your advertisement. Every time you open your mouth, you let me look into your mind."
—Bruce Barton

The present participle of a regular verb is formed by adding *ing* to the present tense of the verb. When used in a sentence as part of a verb phrase, the present participle is always preceded by some form of the helping verb *to be* (*am*, *is*, *are*, *was*, *were*, *be*, *been*).

> I *am printing* the proposal.
> You *are wasting* good paper.

Past Participle

SPOT THE BLOOPER

From a CNN interview: "The warden has came out and gave us his view of the execution."

The past participle of a regular verb is usually formed by adding a *d* or *t* sound to the present tense of the verb. Like present participles, past participles may function as parts of verb phrases.

> Chandra *has checked* her data carefully.
> Her data *has been checked* by Chandra.
> We *should have finished* the project earlier.
> The project *should have been finished* earlier.

IRREGULAR VERBS

Up to this point, we have considered only regular verbs. Regular verbs form the past tense by the addition of *d* or *ed* to the present tense form. Many verbs, however, form the past tense and the past participle irregularly. (More specifically, irregular verbs form the past tense by a variation in the root vowel and, commonly, the past participle by the addition of *en*.) A list of the more frequently used irregular verbs follows. Learn the forms of these verbs by practicing in patterns such as:

PRESENT TENSE:	Today I drive.
PAST TENSE:	Yesterday I drove.
PAST PARTICIPLE:	In the past I have driven.

CAREER TIP

In employment interviews, recruiters listen carefully to a candidate's spoken English. One quick way to be eliminated is to substitute a verb past tense for a past participle. WRONG: *He come over last night* or *I seen them.*

Frequently Used Irregular Verbs

PRESENT	PAST	PAST PARTICIPLE
arise	arose	arisen
be (am, is, are)	was, were	been
become	became	become
begin	began	begun
bite	bit	bitten
blow	blew	blown
break	broke	broken
bring	brought	brought
build	built	built

SPOT THE BLOOPER

From *The New York Times*: "But Van Hellemond said he had blew his whistle . . . ."

SPOT THE BLOOPER

From a Dunkin' Donuts advertisement: "The trouble with supermarket doughnuts is there's no telling how long they've been laying around."

SPOT THE BLOOPER

From the *Arizona Republic*: "The great tree uprooted the back fence, causing it to raise 5 feet in the air."

SPOT THE BLOOPER

From Walt Disney Company: "Honey, I Shrunk the Kids."

SPOT THE BLOOPER

From *The Times-Union* [Albany, NY]: "Jane Fonda's Beverly Hills hairdresser sweared the thick blond braid she's been sporting . . . is her real hair."

Present	Past	Past Participle
choose	chose	chosen
come	came	come
do	did	done
draw	drew	drawn
drink	drank	drunk
drive	drove	driven
eat	ate	eaten
fall	fell	fallen
fly	flew	flown
forbid	forbade	forbidden
forget	forgot	forgotten *or*
forgot		
forgive	forgave	forgiven
freeze	froze	frozen
get	got	gotten or got
give	gave	given
go	went	gone
grow	grew	grown
hang (to suspend)	hung	hung
hang (to execute)	hanged	hanged
hide	hid	hidden *or* hid
know	knew	known
lay (to place)	laid	laid
leave	left	left
lie (to rest)	lay	lain
lie (to tell a falsehood)	lied	lied
pay	paid	paid
prove	proved	proved *or* proven
raise (to lift)	raised	raised
ride	rode	ridden
ring	rang	rung
rise (to move up)	rose	risen
run	ran	run
see	saw	seen
set (to place)	set	set
shake	shook	shaken
shrink	shrank	shrunk
sing	sang	sung
sink	sank	sunk
sit (to rest)	sat	sat
speak	spoke	spoken
spring	sprang	sprung
steal	stole	stolen
strike	struck	struck *or* stricken
swear	swore	sworn
swim	swam	swum
take	took	taken
tear	tore	torn
throw	threw	thrown
wake	woke	woken
wear	wore	worn
write	wrote	written

THREE PAIRS OF FREQUENTLY MISUSED IRREGULAR VERBS

Up to this point, we have considered only regular verbs. Regular verbs form the past tense by the addition of *d* or *ed* to the present tense form. Many verbs, however, form the past tense and the past participle irregularly.

The key to the correct use of the following pairs of irregular verbs lies in developing the ability to recognize the tense forms of each and to distinguish transitive verbs and constructions from intransitive ones.

STUDY TIP

Whenever you use *lay* in the sense of "placing" something, you must provide a receiver of the action: *Please lay the book down.* If nothing receives action, you probably want the verb *lie,* which means "resting."

Lie–Lay

These two verbs are confusing because the past tense of *lie* is spelled in exactly the same way that the present tense of *lay* is spelled. To be safe, you'll want to memorize these verb forms:

	PRESENT	PRESENT PARTICIPLE	PAST	PAST PARTICIPLE
INTRANSITIVE:	lie (to rest)	lying	lay	lain
TRANSITIVE:	lay (to place)	laying	laid (*not layed*)	laid

The verb *lie* is intransitive; therefore, it requires no direct object to complete its meaning.

> I *lie* down for a nap every afternoon. (Note that *down* is not a direct object.)
> "*Lie* down," he told his dog. (Commands are given in the present tense.)
> Yesterday I *lay* down for a nap. (Past tense.)
> The papers are *lying* on the desk. (Present participle.)
> They have *lain* there for some time. (Past participle.)

SPOT THE BLOOPER

From *The Detroit News*: "Emerick allegedly fired one shot in his wife's back as she lied on the floor."

The verb *lay* is transitive and must have a direct object to complete its meaning.

> *Lay* the report over there. (Command in the present tense.)
> The mason is *laying* bricks. (Present participle.)
> He *laid* the handouts on the conference table. (Past tense.)
> He has *laid* bricks all his life. (Past participle.)

STUDY TIP

To help you remember that these verbs are intransitive, look at the second letter of each:
lie
sit
rise
Associate *i* with intransitive.

Sit–Set

Less troublesome than *lie–lay,* the combination of *sit–set* is nevertheless perplexing because the sound of the verbs is similar. The intransitive verb *sit* (past tense, *sat*; past participle, *sat*) means "to rest" and requires no direct object.

> Do you *sit* here often? (Used intransitively; *here* is not an object.)
> Are you *sitting* here tomorrow? (Present participle.)

The transitive verb *set* (past tense, *set*; past participle, *set*) means "to place" and must have a direct object.

> Letty usually *sets* her briefcase there. (*Briefcase* is the direct object.)
> She is *setting* her briefcase here today. (Present participle.)

Rise–Raise

The intransitive verb *rise* (past tense, *rose*; past participle, *risen*) means "to go up" or "to ascend" and requires no direct object.

> He *rises* early every morning. (*Every morning* is an adverbial phrase, not an object.)
> Our elevator is *rising* to the seventh floor. (Present participle.)
> The president *rose* from his chair to greet us. (Past tense.)

Interest rates have *risen* steadily. (Past participle.)

The transitive verb *raise* (past tense, *raised*; past participle, *raised*) means "to lift up" or "to elevate" and must have a direct object.

Please *raise* the blinds after the presentation. (*Blinds* is a direct object.)
The manufacturer is *raising* prices next month. (*Prices* is a direct object.)

PROGRESSIVE AND PERFECT TENSES

The remainder of this chapter focuses on two additional sets of verb tenses: the perfect and the progressive. Most native speakers and writers of English have little difficulty controlling these verb forms because they have frequently heard them used correctly. This largely descriptive section is presented for individuals who are not native speakers and for those who are eager to study the entire range of verb tenses.

Progressive Tenses

PRESENT PROGRESSIVE TENSE

	FIRST PERSON	SECOND PERSON	THIRD PERSON
ACTIVE:	I am asking we are asking	you are asking	he, she, it is asking they are asking
PASSIVE:	I am being asked we are being asked	you are being asked	he, she, it is being asked they are being asked

PAST PROGRESSIVE TENSE

	FIRST PERSON	SECOND PERSON	THIRD PERSON
ACTIVE:	I was asking we were asking	you were asking	he, she, it was asking they were asking
PASSIVE:	I was being asked we were being asked	you were being asked	he, she, it was being asked they were being asked

FUTURE PROGRESSIVE TENSE

	FIRST PERSON	SECOND PERSON	THIRD PERSON
ACTIVE:	I will be asking we will be asking	you will be asking	he, she, it will be asking they will be asking
PASSIVE:	I will be being asked we will be being asked	you will be being asked	he, she, it will be being asked they will be being asked

SPOT THE BLOOPER

In *Skyway News/Freeway News*, describing a restaurant in Mantonville, Minnesota: Proprietor Paul J. Pappas extends his hostility to tour groups. Call for reservations.

We *are sending* the fax right now. (Present progressive tense expresses action in progress.)
Federal Express *was testing* its systems last week. (Past progressive tense indicates action begun in the past.)
They *will be announcing* the winner tomorrow. (Future progressive tense indicates action in the future.)

Perfect Tenses

PRESENT PERFECT TENSE

	FIRST PERSON	SECOND PERSON	THIRD PERSON
ACTIVE:	I have asked we have asked	you have asked	he, she, it has asked they have asked
PASSIVE:	I have been asked	you have been asked	he, she, it has been asked

we have been asked		they have been asked

PAST PERFECT TENSE

	FIRST PERSON	SECOND PERSON	THIRD PERSON
ACTIVE:	I had asked we had asked	you had asked	he, she, it had asked they had asked
PASSIVE:	I had been asked we had been asked	you had been asked	he, she, it had been asked they had been asked

FUTURE PERFECT TENSE

	FIRST PERSON	SECOND PERSON	THIRD PERSON
ACTIVE:	I will have asked we will have asked	you will have asked	he, she, it will have asked they will have asked
PASSIVE:	I will have been asked we will have been asked	you will have been asked	he, she, it will have been asked they will have been asked

Miriam has just *left* the building. (Present perfect tense expresses action just completed or *perfected.*)
The letter *had reached* your office by the time I called. (Past perfect tense shows an action finished before another action in the past.)
The polls *will have been closed* two hours when the results are televised. (Future perfect tense indicates action that will be completed before another future action.)

SUMMARY OF TENSES

The following table summarizes the four sets of tenses.

PRIMARY TENSES	EMPHATIC TENSES
Present	Present emphatic
Past	Past emphatic
Future	

PROGRESSIVE TENSES	PERFECT TENSES
Present progressive	Present perfect
Past progressive	Past perfect
Future progressive	Future perfect

VERB VOICES

A verb expressing an action directed toward a person or thing is said to be transitive. Transitive verbs fall into two categories depending on the receiver of the action of the verbs.

Active Voice

When the verb expresses an action directed by the subject toward the object of the verb, the verb is said to be in the *active voice.*

Stephanie answered the telephone. (Action directed to the object, *telephone.*)

Verbs in the active voice are direct and forceful; they clearly identify the doer of the action. For these reasons, writing that frequently uses the active voice is vigorous and effective. Writers of business communications strive to use the active voice; in fact, it is called the *voice of business.*

STUDY TIP

In the passive voice, verbs always require a *helper*, such as *is, are, was, were, being*, or *been*.

Passive Voice

When the action verb is directed toward the subject, the verb is said to be in the *passive voice.* Study the following pairs:

PASSIVE: Computers are used daily.
ACTIVE: We use computers daily.
PASSIVE: The lottery was won by Mr. Chavez.
ACTIVE: Mr. Chavez won the lottery.
PASSIVE: Three errors were made in the report.
ACTIVE: The accountant made three errors in the report.

Because the passive voice can be used to avoid mentioning the performer of the action, the passive voice is sometimes called the *voice of tact.* Notice how much more tactful the passive version of the last example shown above is. Although directness in business writing is generally preferable, in certain instances the passive voice is used when indirectness is desired.

HOTLINE QUERIES

QUESTION What is the name of a group of initials that form a word? Is it an abbreviation?

ANSWER A word formed from the initial letters of an expression is called an *acronym* (pronounced ACK-ro-nim). Examples: *scuba* from *self-contained underwater breathing apparatus* and *RAM* from *random-access memory.* Acronyms are usually pronounced as a single word and are different from abbreviations. Expressions such as *FBI* and *dept.* are abbreviations, not acronyms. Notice that an abbreviation is pronounced letter by letter (*F, B, I*) while an acronym is pronounced as a word (*MADD*, which stands for *Mothers Against Drunk Driving*).

QUESTION We have a new electronic mail system, and one of the functions is "messaging" people. When folks say, *I'll message you,* it really grates on my nerves. Is this correct?

ANSWER "Messaging" is certainly a hot term with the explosion of e-mail. As to its correctness, we think we've caught language in the act of evolving. What's happened here is the reinstitution of a noun (*message*) as a verb. Converting nouns into verbs is common in English (he *cornered* the market, we *tabled* the motion, I *penciled* it in on my calendar, the farmer *trucked* the vegetables to market). Actually, *message* was sometimes used as a verb nearly a century ago (in 1896 *the bill was messaged over from the house*). However, its recent use has been almost exclusively as a noun. Today, it is increasingly being used again as a verb. New uses of words usually become legitimate when the words fill a need and are immediately accepted. Some word uses, though, appear to be mere fads, like *The homeless child could not language her fears.* Forcing the noun *language* to function as a verb is unnecessary since a good word already exists for the purpose: *express.* But other "nouns-made-verbs" have been in use long enough to sound reasonable: I *faxed* the document, he *videotaped* the program, she *keyed* the report.

QUESTION I'm embarrassed to ask this because I should know the answer—but I don't. Is there an apostrophe in this: *its relevance to our program?*

ANSWER No. Use an apostrophe only for the contraction *it's*, meaning "it is" (*it's a good plan*). The possessive pronoun *its*, as used in your example, has no apostrophe (*the car had its oil changed*).

QUESTION I thought I knew the difference between *principal* and *principle*, but now I'm not so sure. In a report I'm typing I find this: *The principal findings of the research are negative*. I thought principal always meant your "pal," the school principal.

ANSWER You're partly right and partly wrong. *Principal* may be used as a noun meaning "chief" or *head person*. In addition, it may be used as an adjective to mean "chief" or "main." This is the meaning most people forget, and this is the meaning of the word in your sentence. The word *principle* means a "law" or "rule." Perhaps it is easiest to remember *principle = rule*. All other uses require *principal*: the *principal* of the school, the *principal* of the loan, the *principal* reason.

QUESTION Even when I use a dictionary, I can't tell the difference between *affect* and *effect*. What should the word be in this sentence? *Changes in personnel (affected/effected) our production this month*.

ANSWER No words generate more confusion than do *affect* and *effect*. In your sentence use *affected*. Let's see if we can resolve the *affect/effect* dilemma. *Affect* is a verb meaning "to influence" (*smoking affects health*; *government policies affect citizens*). *Affect* may also mean "to pretend or imitate" (*he affected a British accent*). *Effect* can be a noun or a verb. As a noun, it means "result" (*the effect of the law is slight*). As a verb (and here's the troublesome part) *effect* means "to produce a result" (*small cars effect gasoline savings*; *GM effected a new pricing policy*).

QUESTION I'm editing a screenplay for a studio, and I know something is grammatically wrong with this sentence: *The old man left the room hurriedly after discovering a body laying near the window*.

ANSWER As you probably suspected, the verb *laying* should be *lying*. *Lay* means "to place" and requires an object (*he is laying the report on your desk now*). *Lie* means "to rest" and requires no object (*the document is lying on your desk*).

QUESTION As the holiday season approaches, I'm wondering whether it's *Season's Greetings* or *Seasons' Greetings*.

ANSWER If you are referring to one season, it's *Season's Greetings*.

QUESTION I learned that the verb *set* is transitive and requires an object. If that's true, how can we say that the sun *sets* in the west?

ANSWER Good question! The verb *set* is generally transitive, but it does have some standardized intransitive uses, such as the one you mention. Here's another: *Glue sets up quickly*. I doubt that anyone would be likely to substitute *sit* in either of these unusual situations. While we're on the subject, the verb *sit* also has some exceptions. Although generally intransitive, *sit* has a few transitive uses: *Sit yourself down* and *The waiter sat us at Table 1*.

NAME ____________________

5 REINFORCEMENT EXERCISES

A. (Self-check) Write the correct verb. Do not add a helper verb.

EXAMPLE: He wished he had (eat) before he left. ______eaten______

1. I have (fly) over the Grand Canyon in a helicopter. ____________

2. If she had (know) about the problem, she might have been able to solve it. ____________

3. Isabel (become) president last year. ____________

4. When is the last time you (speak) with your manager? ____________

5. She (begin) to design her Web site yesterday. ____________

6. His attorney (come) to see him yesterday to discuss the case. ____________

7. Have you (see) the Miami contract anywhere? ____________

8. Three e-mail messages were (write) by Ms. Shapiro. ____________

9. Over the past year Dr. Nakajima (give) freely of his services. ____________

10. All employees should have (go) to the computer demonstration. ____________

Check your answers below.

B. Underline any verb errors you find in the following sentences. Write the correct forms in the spaces provided. Do not add helper verbs. Write *C* if the sentence is correct as it stands.

EXAMPLE: Janet said she <u>seen</u> the accident. ______saw______

1. Because of advances in technology, the world has shrank. ____________

2. Real estate sales sunk to an all-time low. ____________

3. The office staff must chose a new letterhead stationery. ____________

4. President Meyers has wore the same suit for the last two presentations. ____________

5. Leslie and he have went to the seminar in Royce Hall. ____________

6. Her friend asked if she had ate lunch yet. ____________

7. His car was stole over the weekend. ____________

8. She had drank her entire iced tea by the time her colleague arrived. ____________

9. Our telephone bill was not payed last month. ____________

10. The building plans were drew up by a well-known architect firm. ____________

11. An agreement binding both parties was recently wrote. ____________

12. The telephone has rang only twice in the past hour. ____________

13. Mark brang his laptop to the meeting so that he could show his PowerPoint slides. ____________

14. Howling winds have blown all day, making outside work difficult. ____________

15. The first pitch of the season was threw out by the president. ____________

1. flown, 2. known, 3. became, 4. spoke, 5. began, 6. came, 7. seen, 8. written, 9. gave, 10. gone

C. Lie–Lay. Select the correct verb.

1. Norma had to (lay, lie) down until the dizziness passed. ______
2. She (lay, laid) the mail on Ms. Tong's desk. ______
3. The contracts have been (lying, laying) there for some time. ______
4. In fact, they have (laid, lain) there over a week. ______
5. After lunch she (lay, laid) down for a nap. ______

D. Sit–Set; Rise–Raise. Select the correct verb.

1. Please (raise, rise) the windows to let in fresh air. ______
2. We'll never finish if Marcy (sits, sets) there all day. ______
3. Working computers (raise, rise) the temperature in a room. ______
4. Don't (set, sit) the vase so close to the edge of the desk. ______
5. The value of gold (raises, rises) or falls in relation to the dollar. ______
6. Our office building (sits, sets) on the corner of California and Pine. ______
7. Who (rose, raised) the question of salary? ______
8. Maverick refused to (set, sit) with his back to the door. ______
9. Luis Suarez always (rises, raises) first to signal that a meeting is over. ______
10. Have you been (setting, sitting) goals for your future? ______

E. Write the proper verb form.

EXAMPLE: They (drive) all night before they found a place to stay. (Past perfect) **had driven**

1. Before the meeting was held, we (know) an announcement would be made. (Past perfect) ______
2. Perhaps you (hear) from the human resources director soon. (Future progressive) ______
3. Plans (develop) to reduce administrative costs. (Present progressive, passive) ______
4. I'm sure they (receive) the message by now. (Present perfect) ______
5. By Friday the checks (sign) and put in the mail. (Past perfect, passive) ______

F. In the spaces provided, write *active* or *passive* to indicate the voice of the italicized verbs in the following sentences.

1. Judy Welch *prepared* the certified check. ______
2. The certified check *was prepared* by Judy Welch. ______
3. Intranets *are being used* in many companies. ______
4. You *withdrew* the funds in question on May 29. ______
5. From his gross income, Amir Liba *deducts* medical expenses and contributions. ______
6. Jim Perez *was told* to visit the Human Resources Department. ______
7. Contract arbitration *will be conducted* by the union and the manufacturer. ______

8. Pollution *was* greatly *reduced* by General Motors when the company built its new plant. ____________

9. Net income before taxes *must be calculated* carefully when you fill out your tax return. ____________

10. The investigators carefully *reviewed* the documents during the audit. ____________

6 Verb and Subject Agreement

OBJECTIVES When you have completed the materials in this chapter, you will be able to do the following:

- Make verbs agree with true subjects.
- Make verbs agree with subjects joined by *and.*
- Make verbs agree with subjects joined by *or* or *nor.*
- Select the correct verbs to agree with collective nouns and indefinite pronouns.
- Make verbs agree with quantities, fractions, portions, clauses, and *a number/the number.*
- Achieve subject–verb agreement within *who* clauses.

SPOT THE BLOOPER

On the label of Heinz 57 sauce: "Its' unique tangy blend of herbs and spices bring out the natural taste of steak." (Did you spot two bloopers?)

Subjects must agree with verbs in number and person. Beginning a sentence with *He don't* damages a speaker's credibility and limits a communicator's effectiveness.

If an error is made in subject–verb agreement, it can generally be attributed to one of three lapses: (a) failure to locate the subject, (b) failure to recognize the number (singular or plural) of the subject after locating it, or (c) failure to recognize the number of the verb. Suggestions for locating the true subject and determining the number of the subject and its verb follow.

LOCATING SUBJECTS

Prepositional Phrases

All verbs have subjects. Locating these subjects can be difficult, particularly if a prepositional phrase comes between the verb and its subject. Subjects of verbs are not found in prepositional phrases. Therefore, you must learn to ignore such phrases in identifying subjects of verbs. Some of the most common prepositions are *of, to, in, from, for, with, at,* and *by.* Notice in these sentences that the italicized prepositional phrases do not contain the subjects of the verbs.

SPOT THE BLOOPER

Headline in *The Democrat and Chronicle* [Rochester, NY]: "In Keshequa, Drop in Scores Are No Surprise."

Each *of our products* is unconditionally guaranteed. (The verb *is* agrees with its subject, *each.*)

I asked whether her report *on the benefits* was copied. (The verb *was* agrees with its subject, *report.*)

The variety *of papers and inks available* makes choosing letterhead difficult. (The verb *makes* agrees with the subject, *variety.*)

Some of the less easily recognized prepositions are *except, but, like,* and *between.* In the following sentences, distinguish the subjects from the italicized prepositional phrases.

All employees *but Scott* are to report early. (The verb *are* agrees with its subject, *employees.*)

Everyone *except the managers* is expected to attend. (The verb *is* agrees with its subject, *everyone.*)

Intervening Elements

SPOT THE BLOOPER

From *The Erie* [PA] *Daily Times*: "Some comput-ers—and we don't know what else—is showing up in previously scanned rooms."

Groups of words introduced by *as well as, in addition to, such as, including, together with,* and *other than* do *not* contain sentence subjects.

Our favorite speaker, *in addition to the other presenters,* is scheduled to appear.

In this sentence the writer has elected to emphasize the subject *speaker* and to deemphasize *other presenters.* The writer could have given equal weight to these elements by writing *Our favorite speaker and other presenters are scheduled to appear.* Notice that the number (singular or plural) of the verb changes when both *speaker* and *presenters* are given equal emphasis. Here are additional examples involving intervening elements:

Our president, *together with her entire staff of employees,* sends her greetings. (The singular subject *president* agrees with the singular verb *sends.*)

Some entrepreneurs *such as Bill Gates* have started companies based on a single idea. (The plural subject *entrepreneurs* agrees with the plural verb *have.*)

The Adverbs *there* and *here*

SPOT THE BLOOPER

Sign above a group of photographs in a Service Merchandise store, Ft. Myers, Florida: "HERE'S OUR STORE MANAGERS."

In sentences beginning with *there* or *here,* look for the true subject *after* the verb. As adverbs, *here* and *there* cannot function as subjects.

There are many ways to approach the problem. (The subject *ways* follows the verb *are.*)

Here is my application for the position. (The subject *application* follows the verb *is.*)

Inverted Sentence Order

Look for the subject after the verb in inverted sentences and in questions.

On our board of directors are three prominent scientists. (Verb precedes subject.)

Has your tax refund been received? (Subject separates verb phrase.)

How do law and ethics relate to everyday business? (Verb precedes subjects.)

BASIC RULES FOR VERB–SUBJECT AGREEMENT

SPOT THE BLOOPER

From *The Saint John's* [Newfoundland] *Evening* *Telegram*: "It's important that we have in that position someone who's judgment, integrity, and incompetence is beyond question." (Did you spot three bloopers?)

Once you have located the sentence subject, decide whether the subject is singular or plural and select a verb that agrees in number.

Subjects Joined by *and*

When one subject is joined to another by the word *and,* the subject is plural and requires a plural verb.

Steve Case and Bill Gates are two influential people in the world of technology.

The proposed law and its amendment are before the legislature.

STUDY TIP

To help you select correct verbs, temporarily substitute *it* for singular subjects or *they* for plural subjects. Then you can more easily make verbs agree with their subjects.

Company Names and Titles

Even though they may appear to be plural, company names and titles of publications are singular; therefore, they require singular verbs.

> *Fast Companies* is the only magazine I read.
> American Airlines is advertising the lowest fare to Washington, D.C.
> Milberg, Weiss, and Lerach, Inc., is offering the bond issue.

SPECIAL RULES FOR VERB–SUBJECT AGREEMENT

STUDY TIP

Unlike subjects joined by *and*, subjects joined by *or*/*nor* require a choice between Subject No. 1 and Subject No. 2.

Subjects Joined by *or* or *nor*

When two or more subjects are joined by *or* or *nor*, the verb should agree with the closer subject.

> Neither the clerks nor the supervisor knows the order number.
> Either Leslie or you are in charge of ordering supplies.
> Either the mayor or his constituents were bound to be unhappy with the results.

Indefinite Pronouns as Subjects

As you may recall from Chapter 4, some indefinite pronouns are always singular, while other indefinite pronouns are always plural. In addition, some may be singular or plural depending on the words to which they refer.

Always Singular			Always Plural	Singular or Plural
anyone	every	nobody	both	all
anybody	everyone	nothing	few	more
anything	everybody	someone	many	most
each	everything	somebody	several	some
either	many a	something		any
	neither			none

SPOT THE BLOOPER

Headline in *The San Francisco Chronicle*: "One in 11 Have Trouble Speaking California's Official Language."

> *Either* of the candidates *is* qualified.
> *Anybody* who returns merchandise *is reimbursed.*
> *Many* of the workers *are attending* the seminar.
> *Neither* of the Web sites *is* particularly helpful.

Indefinite pronouns such as *all*, *more*, and *most* provide one of the few instances in which prepositional phrases become important in determining agreement. Although the prepositional phrase does not contain the subject of the sentence, it does contain the noun to which the indefinite pronoun refers.

> *Most* of the letters *are* finished. (*Most* is plural because it refers to *letters.*)
> *Most* of the work *is* completed. (*Most* is singular because it refers to *work.*)

STUDY TIP

This use of a singular verb for two or more subjects joined by *and* is the only exception to the general rule presented earlier in the chapter.

If the indefinite pronouns *each*, *every*, or *many a* are used to describe two or more subjects joined by *and*, the subjects are considered separate. Therefore, the verb is singular.

> Many a semicolon and colon *is* misused.
> Every man, woman, and child *is* affected by the tax cut.

The indefinite pronouns *anyone*, *everyone*, and *someone* should be spelled as two words when followed by *of* phrases.

Every one of us should commit to learning the new software package.
Any one of those Web sites can give us the information we need.

Collective Nouns as Subjects

DID YOU KNOW

In America collective nouns are almost always considered to be singular (*The staff is . . .*) In Britain, however, collective nouns are usually plural (*The staff are . . .*).

Words such as *faculty, committee,* and *council* may be singular or plural depending on their mode of operation. When a collective noun operates as a single unit, its verb should be singular. When the elements of a collective noun operate separately, the verb should be plural.

Our staff *has* unanimously *adopted* the board's proposal. (*Staff* is acting as a single unit.)
The council *were* sharply *divided* over the budget. (*Council* members were acting separately. While technically correct, the sentence would be less awkward if it read *The council members* were sharply . . .)

SPOT THE BLOOPER

From the *Evansville* [IN] *Press*: "Although a large crowd were gathered . . ."

ADDITIONAL RULES FOR VERB–SUBJECT AGREEMENT

The Distinction Between *the number* and *a number*

When the word *number* is the subject of a sentence, its article (*the* or *a*) becomes significant. *The* is specific and therefore implies *singularity*; *a* is general and therefore implies *plurality.*

The number of managers *is* declining. (Singular)
A number of e-mail messages *were* lost. (Plural)

Quantities, Measures

When they refer to *total* amounts, quantities and measures are singular. If they refer to individual units that can be counted, quantities and measures are plural.

Two years *is* the period of the loan. (Quantity as a total amount.)
Two years *are* required to complete the program. (Quantity as individual units.)

Fractions, Portions

Fractions and portions may be singular or plural depending on the nouns to which they refer.

Three-fourths of the applications *were accepted.*
Over half of the contract *was* ratified.
A majority of employees *agree* with the proposal.
A minimum of work *is* required to receive approval.
Part of the problems *were caused* by miscommunication.
Part of the proposal *is* ambiguous.

Who Clauses

STUDY TIP

For sentences with *one of those who* clauses, begin reading with the word *of*: *Of those people who give 100 percent, Richard is one.* The verb will always be plural. However, if the sentence is limited by *only one*, the verb is always singular.

Verbs in *who* clauses must agree in number and person with the nouns to which they refer. In *who* clauses introduced by *one of*, the verb is usually plural because it refers to a plural antecedent. In *who* clauses introduced by *the only one of*, the verb is singular.

Richard is *one of* those people who always give 100 percent.

Rachel is *one of* those employees who are technical experts.

Pamela is *the only one* of the managers who is prepared.

Verbs must agree in person with the nouns or pronouns to which they refer.

It is you who are responsible for security.
Was it you who were on the phone?

Phrases and Clauses as Subjects

Use a singular verb when the subject of a sentence is a phrase or clause.

To learn about the stock market is fascinating.
That we will design our own Web site is understood.

Subject Complements

SPOT THE BLOOPER

From *The Atlanta Journal and Constitution*: "Initia-tion fee and dues information also is top secret."

Linking verbs are followed by complements. Although a complement may differ from the subject in number, the linking verb should always agree with the subject.

The best part of the Web site is the graphics and video. (The singular subject *part* agrees with the singular verb *is* despite the plural complement *graphics and video*.)
The reason for his bankruptcy is poor investments in stocks.

To avoid awkwardness, it may be better to reconstruct such sentences so that the plural element is first: *The graphics and video are the best part of the Web site.*

HOTLINE QUERIES

QUESTION My uncle insists that *none* is singular. My English book says that it can be plural. Who's right?

ANSWER Times are changing. Thirty years ago *none* was almost always used in a singular sense. Today, through usage, *none* may be singular or plural depending on what you wish to emphasize. For example, *None are more willing than we.* But, *None of the students is* (or *are* if you wish to suggest many students) *failing.*

QUESTION When do you use *all together*, and when do you use *altogether*?

ANSWER *All together* means "collectively" or "all the members of a group" (*we must work all together to reach our goal*). *Altogether* means "entirely" (*he was altogether satisfied*).

QUESTION Please help me with this sentence that I'm transcribing for a medical laboratory: *A copy of our analysis, along with our interpretation of its results, (has or have) been sent to you.*

ANSWER The subject of your sentence is *copy*; thus the verb must be *has.* Don't let interrupting elements obscure the real sentence subject.

QUESTION After looking in the dictionary, I'm beginning to wonder about this: *We have alot of work yet to do.* I can't find the word *alot* in the dictionary, but it must be there. Everyone uses it.

ANSWER The two-word phrase *a lot* is frequently used in conversation or in very informal writing (*the copier makes a lot of copies*). *Alot* as one word does not exist. Don't confuse it with *allot*, meaning "to distribute" (*the company will allot to each department its share of supplies*).

QUESTION Should *reevaluate* be hyphenated?

ANSWER No. It is not necessary to use a hyphen after the prefix *re* unless the resulting word may be confused with another word (*to re-mark the sales ticket, to re-cover the chair*).

QUESTION I'm totally confused by job titles for women today. What do I call a woman who is a *fireman*, a *policeman*, a *chairman*, or a *spokesman*? And what about the word *mankind*?

ANSWER As more and more women enter nontraditional careers, some previous designations are being replaced by neutral, inclusive titles. Here are some substitutes:

actor	for *actress*
firefighter	for *fireman*
mail carrier	for *mailman*
police officer	for *policeman*
flight attendant	for *steward* or *stewardess*
reporter or journalist	for *newsman*

Words like *chairman*, *spokesman*, and *mankind* traditionally have been used to refer to both men and women. Today, though, sensitive writers strive to use more inclusive language. Possible substitutes are *chair*, *spokesperson*, and *humanity*.

QUESTION I'm never sure how to handle words that are used to represent quantities and proportions in sentences. For example, what verb is correct in this sentence: *A large proportion of voters (was or were) against the measure.*

ANSWER Words that represent fractional amounts (such as *proportion*, *fraction*, *minimum*, and *majority*) may be singular or plural depending on the words they represent. In your sentence *proportion* represents *voters*, which is plural. Therefore, use the plural verb *were*.

QUESTION Is *every day* one word or two in this case? *We encounter these problems every day.*

ANSWER In your sentence it is two words. When it means "ordinary," it is one word (*she wears everyday clothes to work*). If you can insert the word *single* between *every* and *day* without altering your meaning, you should be using two words.

NAME ______________________________

6 REINFORCEMENT EXERCISES

A. (Self-check) Select the correct word to complete each sentence below. Write it in the space provided.

1. Everyone except those three employees (was, were) at the meeting. ________
2. (Has, Have) any of your grant applications been approved? ________
3. Preparing the dinner for the awards banquet (is, are) gourmet chefs from around the world. ________
4. Wallace Publishers (is, are) offering a discount on its Web design series of books. ________
5. A group of technicians (was, were) challenged by the problem for three days. ________
6. A staff of two managers and three salespeople (is, are) to be added to the company. ________
7. Each of the contracts (requires, require) a signature. ________
8. Many a worker and supervisor (has, have) disagreed over benefits. ________
9. (Everyone, Every one) of our demands was met by management. ________
10. Each member and officer (was, were) required to cast a vote. ________
11. Part of his losses (was, were) caused by poor management. ________
12. Did they tell you it is he who (is, are) to be laid off this summer? ________
13. A number of issues (is, are) still open for discussion. ________
14. Leslie is the only one of the engineers who (has, have) filed a report. ________
15. About one third of the documents (is, are) available on the company Web site. ________

Check your answers below.

B. For each of the following sentences, circle the sentence subject. Then, cross out any phrases that separate the verb from its subject. Choose the correct verb and write it in the space provided.

EXAMPLE: Our manager, ~~along with her staff,~~ (is, are) available to meet with us. ____is____

EXAMPLE: Our catalog ~~of gift ideas~~ (is, are) being sent to you. ____is____

1. A sound education, along with several years of experience (is, are) necessary for this position. ________
2. The range of prices for these models, (make, makes) it difficult to fill telephone orders. ________
3. All participants except Marcus (has, have) submitted their expense statements. ________
4. Only one of the many candidates (has, have) taken a position on that issue. ________
5. One of your duties, in addition to the tasks already described, (is, are) the budgeting of funds for both departments. ________

1. was, 2. Have, 3. are, 4. is, 5. was, 6. is, 7. requires, 8. has, 9. Every one, 10. was, 11. were, 12. is, 13. are, 14. has, 15. are.

C. Select the correct verb and write it in the space provided.

1. Here (is, are) the keys to your new office. ______________
2. Outside of Phoenix (is, are) several new office complexes. ______________
3. Our governor, along with top congressional leaders, (is, are) protesting the budget cuts. ______________
4. General Motors (is, are) offering a substantial rebate on last year's models. ______________
5. Sitting at that table (is, are) both award recipients. ______________
6. Redfern and Sons (is, are) this town's oldest manufacturing firm. ______________
7. Considerable time and money (was, were) spent on the plans. ______________
8. How essential (is, are) experience and education in this field? ______________
9. Neither Brad nor Janet (is, are) able to attend our meeting. ______________
10. (Everyone, Every one) of our staff members was able to attend the training seminar. ______________
11. Either the owner or her partners (is, are) responsible for the taxes. ______________
12. Our staff of counselors, therapists, and mediators (is, are) here to help solve the grievance. ______________
13. Either of those candidates (is, are) equally qualified. ______________
14. In the first-class section (was, were) all the employees of the airline. ______________
15. Either of the Web site designs (is, are) acceptable for our purposes. ______________
16. A calendar showing all the proposed events (is, are) available from the receptionist. ______________
17. Both a written report and an oral presentation (is, are) required for this proposal. ______________
18. Any one of the employees (has, have) the right to see the records. ______________
19. Seventy pounds (is, are) the limit for a package shipped by UPS. ______________
20. The Marriott was the only one of the hotels in the area that (was, were) available. ______________
21. (Is, Are) either of the clients satisfied with our campaign? ______________
22. A portion of the contributions (goes, go) to the American Red Cross. ______________
23. Attending the convention (is, are) a delegation from South Carolina. ______________
24. Neither the employees nor their manager (wants, want) an investigation. ______________
25. Supplying our office with temporary personnel (is, are) a company with a solid reputation. ______________
26. Clark, Widman, and McCollum, with offices in Macon and Atlanta, (has, have) been our law firm for years. ______________
27. One of the representatives, in addition to several members of her staff, (has, have) been charged with fraud. ______________
28. Mr. Broom is one of those accountants who (has, have) earned the respect of his clients. ______________
29. There (is, are) many firms we can use to design our new Web site. ______________
30. To take night classes while working (is, are) challenging. ______________

7 Verbals

OBJECTIVES When you have completed the materials in this chapter, you will be able to do the following:

- Recognize gerunds and supply appropriate modifiers of gerunds.
- Identify and remedy split infinitives that result in awkward sentences.
- Correctly punctuate introductory and other verbal phrases.
- Avoid writing awkward participial phrases.
- Spot dangling verbal phrases and other misplaced modifiers.
- Rewrite sentences to avoid misplaced verbal phrases and modifiers.

As you learned earlier, English is a highly flexible language in which a given word may have more than one grammatical function. In this chapter you will study verbals. Derived from verbs, *verbals* are words that function as nouns, adjectives, or adverbs. Three kinds of verbals are gerunds (verbal nouns), infinitives, and participles (verbal adjectives).

GERUNDS

A verb form ending in *ing* and used as a noun is called a *gerund.*

> *Advertising* is necessary. (Gerund used as the subject.)
> Amarjit enjoys *computing.* (Gerund used as the direct object.)

Using Gerunds Correctly

STUDY TIP

To distinguish between *ing* forms used as nouns and those used as adjectives, try the *what*? question approach. In the sentence *I admired Sara's programming*, say to yourself, "I admired what?" Answer: "I admired Sara's *programming*, not Sara." Therefore, *programming* is the object and functions as an *ing* noun.

In using gerunds, follow this rule: Make any noun or pronoun modifying a gerund possessive, as in *Karen's keyboarding* or *Dale's computing*. Because we sometimes fail to recognize gerunds as nouns, we fail to make their modifiers possessive:

> WRONG: The staff objects to *Kevin smoking.*
> RIGHT: The staff objects to *Kevin's smoking.*

The staff does not object to Kevin, as the first version states; it objects to his smoking. If we substitute a more easily recognized noun for *smoking*, the possessive form seems more natural: *The staff objects to Kevin's behavior. Behavior* is a noun, just as *smoking* is a noun; the noun or pronoun modifiers of both must be possessive.

> The manager appreciated *his* working late. (The gerund *working* requires the possessive pronoun *his*, not the objective case pronoun *him*.)
> I resent *your complaining* to my boss. (Not *you complaining*.)

SPOT THE BLOOPER

From a notice to holders of Exxon credit cards: "We appreciate you choosing Exxon . . ."

Not all verbs ending in *ing* are, of course, gerunds. Some are elements in verb phrases and some act as adjectives. Compare these three sentences:

> I saw Kelli programming. (The word *programming* functions as an adjective describing Kelli.)
>
> I admired Kelli's programming. (As the object of the verb, *programming* acts as a gerund.)
>
> Kelli is programming. (Here is *programming* is a verb phrase.)

INFINITIVES

When the present form of a verb is preceded by *to*, the most basic verb form results: the *infinitive*. The sign of the infinitive is the word *to*.

> She tried *to follow* your instructions exactly.
>
> *To write* effectively requires great skill.

Using Infinitives Correctly

SPOT THE BLOOPER

Headline from *The Urbana* [OH] *Daily Citizen*: "Volunteers Use Sandbags to Try and Save Water Plant." (What's wrong with using *and*?)

In certain expressions infinitives may be misused. Observe the use of the word *to* in the following infinitive phrases. Do not substitute the conjunction *and* for the *to* of the infinitive.

> Try *to call* when you arrive. (Not *try and call.*)
>
> Be sure *to put* your initials on the letter. (Not *be sure and put.*)
>
> Check *to see* when the flight is due to arrive. (Not *check and see.*)

When any word appears between *to* and the verb (*to* carefully *prepare*), an infinitive is said to be split. At one time split infinitives were considered great grammatical sins. Today most authorities agree that infinitives may be split if necessary for clarity and effect. Avoid, however, split infinitives that result in awkward sentences.

AWKWARD:	Mr. Stokes wanted *to*, if he could find time, *recheck* his figures.
BETTER:	If he could find time, Mr. Stokes wanted *to recheck* his figures.
AWKWARD:	Our manager had *to*, when budget cuts were announced, *lay off* several salespeople.
BETTER:	When budget cuts were announced, our manager had *to lay off* several salespeople.
ACCEPTABLE:	*To* honestly *state* the facts is the job of the prosecutor. (No awkwardness results from split infinitive.)
ACCEPTABLE:	Ms. Gomez expects you *to* really *work* hard. (No awkwardness results from split infinitive.)

PARTICIPLES

You have already studied the present and past forms of participles functioning as parts of verb phrases. You will recall that in such constructions present and past participles always require helping verbs: *is working, was seen, had broken.*

In this chapter we are concerned with a second possible function of participles. Participles can function as adjectives. As adjectives, participles modify nouns or pronouns, and they do not require helping verbs.

Participles used as adjectives have three tenses and two voices:

	PRESENT TENSE	PAST TENSE	PERFECT TENSE
ACTIVE VOICE:	selling	sold	having sold
PASSIVE VOICE:	being sold	sold	having been sold

A participle in the present tense is used to show additional action occurring at the time of the action expressed by the main verb in the sentence (such main verbs may be present, past, or future).

> The company *is recruiting* applicants on the Web. (Present participle.)

A participle in the past or perfect tense is used to show other action completed *before* the action expressed by the main verb in the sentence.

> *Having completed* the interview, Gary felt relief. (Perfect participle used to show action completed prior to action of main verb *felt*.)
>
> The *broken* chair had to be discarded. (Past participle shows that the chair was broken before it was discarded.)

Using Participles Correctly

Avoid using participial phrases that sound awkward, such as these:

AWKWARD:	Brian's having been absent was a coincidence.
BETTER:	Brian's absence was a coincidence.
AWKWARD:	Being as you live nearby, should we carpool?
BETTER:	Since you live nearby, should we carpool?

PUNCTUATING VERBAL FORMS

Determining whether verbal forms require commas often causes difficulty. Let's try to clear up this difficulty with explanations and examples.

Punctuating Introductory Verbal Forms

SPOT THE BLOOPER

From *Country Collectibles*: "Sitting by a blazing fire, reading a good mystery novel, a dog can jump into your lap and beg for a few playful pats on the head."

When verbal forms are used in introductory words or expressions, there's no question about punctuating them. A comma should be placed between an introductory verbal form and the main clause of a sentence.

> *Amazed*, we wanted to hear her explanation. (Introductory verbal form.)
>
> *To increase productivity*, our manager hired a management consultant. (Introductory verbal phrase.)
>
> *Filing the correspondence*, Andy found the lost Harrison papers. (Introductory verbal phrase.)
>
> *Completing forty-three years*, Lynn Reynolds retired. (Introductory verbal phrase.)

Not all verbal phrases that begin sentences, however, are considered introductory. If the verbal phrase represents the subject or part of the predicate of the sentence, *no* comma should separate it from the rest of the sentence.

STUDY TIP

To help you understand the use of commas in dealing with nonessential (nonrestrictive) information, think of a window shade. Use commas to lower the window shade and cover the words enclosed. If words in a verbal phrase are not essential to the meaning of a sentence, use a "comma window shade" to obscure them.

> *Filing the correspondence* is Andy's responsibility. (Verbal phrase used as subject; no comma.)
>
> *To alter the schedule* at this point would be difficult. (Verbal phrase used as subject; no comma.)
>
> *Offering an incentive* is the best way to motivate workers. (Verbal phrase used as part of predicate; no comma.)

Punctuating Nonessential Verbal Phrases*

Essential (restrictive) information is needed for the reader to understand the sentence. Verbal phrases often help identify the subject. These phrases require no

*Many people find it easier to work with the words *essential* and *nonessential* than with the more traditional grammatical terms *restrictive* and *nonrestrictive*; therefore, the easier terminology is used here.

commas. Nonessential information could be omitted without altering the basic meaning of the sentence; thus, nonessential phrases are set off by commas.

> Ms. Ramirez, *working late at the office*, was able to meet the deadline. (The verbal phrase *working late at the office* adds additional information, but it is not essential. The subject is fully identified by name. Use commas to set off the nonessential phrase.)
>
> The woman *working late at the office* was able to meet the deadline. (In this sentence the verbal phrase *working late at the office* is essential; it is needed to identify the subject. *Which* woman was able to meet the deadline? The woman *working late at the office*. No commas separate this essential verbal phrase.)
>
> Talleyrand Corporation, *offering services in 50 states*, is a leading real estate firm. (The verbal phrase is not essential because there is only one Talleyrand Corporation, and it has been identified. Commas enclose this nonessential verbal phrase.)
>
> A corporation *offering services in 50 states* would be ideal for our needs. (This verbal phrase is essential to identify *which* corporation would be ideal. No commas are needed. *Note:* Even though you pause when you reach the end of the verbal phrase, don't be tempted to add a comma.)

Notice in the preceding sentences that whenever a nonessential verbal phrase interrupts the middle of a sentence, two commas set it off.

AVOIDING MISPLACED VERBAL MODIFIERS

Introductory Verbal Phrases

SPOT THE BLOOPER

From the *Sun Cities* [AZ] *Independent*: "While pumping gas, an unoccupied car rolled into the victim's car."

Introductory verbal phrases must be followed by the words they can logically modify. Such phrases can create confusion or unintended humor when placed incorrectly in a sentence. Consider this sentence: *Sitting in the car, the mountains were breathtaking*. The introductory participial phrase in this sentence is said to *dangle* because it is not followed immediately by a word it can logically modify. The sentence could be improved by revising it to read: *Sitting in the car, we saw the breathtaking mountains*. Observe how the following illogical sentences have been improved:

STUDY TIP

After reading an introductory verbal phrase, ask the question *who*? The answer to that question must immediately follow the introductory phrase. For example, *To find a good job, who?* Answer: *To find a good job, Derek wrote to many companies.*

ILLOGICAL:	Slipping on the stairs, his back was injured.
LOGICAL:	Slipping on the stairs, he injured his back.
ILLOGICAL:	Turning on the fan, papers flew about the office.
LOGICAL:	Turning on the fan, I caused papers to fly about the office.
ILLOGICAL:	To receive a free CD, the enclosed card must be returned.
LOGICAL:	To receive a free CD, you must return the enclosed card.
ILLOGICAL:	Skilled with computers, the personnel director hired Chae Lee.
LOGICAL:	Skilled with computers, Chae Lee was hired by the personnel director.
BUT:	To master the language, listen carefully to native speakers.
	To master the language, (you) listen carefully. (In commands, the understood subject is *you*. Therefore, this sentence is correctly followed by the word to which it refers.)

SPOT THE BLOOPER

From the *Tri-Cities Herald* [Richland, WA]: "He laid there for 23 hours critically injured. . . . After lingering close to death for many days, newspaper reporters were allowed to visit him." [Did you spot two bloopers?]

Verbal Phrases in Other Positions

In other positions within sentences, verbal phrases must also be placed in logical relation to the words they modify.

SPOT THE BLOOPER

From *The Ft. Lauderdale [FL] Sun Sentinel*: "Architect Barry Sugerman of North Miami designed this pergola to divert attention from the garage, which is seen walking up to the house from the motorcourt."

ILLOGICAL: The missing purchase orders were found by Mrs. Seldon's secretary lying in her top desk drawer.

LOGICAL: Mrs. Seldon's secretary found the missing purchase orders lying in her top desk drawer.

ILLOGICAL: Mr. Yoneji returned the envelope and its contents, recognizing his error.

LOGICAL: Mr. Yoneji, recognizing his error, returned the envelope and its contents.

HOTLINE QUERIES

QUESTION Are there two meanings for the word *discreet*?

ANSWER You are probably confusing the two words *discreet* and *discrete*. *Discreet* means "showing good judgment" and "prudent" (*the witness gave a discreet answer, avoiding gossip and hearsay*). The word *discrete* means "separate" or "noncontinuous" (*Alpha, Inc., has installed discrete computers rather than a network computer system*). You might find it helpful to remember that the *e's* are separate in *discrete*.

QUESTION Should I use *complimentary* or *complementary* to describe free tickets?

ANSWER Use *complimentary*, which can mean "containing a compliment, favorable, or free" (*the dinner came with complimentary wine*; *he made a complimentary remark*). *Complementary* means "completing or making perfect" (*the complementary colors enhanced the room*). An easy way to remember *compliment* is by thinking "*I* like to receive a *compliment*."

QUESTION I confuse *i.e.* and *e.g.* What's the difference?

ANSWER The abbreviation *i.e.* stands for the Latin *id est*, meaning "that is" (*the package exceeds the weight limit, i.e., 5 pounds*). Notice the use of a comma after *i.e.* The abbreviation *e.g.* stands for the Latin *exempli gratia*, meaning "for the sake of example" or "for example" (*the manufacturer may offer a purchase incentive, e.g., a rebate or discount plan*).

QUESTION We're having an argument in our office about abbreviations. Can *department* be abbreviated *dep't*? How about *manufacturing* as *mf'g*? Where could we find a correct list of such abbreviations?

ANSWER In informal writing or when space is limited, words may be contracted or abbreviated. If a conventional abbreviation for a word exists, use it instead of a contracted form. Abbreviations are simpler to write and easier to read. For example, use *dept.* instead of *dep't*; use *natl.* instead of *nat'l*; use *cont.* instead of *cont'd*. Other accepted abbreviations are *ins.* for *insurance*; *mfg.* for *manufacturing*; *mgr.* for *manager*; and *mdse.* for *merchandise*. Notice that all abbreviations end with periods. Some dictionaries show abbreviations of words along with their definitions. Other dictionaries alphabetize abbreviations within the main entries, so that a reader must know how to spell an abbreviation in order to be able to locate it. Reference manuals often have lists of abbreviations that are very helpful.

QUESTION I'm not sure which word to use in this sentence: *They have used all (they're, their, there) resources in combating the disease.*

ANSWER Use *their*, which is the possessive form of *they*. The adverb *there* means "at that place or at that point" (*we have been there before*). *There* is also used as an expletive or filler preceding a linking verb (*there are numerous explanations*). *They're* is a contraction of *they* and *are* (*they're coming this afternoon*).

QUESTION In a letter written by my boss, how should we spell *there*: *We do not want an open invoice without there being justifiable reasons.*

ANSWER *There* is spelled correctly, but its use creates an awkward verbal form. If your boss agrees, revise the sentence to read: *We do not want an open invoice without justification.*

QUESTION Which word should I use in this sentence? *Our department will* disburse *or* disperse *the funds shortly.*

ANSWER Use *disburse. Disperse* means to "scatter" or "to distribute" (*information will be dispersed to all divisions*). *Disburse* means to "pay out." Perhaps this memory device will help you keep them straight: associate the *b* in *disburse* with *bank* (*banks dispurse money*).

QUESTION What's the difference between *toward* and *towards*?

ANSWER None. They are interchangeable in use. However, it's more efficient to use the shorter word *toward.*

7 REINFORCEMENT EXERCISES

A. (Self-check) In the following sentences gerunds are italicized. Other *ing* words that are not italicized are not functioning as gerunds. Select appropriate modifiers.

1. We noticed (Evelyn, Evelyn's) *leaving* the office early. ______________

2. Sherry suggested (us, our) *arriving* half an hour early. ______________

3. Can you believe (Katie, Katie's) *missing* the plane? ______________

4. (Him, His) *completing* the assignment surprised us all. ______________

5. We appreciate (you, your) *picking* up our mail last week. ______________

From each of the sets of sentences that follow, select the sentence that is stated in the most logical manner. Write its letter in the space provided.

6. **(a)** To impress his employer, many extra hours were logged. ____
(b) To impress his employer, he logged many extra hours.

7. **(a)** Plunging 1,000 feet into the gorge, we saw Yosemite Falls. ____
(b) Plunging 1,000 feet into the gorge, Yosemite Falls was a beautiful sight.

8. **(a)** To choose the best candidate, you must check references carefully. ____
(b) To choose the best candidate, references must be checked carefully.

9. **(a)** Before approving the proposal, all bids must be received. ____
(b) Before approving the proposal, we must receive all bids.

10. **(a)** In registering the trademark, the inventor must contact the patent office. ____
(b) In registering the trademark, the patent office must be contacted.

11. **(a)** To earn your salary, hard work is essential. ____
(b) To earn your salary, you must work hard.

12. **(a)** Having completed the project, a bonus was given to the entire team. ____
(b) Having completed the project, the entire team was given a bonus.

13. **(a)** After raising the money, Sheryl put it in a safe place. ____
(b) After raising the money, it was put in a safe place.

14. **(a)** To complete the accounting equation, one must add liabilities to equity. ____
(b) To complete the accounting equation, it is necessary to add liabilities to equity.

15. **(a)** To qualify for the certification, a three-part test must be passed. ____
(b) To qualify for the certification, one must pass a three-part test.

Check your answers below.

B. In the following sentences gerunds are italicized. Choose the correct modifier.

1. Our success depends on (you, your) *making* the best investments. ______________

2. (Us, Our) *videotaping* the sales meeting will allow all employees to participate. ______________

3. Do you recommend (me, my) *attending* the briefing? ______________

1. Evelyn, 2. our, 3. Katie's, 4. his, 5. your, 6. b, 7. b, 8. a, 9. b, 10. a, 11. b, 12. b, 13. a, 14. a, 15. b.

4. (Him, His) *declining* the award surprised some of his colleagues. ____________

5. They said (you, your) *printing* of the brochures was excellent. ____________

6. (You, Your) *being* at the workshop is very important to the company. ____________

7. The (person, person's) *submitting* the winning proposal will receive the contract. ____________

8. Did (Marian, Marian's) *explaining* the concept help you to understand? ____________

9. (Him, His) *accepting* the position will depend on the salary. ____________

10. (Me, My) *being* on time for the appointment is very important. ____________

C. From each of the pairs of sentences shown, select the more acceptable version and write its letter in the space provided.

1. **(a)** Christine Bolt was asked to, as soon as possible, develop a Web site. ____
   (b) Christine Bolt was asked to develop a Web site as soon as possible.

2. **(a)** Hurriedly, Vicente Aguilar began to scan his e-mail messages. ____
   (b) Vicente Aguilar began to hurriedly scan his e-mail messages.

3. **(a)** Be sure and stop by our booth at the trade show. ____
   (b) Be sure to stop by our booth at the trade show.

4. **(a)** We wondered about his ordering so few office supplies. ____
   (b) We wondered about him ordering so few office supplies.

5. **(a)** The administrative assistant started to, as the deadline approached, check the names and addresses. ____
   (b) As the deadline approached, the administrative assistant started to check the names and addresses.

6. **(a)** Try to find when the meeting is scheduled. ____
   (b) Try and find when the meeting is scheduled.

7. **(a)** I think their being present at the hearing is crucial. ____
   (b) I think them being present at the hearing is crucial.

8. **(a)** Please check to see whether the contract is ready. ____
   (b) Please check and see whether the contract is ready.

9. **(a)** You may wish to, if you have time, contact your broker. ____
   (b) You may wish to contact your broker if you have time.

10. **(a)** The travel agent recommends us arriving one hour before the flight. ____
    (b) The travel agent recommends our arriving one hour before the flight.

D. Selected verbal words and phrases have been italicized in the following sentences. Insert commas if needed. In the space provided at the right, write the number of commas that you insert for each sentence. If no commas are added, write *0*.

EXAMPLE: *To complete the report before the deadline*, we worked late. 1

1. *To further the cause of medicine* he donated his body to science. ____

2. *Providing housing to people in need* is the mission of Habitat for Humanity. ____

3. *Accepting ABC's offer to co-anchor the evening news* Barbara Walters became the first anchorwoman in network television. ____

4. *Startled* Bridget dropped her papers when the alarm sounded. ____

5. *Working in another office* are the paralegals who specialize in contracts. ____

6. *Founding International Business Machines* was Thomas Watson's claim to fame. ______
7. *To improve the writing of government employees* consultants were hired. ______
8. *Fearing detection* the embezzler could never take a day off. ______
9. *Beginning as a sole proprietor* H. J. Heinz eventually built a large corporation. ______
10. *Breaking down a job cycle into separate units of work* is the first task in a time-and-motion study. ______
11. *Hoping to increase sales* the company began selling its product on the Web. ______
12. *Confused by the instructions* Darrell asked for help to download the software. ______
13. *Writing a weekly news column* left Lisa little time for exercise. ______
14. *Sweating and panting* the attorney ran into the courtroom late for the trial. ______
15. *Convincing her boss to adopt her idea* is the hardest task she has ever faced. ______

E. Selected verbal phrases have been italicized in the following sentences. Insert commas if the phrases are nonessential. In the space provided, write the number of commas that you insert for each sentence. If no commas are added, write *0*.

1. Darshan Kaur *recently assigned to this project* will share in the completion bonus. ______
2. Employees *participating in our profit-sharing plan* will benefit from the stock split. ______
3. Terri *hoping for a position in marketing* left her job in the sales department. ______
4. Anyone *seeking a promotion* should consider taking technical courses. ______
5. Those employees *expecting a raise* will have to work extra hours. ______

F. If needed, insert commas to punctuate verbal forms in the following sentences. In the space provided, indicate the number of commas added. If no commas are added, write *0*.

1. To work efficiently employees need the correct tools. ______
2. Anyone possessing the necessary skills may apply for the position. ______
3. Our CEO facing another year of intense pressure resigned her post. ______
4. All employees interested in improving their jobs skills are invited to attend the in-service programs. ______
5. General Motors facing unexpected competition from foreign suppliers decided to close the small fabrication plant. ______

NAME ______________________________

UNIT 2 REVIEW ■ Chapters 5–7 (Self-Check)

Begin your review by rereading Chapters 5–7. Then test your comprehension of those chapters by completing the exercises that follow. Compare your responses with those at the end of the review.

In the blank provided, write the letter of the word or phrase that correctly completes each of the following sentences.

1. Is there any possibility of (a) Laura, (b) Laura's making payment in the next two days? _____

2. Here (a) is, (b) are my proposal for recycling paper and aluminum in the office. _____

3. Our list of customer names and addresses (a) has, (b) have to be updated before the next mailing. _____

4. The president, together with her entire staff of employees, (a) hope, (b) hopes to resolve the budget problems before the next quarter. _____

5. The president and her entire staff (a) hope, (b) hopes to resolve the budget problems before the next quarter. _____

6. Be sure (a) to record, (b) and record all your trip expenses. _____

7. Wilson, Rivers, and Watson, Inc., (a) is, (b) are hiring new employees. _____

8. I certainly appreciate (a) you, (b) your answering my e-mail while I was gone. _____

9. A complete inventory of all merchandise (a) is, (b) are necessary before we close the books. _____

10. When converting a verb from the passive to the active voice, the writer must make the doer of the action the (a) subject, (b) object of the active voice verb. _____

11. In the sentence *Two mistakes were made in our order*, the verb is in the (a) active, (b) passive voice. _____

12. In the sentence *The chairperson called the meeting to order*, the verb is in the (a) active, (b) passive voice. _____

13. Their newspapers have (a) laid, (b) lain, (c) lay in the break room for the past two weeks. _____

14. Everyone ignores that car's alarm because it has (a) rang, (b) rung too often in the past. _____

15. The purse (a) lying, (b) laying on the floor apparently was left by a customer. _____

16. Neither the owner nor the renters (a) is, (b) are willing to pay the damages. _____

17. Do you know if (a) anyone, (b) any one of the part-time employees is able to work Saturday night? _____

Insert commas where necessary in the next group of sentences. Indicate the number of commas that you added. Write *0* for none.

18. Parking close to the building Carolyn was able to carry the boxes inside without help. _____

19. Accessing thousands of customer files became much easier when we installed an electronic database. _____

20. Jeremy and Lisa working late to complete their brief ordered pizza at 11 p.m. _____

In the blank provided, write the letter of the word or phrase that correctly completes each sentence.

21. Many of our clients (a) is, (b) are from out of the country. _____

22. Somebody (a) is, (b) are responsible for the conflict in the agenda. ____

23. A number of employees (a) has, (b) have complained about drug testing. ____

24. Did you know it is you who (a) is, (b) are presenting at the sales meeting? ____

25. Only one third of the stockholders (a) has, (b) have voted thus far. ____

26. He is one of those people who always (a) keep, (b) keeps a clean desk. ____

Hotline Review

27. One of the (a) principal, (b) principle reasons for becoming a hotel manager is the possibility of a pleasant working environment. ____

28. These new taxes will negatively (a) effect, (b) affect small businesses. ____

29. The president was (a) all together, (b) altogether pleased with the vote of Congress. ____

30. Robert Cannon was quite (a) complementary, (b) complimentary in discussing the other team members. ____

1. b, 2. a, 3. a, 4. b, 5. a, 6. a, 7. a, 8. b, 9. a, 10. a, 11. b, 12. a, 13. b, 14. b, 15. a, 16. b, 17. b, 18. 1, 19. 0, 20. 2, 21. b, 22. a, 23. b, 24. b, 25. b, 26. a, 27. a, 28. b, 29. b, 30. b.

UNIT 3

Modifying and Connecting Words

8 Modifiers: Adjectives and Adverbs

OBJECTIVES When you have completed the materials in this chapter, you will be able to do the following:

- Form the comparative and superlative degrees of regular and irregular adjectives and adverbs.
- Use articles correctly and avoid double negatives.
- Use adjectives after linking verbs and use adverbs to modify verbs, adjectives, and other adverbs.
- Punctuate compound and successive independent adjectives correctly.
- Compare degrees of absolute adjectives and make comparisons within a group.
- Place adverbs and adjectives close to the words they modify.

SPOT THE BLOOPER

Headline in Florida newspaper: "MAN EATING PI-RANHA SOLD AS PET FISH" (How does a missing hyphen alter the meaning?)

Both adjectives and adverbs act as modifiers; that is, they describe or limit other words. Since many of the forms and functions of adjectives and adverbs are similar and since faulty usage often results from the confusion of these two parts of speech, adjectives and adverbs will be treated together in this chapter.

BASIC FUNCTIONS OF ADJECTIVES AND ADVERBS

NOTABLE QUOTABLE

"The difference between the almost-right word and the right word is . . . [like] the difference between the lightning bug and the lightning."
—Mark Twain

Adjectives describe or limit nouns and pronouns. They often answer the questions *what kind? how many?* or *which one?* Adjectives in the following sentences are italicized.

> *Short* meetings are *the best* meetings.
> *Large government* grants were awarded to *the eight top* institutions.

Adverbs describe or limit verbs, adjectives, or other adverbs. They often answer the questions *when? how? where?* or *to what extent?*

> *Today* we left work *early.*
> He answered *quite decisively.*

Comparative and Superlative Forms

Most adjectives and adverbs have three forms, or degrees: positive, comparative, and superlative. The following examples illustrate how the comparative and superlative degrees of regular adjectives and adverbs are formed.

	POSITIVE	COMPARATIVE	SUPERLATIVE
ADJECTIVE:	warm	warmer	warmest
ADVERB:	warmly	more warmly	most warmly
ADJECTIVE:	careful	more careful	most careful
ADVERB:	carefully	more carefully	most carefully

SPOT THE BLOOPER

ABC-TV anchor, quoted in *The San Jose Mercury News*: "They're a lot smarter and a lot savvier in the way they're handling the press now, which means we'll have to be even smarter and a lot more savvier ourselves."

The positive degree of an adjective or an adverb is used in merely describing or in limiting another word. The comparative degree is used to compare two persons or things. The superlative degree is used in the comparison of three or more persons or things.

The comparative degree of short adjectives (nearly all one-syllable and most two-syllable adjectives ending in *y*) is formed by adding *r* or *er* (*warmer*). The superlative degree of short adjectives is formed by the addition of *st* or *est* (*warmest*). Long adjectives, and those difficult to pronounce, form the comparative and superlative degrees, as do adverbs, with the addition of *more* and *most* (*more careful, most beautiful*). The following sentences illustrate degrees of comparison for adjectives and adverbs.

ADJECTIVES:	Sales are unusually *high*.	(Positive degree)
	Sales are *higher* than ever before.	(Comparative degree)
	Sales are the *highest* in years.	(Superlative degree)
ADVERBS:	He works *quickly*.	(Positive degree)
	He works *more quickly* than his partner.	(Comparative degree)
	He works *most quickly* under pressure.	(Superlative degree)

SPOT THE BLOOPER

From an editorial in *U.S. News & World Report*: "Of two interpretations of conduct, they prefer the worst."

Do not create a double comparative form by using *more* and the suffix *er* together (such as *more neater*) or by using *most* and the suffix *est* together (such as *most fastest*).

A few adjectives and adverbs form the comparative and superlative degrees irregularly. Some common irregular adjectives are *good* (*better, best*); *bad* (*worse, worst*); and *little* (*less, least*). Some common irregular adverbs are *well* (*better, best*); *many* (*more, most*); and *much* (*more, most*).

MODIFIERS THAT DESERVE SPECIAL ATTENTION

Adjectives as Articles

STUDY TIP

The sound, not the spelling, of a word governs the choice between *a* and *an*. When the letter *u* sounds like a *y*, it is treated as a consonant: a *u*tility, a *u*sed car.

The articles *a*, *an*, and *the* merit special attention. When describing a specific person or thing, use the article *the*, as in *the firm*. When describing persons or things in general, use *a* or *an*, as in *a firm* (meaning *any firm*). The choice of *a* or *an* is determined by the initial sound of the word modified. *A* is used before consonant sounds; *an* is used before vowel sounds.

BEFORE VOWEL SOUNDS		BEFORE CONSONANT SOUNDS	
an operator an executive		a printer a plan	
an hour an honor	*h* is not voiced; vowel is heard	a hook a hole	*h* is voiced
an office an opinion	*o* sounds like a vowel	a one-year contract a one-week trip	*o* sounds like the consonant *w*
an urgent request an undertaking	*u* sounds like a vowel	a union a unit	*u* sounds like the consonant *y*
an X-ray an M.D.	*x* and *m* sound like vowels		

SPOT THE BLOOPER

From a Citibank brochure: "Your Citibank card will only access your checking account for these type purchases."

The Adjectives *this/that* and *these/those*

The adjective *this*, and its plural form *these*, indicates something nearby. The adjective *that*, and its plural form *those*, indicates something at a distance. Be careful to use the singular forms of these words with singular nouns and the plural forms with plural nouns: *this company, that presentation, these accounts, those records.* Pay special attention to the nouns *kind, type,* and *sort.* Match singular adjectives to the singular forms of these nouns (for example, *this kind* of question, *that sort* of person; but *these kinds* of questions, *those sorts* of people).

PROBLEMS WITH ADJECTIVES AND ADVERBS

Confusion of Adjectives and Adverbs

Because they are closely related, adjectives are sometimes confused with adverbs. Here are guidelines that will help you avoid common adjective–adverb errors.

SPOT THE BLOOPER

From the *Daily News Tribune* [Tempe, AZ]: "People with 'week' wills can lose weight easy."

- Use adjectives to modify nouns and pronouns. Note particularly that adjectives (not adverbs) should follow linking verbs.
- Use adjectives to modify nouns and pronouns. Note particularly that adjectives (not adverbs) should follow linking verbs.

  This pasta tastes *delicious.* (Not *deliciously.*)
  I feel *bad* about the loss. (Not *badly.*)
  He looks *good* in his uniform. (Not *well.*)

STUDY TIP

The misuse of *badly* for *bad* is one of the most frequent errors made by educated persons. Following the linking verb *feel*, use the adjective *bad*, not the adverb *badly*.

- Use adverbs to describe verbs, adjectives, or other adverbs.

  The engine runs *smoothly.* (Not *smooth.*)
  It runs *more smoothly* than before. (Not *smoother.*)
  Listen *carefully* to the directions. (Not *careful.*)
  Time passes *quickly.* (Not *quick.*)

It should be noted that a few adverbs have two acceptable forms: *slow, slowly; deep, deeply; direct, directly;* and *close, closely.*

Drive *slowly.* (Or, less formally, *slow.*)
You may dial us *directly.* (Or, less formally, *direct.*)

Compound Adjectives

Writers may form their own adjectives by joining two or more words. When these words act as a single modifier preceding a noun, they are temporarily hyphenated. If these same words appear after a noun, they are generally not hyphenated.

Words Temporarily Hyphenated Before a Noun	Same Words Not Hyphenated After a Noun
never-say-die attitude	attitude of never say die
eight-story building	building of eight stories
state-sponsored program	program that is state sponsored
a case-by-case analysis	analysis that is case by case
high-performance computer	computer that has high performance
income-related expenses	expenses that are income related
government-subsidized loan	loan that is government subsidized
home-based business	business that is based at home

SPOT THE BLOOPER

Headline in *The Milwaukee Sentinel*: "Police killing suspect to be tried as an adult." [What unintended meaning resulted from the omission of a hyphen?]

SPOT THE BLOOPER

Under a photograph in *Science* magazine: "Museum staffer Ed Rodley checks out 65 million year-old eggs." (How does the missing hyphen alter the meaning?)

Compound adjectives shown in your dictionary with hyphens are considered permanently hyphenated. Regardless of whether the compound appears before or after a noun, it retains the hyphens. Use a current dictionary to determine what expressions are always hyphenated. Be sure that you find the dictionary entry that is marked *adjective.* Here are samples:

Permanent Hyphens Before Nouns	Permanent Hyphens After Nouns
first-class seats	seats that are first-class
up-to-date information	information that is up-to-date
old-fashioned attitude	attitude that is old-fashioned
short-term goals	goals that are short-term
well-known expert	expert who is well-known
out-of-pocket expenses	expenses that are out-of-pocket

Don't confuse adverbs ending in *ly* with compound adjectives: *newly appointed judge* and *highly regarded entrepreneur* would not be hyphenated.

As compound adjectives become more familiar, they are often simplified and the hyphen is dropped. Some familiar compounds that are not hyphenated are *high school student, charge account balance, income tax refund, home office equipment,* and *data processing center.*

Independent Adjectives

STUDY TIP

To determine whether successive adjectives are independent, mentally insert the word *and* between them. If the insertion makes sense, the adjectives are probably independent and require a comma.

Two or more successive adjectives that independently modify a noun are separated by commas. No comma is needed, however, when the first adjective modifies the combined idea of the second adjective and the noun.

Two Adjectives Independently Modifying a Noun	First Adjective Modifying a Second Adjective Plus a Noun
productive, reliable employee	efficient administrative assistant
economical, efficient car	blue sports car
stimulating, provocative book	assistant deputy director

Special Cases

The following adjectives and adverbs cause difficulty for some writers and speakers. With a little study, you can master their correct usage.

almost (adv.—nearly): *Almost* (not *Most*) everybody wants to work.
most (adj.—greatest in amount): *Most* people want to work.
farther (adv.—actual distance): How much *farther* is the airport?
further (adv.—additionally): Let's discuss the issue *further.*
sure (adj.—certain): She is *sure* of her decision.
surely (adv.—undoubtedly): He will *surely* be chosen for the position.
later (adv.—after expected time): The contract arrived *later* in the day.
latter (adj.—the second of two things): Of the two options, I prefer the *latter.*
fewer (adj.—refers to numbers): *Fewer* than 50 people applied for the position.
less (adj.—refers to amounts or quantities): *Less* time remains than we anticipated.
real (adj.—actual, genuine): The *real* power in the company lies with the board of directors.
really (adv.—actually, truly): Jan wondered if she could *really* learn to operate the equipment in five hours.
good (adj.—desirable): A number of *good* plans were submitted.
well { (adv.—satisfactorily): Jeff did *well* on his evaluation.
(adj.—healthy): Jamal feels *well* enough to go back to work.

OTHER USES OF ADJECTIVES AND ADVERBS

Absolute Modifiers

SPOT THE BLOOPER

Advertisement in a national magazine: "Quaker Oats is one of nature's most perfect foods."

Adjectives and adverbs that name perfect or complete (absolute) qualities cannot logically be compared. For example, to say that one ball is more *round* than another ball is illogical. Here are some absolute words that should not be used in comparisons.

round	dead	complete
perfect	true	right
unique	correct	straight
perpendicular	endless	unanimous

Authorities suggest, however, that some absolute adjectives may be compared by the use of the words *more nearly* or *most nearly.*

Ron's account of the disagreement was *more nearly accurate* than Sue's version. (Not *more accurate.*)
Kris's project is *more nearly complete* than mine (Not *more complete.*)

Comparisons Within a Group

SPOT THE BLOOPER

From a radio commercial for The Club, a device to prevent auto theft: "The Club works where other cheap imitations fail." [Does this statement say that The Club is a cheap imitation?]

When the word *than* is used to compare a person, place, or thing with other members of a group to which it belongs, be certain to include the words *other* or *else* in the comparison. This inclusion ensures that the person or thing being compared is separated from the group with which it is compared.

ILLOGICAL: Alaska is larger than any state in the U.S. (This sentence suggests that Alaska is larger than itself.)
LOGICAL: Alaska is larger than any *other* state in the U.S.
ILLOGICAL: Our team had better results than any team in the company.
LOGICAL: Our team had better results than any *other* team in the company.
ILLOGICAL: Alex works harder than anyone in the office.
LOGICAL: Alex works harder than anyone *else* in the office.

Placing Adverbs and Adjectives

NOTABLE QUOTABLE

"A determined person is one who, when he or she gets to the end of the rope, ties a knot and hangs on."
—Joe L. Griffith

The position of an adverb or adjective can seriously affect the meaning of a sentence. Study these examples.

Only Mike Mixon can change the password. (No one else can change it.)
Mike Mixon can *only* change the password. (He can't do anything else to it.)
Mike Mixon can change *only* the password. (He can't change anything else.)

To avoid confusion, adverbs and adjectives should be placed close to the words they modify. In this regard, special attention should be given to the words *only, merely, first,* and *last.*

CONFUSING: He *merely* said that the report could be improved.
CLEAR: He said *merely* that the report could be improved.
CONFUSING: Seats in the five *first* rows have been reserved.
CLEAR: Seats in the *first* five rows have been reserved.

HOTLINE QUERIES

QUESTION One of my favorite words is *hopefully*, but I understand that it's often used improperly. How should it be used?

ANSWER Language purists insist that the word *hopefully* be used to modify a verb (*We looked at the door hopefully, expecting Mr. Guerrero to return momentarily*). The word *hopefully* should not be used as a substitute for *I hope that* or *We hope that*. Instead of saying *Hopefully, interest rates will decline*, one should say *I hope that interest rates will decline.*

QUESTION Is it necessary to hyphenate a *25 percent* discount?

ANSWER No. Percents are not treated in the same way that numbers appearing in compound adjectives are treated. Thus, you would not hyphenate a *15 percent* loan, but you would hyphenate a *15-year* loan.

QUESTION Should hyphens be used in *a point-by-point analysis?*

ANSWER Yes. When words are combined in order to create a single adjective preceding a noun, these words are temporarily hyphenated (*last-minute decision, two-semester course, step-by-step procedures*).

QUESTION In my writing I want to use *firstly* and *secondly*. Are they acceptable?

ANSWER Both words are acceptable, but most good writers prefer *first* and *second*, because they are more efficient and equally accurate.

QUESTION How many hyphens should I use in this sentence? *The three, four, and five year plans continue to be funded.*

ANSWER Three hyphens are needed: *three-, four-, and five-year plans.* Hyphenate compound adjectives even when the parts of the compound are separated or suspended.

QUESTION Why can't I remember how to spell *already*? I want to use it in this sentence: *Your account has <u>already</u> been credited with your payment.*

ANSWER You—and many others—have difficulty with *already* because two different words (and meanings) are expressed by essentially the same sounds. The adverb *already* means "previously" or "before this time," as in your sentence. The two-word combination *all ready* means "all prepared," as in *The club members are all ready to board the bus.* If you can logically insert the word *completely* between *all* and *ready*, you know the two-word combination is needed.

QUESTION I never know how to write *part time.* Is it always hyphenated?

ANSWER The dictionary shows all of its uses to be hyphenated. *She was a part-time employee* (used as adjective). *He worked part-time* (used as adverb).

QUESTION Here are some expressions that caused us trouble in our business letters. We want to hyphenate all of the following. Right? *Well-produced play, awareness-generation film, decision-making tables, one-paragraph note, swearing-in ceremony, commonly-used book.*

ANSWER All your hyphenated forms are correct except the last one. Don't use a hyphen with an *ly*-ending adverb.

QUESTION Why are these two expressions treated differently: *two-week* vacation and *two weeks'* vacation?

ANSWER Although they express the same idea, they represent two different styles. If you omit the *s*, *two-week* is hyphenated because it is a compound adjective. If you add the *s*, as in *two weeks' vacation*, the expression becomes possessive and requires an apostrophe. Don't use both styles together (not *two-weeks' vacation*).

QUESTION Help! How do I write *fax*? Small letters? Capital letters? Periods? And is it proper to use it as a verb, such as *May we fax the material to you*?

ANSWER The shortened form of *facsimile* is *fax*, written in small letters without periods. Yes, it may be used as a verb, as you did in your sentence.

QUESTION How should I address a person who signed a letter *J. R. Henderson*? I'm not sure of the gender.

ANSWER Use *Dear J. R. Henderson*.

QUESTION I work in an office where we frequently send letters addressed to people on a first-name basis. Should I use a comma or a colon after a salutation like *Dear Chip*?

ANSWER The content of the letter, not the salutation (greeting), determines the punctuation after the salutation. If the letter is a business letter, always use a colon. If the letter is totally personal, a comma may be used, although a colon would also be appropriate.

QUESTION This sentence doesn't sound right to me, but I can't decide how to improve it: *The reason I'm applying is because I enjoy accounting.*

ANSWER The problem lies in this construction: *the reason . . . is because . . . .* Only nouns, pronouns, or adjectives may act as complements following linking verbs. In your sentence an adverbial clause follows the linking verb and sounds awkward. One way to improve the sentence is to substitute a noun clause beginning with *that*: *The reason I'm applying is that I enjoy accounting.* An even better way to improve this sentence would be to make it a direct statement: *I'm applying because I enjoy accounting.*

NAME ____________________

8 REINFORCEMENT EXERCISES

A. (Self-check) Select the correct forms.

1. This is the (worse, worst) performance evaluation I have ever received. ______

2. (This, These) type of problem can be avoided with more careful planning. ______

3. Do you think (this, these) pair of pants will be appropriate for the banquet? ______

4. All that is required is (a, an) honest day's work. ______

5. Thursday's debate between Carol and Mitch will determine the (better, best) candidate. ______

6. The airport was (farther, further) away than it appeared on our map. ______

7. A chief operating officer must be concerned with the (day to day, day-to-day) operations of the organization. ______

8. Companies reported (fewer, less) security breaches last year. ______

9. Can you tabulate the survey results (quicker, more quickly) than they? ______

10. I was (sure, surely) glad that you were able to make it to the meeting on time. ______

11. Greg felt (bad, badly) about missing the presentation. ______

12. Of earned and accrued vacation, only the (later, latter) can be taken before one year. ______

13. Leslie looked (calm, calmly) as she approached the podium. ______

14. It only takes (a, an) hour to download and install the new software. ______

15. The board of directors made a (real, really) bad decision. ______

Underline any errors in the following sentences and write their corrected forms in the spaces provided. If a sentence is correct as it is written, write *C*.

EXAMPLE: Our office is in the <u>most square</u> building on the street. **most nearly square**

16. That software developer claims to sell the most perfect browser available. ______

17. Warren Buffett is more famous than any investor in the nation. ______

18. Mark merely said he needed a short break before continuing the meeting. ______

19. The witness's account of the accident sounds more accurate than the victim's. ______

20. New York is larger than any city in the United States. ______

Check your answers below.

B. Select the correct forms.

1. (This, These) kinds of rumors can cause stock prices to plunge. ______

2. The health care industry is growing at (a, an) unusually fast pace. ______

1. worst, 2. This, 3. this, 4. an, 5. better, 6. farther, 7. day-to-day, 8. fewer, 9. more quickly, 10. surely, 11. bad, 12. latter, 13. calm, 14. an, 15. really, 16. most nearly perfect, 17. any other investor, 18. he merely needed or he needed merely, 19. more nearly accurate, 20. any other city.

3. Which of these three ad campaigns do you like (better, best)? ____________

4. Our part of the project ran even (smoother, more smoothly) than we had hoped. ____________

5. Having practiced every day for weeks, they won the debate (easy, easily). ____________

6. Upon (further, farther) examination, our technician discovered several serious problems. ____________

7. She felt (strong, strongly) about living by her principles. ____________

8. The new policy affects new employees (different, differently) from those who have worked here for more than a year. ____________

9. Ellen had (less, fewer) trouble with the task than Scott. ____________

10. Please don't take this criticism (personal, personally). ____________

11. We must look (further, farther) into this matter before making a decision. ____________

12. Do you think you did (good, well) on the performance evaluation? ____________

13. Beverly's work is (more accurate, more nearly accurate) than Marnie's. ____________

14. Our company has sold more computer peripherals than (any company, any other company) in the industry. ____________

15. Barrie (has only one, only has one) class left in her MBA program. ____________

C. Select the correct group of words below. Write its letter in the space provided.

1. **(a)** state-of-the-art equipment **(b)** state of the art equipment ____
2. **(a)** well-documented report **(b)** well documented report ____
3. **(a)** up to date news **(b)** up-to-date news ____
4. **(a)** vehicle that is fully-equipped **(b)** vehicle that is fully equipped ____
5. **(a)** two-year contract **(b)** two year contract ____
6. **(a)** first-class accommodations **(b)** first class accommodations ____
7. **(a)** word-processing program **(b)** word processing program ____
8. **(a)** strong arm tactics **(b)** strong-arm tactics ____
9. **(a)** well-regarded leader **(b)** well regarded leader ____
10. **(a)** highly-recommended candidate **(b)** highly recommended candidate ____

D. Place commas where needed in the following groups of words.

1. red sports car
2. frank honest appraisal
3. concise courteous letter
4. snug cheerful apartment
5. progressive political party
6. economical efficient procedure

E. Review. For each sentence below, underline any error. Then write a corrected form in the space provided.

1. Of those two computers, our office manager thinks the IBM is best for our needs. ____________

2. The express lane is for shoppers with less than ten items. ____________

3. Investors were looking for a Internet company with solid profits. ______________
4. This new program is designed to make calculations more quicker. ______________
5. Did everything go good in your interview? ______________
6. My performance review was better than any review I've had at this company. ______________
7. Our first two attempts at negotiation failed. ______________
8. After the tune-up, the engine runs smoother than before. ______________
9. Alex works harder than anyone in this department. ______________
10. Are you real sure about turning down the job offer? ______________

9

Prepositions

OBJECTIVES When you have completed the materials in this chapter, you will be able to do the following:

- Use objective case pronouns as objects of prepositions.
- Avoid using prepositions in place of verbs and adverbs.
- Use eight troublesome prepositions correctly.
- Omit unnecessary prepositions and retain necessary ones.
- Construct formal sentences that avoid terminal prepositions.
- Recognize those words and constructions requiring specific prepositions (idioms).

Prepositions are connecting words. They show the relationship of a noun or pronoun to another word in a sentence. This chapter reviews the use of objective case pronouns following prepositions. It also focuses on common problems that communicators have with troublesome prepositions. Finally, it presents many words in our language that require specific prepositions (idiomatic expressions) to sound "right."

COMMON USES OF PREPOSITIONS

SPOT THE BLOOPER

Photo caption in *The Tribune* [Greeley, CO]: "West's David Shaw hits the winning shot for he and Tom White."

SPOT THE BLOOPER

From *The New York Times*: ". . . reflecting on the hardships that pupils like she and Lakesha Perry face in Brownsville, Brooklyn . . . ."

In the following list, notice that prepositions may consist of one word or several.

about	below	from	on
according to	beside	in	on account of
after	between	in addition to	over
along with	but	in spite of	to
among	by	into	under
around	during	like	until
at	except	of	upon
before	for	off	with

Fundamental Problems With Prepositions

In even the most casual speech or writing, the following misuses of prepositions should be avoided.

- ***Of* for *have*.** The verb phrases *should have* and *could have* should never be written as *should of* or *could of*. The word *of* is a preposition and cannot be used in verb phrases.

Juan *should have* called first. (Not *should of*.)
He *could have* given some advance notice. (Not *could of*.)

■ ***Off* for *from*.** The preposition *from* should never be replaced by *off* or *off of.*

> Marsha borrowed money *from* him. (Not *off of.*)
> Shannon said she got the book *from* you. (Not *off* or *off of.*)

■ ***To* for *too*.** The preposition *to* means "in a direction toward." Do not use the word *to* in place of the adverb *too*, which means "additionally," "also," or "excessively."

> Dividends are not distributed *to* stockholders unless declared by the directors.
> No dividends were declared because profits were *too* small.
> Contributions of services will be accepted *too.*

You will recall that the word *to* may also be part of an infinitive construction.

> She is learning *to* program the computer.

TROUBLESOME PREPOSITIONS

Be particularly careful to use the following prepositions properly.

■ ***Among, between*.** *Among* is usually used to speak of three or more persons or things; *between* is usually used for two.

> The disagreement was *between* Mohammad Khan and his partner.
> Supplies were distributed *among* the four divisions.

■ ***Beside, besides*.** *Beside* means "next to"; *besides* means "in addition to."

> The woman sitting *beside* me on the plane is the CEO of Hewlett-Packard.
> *Besides* an executive summary, you must write an introduction.

■ ***Except*.** The preposition *except*, meaning "excluding" or "but," is sometimes confused with the verb *accept*, which means "to receive."

> Everyone *except* Laurie Adamski was able to come.
> Did you *accept* the job offer from PeopleSoft?

NOTABLE QUOTABLE

"Anyone who says the days of opportunity are over is copping out."
—Ann Landers

■ ***In, into*.** *In* indicates a position or location. *Into* indicates direction or movement to an interior location.

> The meeting will be held *in* the conference room. (Preposition *in* indicates location.)
> Come *into* my office to see my new monitor. (Preposition *into* indicates movement to an interior location.)

Some constructions may employ *in* as an adverb preceding an infinitive:

> They went *in* to see the manager. (Adverb *in* precedes infinitive *to see.*)

STUDY TIP

Look at the word(s) following *like*. If many words follow, chances are they function as a clause; use *as*, *as if*, or *as though* instead of *like*.

■ ***Like*.** The preposition *like* should be used to introduce a noun or pronoun. Do not use *like* to introduce a clause (a group of words with a subject and a predicate). To introduce clauses, use *as*, *as if*, or *as though*.

> She looks *like* her sister. (*Like* used as a preposition to introduce the object, *her sister.*)
> She looks *as if* she is tired. (*As if* used to introduce the clause *she is tired.*)
> *As* I said in my letter, I have experience in this field. (Do not use *like* to introduce the clause *I said in my letter.*)

NECESSARY PREPOSITIONS

Don't omit those prepositions necessary to clarify a relationship. Be particularly careful when two prepositions modify a single object.

> We have every desire *for* and anticipation *of* an early settlement. (Do not omit *for*.)
> What type *of* certification are you working toward? (Do not omit *of*.)
> Don Foster is unsure *of* where to place the machine. (Do not omit *of*.)
> Benefits are better for exempt employees than *for* nonexempt employees. (Do not omit *for*.)
> When did you graduate *from* college? (Do not omit *from*.)*

UNNECESSARY PREPOSITIONS

SPOT THE BLOOPER

From an Ann Landers column: ". . . [They] might get their eyes opened up." [Is up a needed preposition?]

Omit unnecessary prepositions, particularly the word *of*.

> Leave the package *inside* the door. (Not *inside of*.)
> Both Web sites are useful. (Not *of the Web sites*.)
> All participants must sign a waiver. (Not *of the*.)
> Where is the meeting? (Not *meeting at*.)
> She could not help agreeing. (Rather than *help from*.)
> Keep the paper near the printer. (Not *near to*.)

ENDING A SENTENCE WITH A PREPOSITION

In the past, language authorities warned against ending a sentence (or a clause) with a preposition. In formal writing today most careful authors continue to avoid terminal prepositions. In conversation, however, terminal prepositions are acceptable.

INFORMAL:	What organization is he a member *of*?
FORMAL:	*Of* what organization is he a member?
INFORMAL:	What is your proposal *about*?
FORMAL:	*About* what is your proposal?
INFORMAL:	How many forms did you write *on*?
FORMAL:	*On* how many forms did you write?
INFORMAL:	We don't know whom you spoke *to* when you called.
FORMAL:	We don't know *to* whom you spoke when you called.

IDIOMATIC USE OF PREPOSITIONS

Every language has idioms (word combinations that are peculiar to that language). These combinations have developed through usage and often cannot be explained rationally. A native speaker usually is unaware of idiom usage until a violation jars his or her ear, such as "He is capable *from* (rather than *of*) violence."

The following list shows words that require specific prepositions to denote precise meanings. This group is just a sampling of the large number of English idioms. Consult a dictionary when you are unsure of the correct preposition to use with a particular word.

acquainted with	Are you *acquainted with* our new manager?
addicted to	Jennifer is *addicted to* surfing the Web.

*See the second Hotline Query in this chapter. (Graduate from college.)

adept in	Are you *adept in* programming?
adhere to	All employees must *adhere to* certain personnel policies.
agree to (a proposal)	Can you *agree to* the terms of the contract?
agree with (a person)	I *agree with* you on this issue.
angry at (a thing)	Many employees are *angry at* the change in vacation policy.
angry with (a person)	Are you *angry with* me for being late?
buy from	You may *buy from* any one of several vendors.
capable of	We had no idea he was *capable of* such leadership.
comply with	We must *comply with* governmental regulations.
concur in (an action)	The directors were able to *concur in* a new business plan.
concur with (a person)	Do you *concur with* the vice president in his analysis?
conform to	Your products do not *conform to* our specifications.
contrast with	The angles *contrast with* the curves in that logo design.
correspond to (match)	A company's success *corresponds to* a company's leadership.
correspond with (write)	We *correspond with* our clients regularly.
desire for	The *desire for* success drives many people.
desirous of	Peter Churchill is *desirous of* acquiring Internet stocks.
differ from (things)	How does your calling plan *differ from* Cellular One's?
differ with (person)	I *differ with* you in small points only.
different from (not <u>than</u>)	This product is *different from* the one I ordered.
disagree with	Ron *disagrees with* me on just about everything.
expert in	Tim Murphy is an *expert in* the stock market.
guard against	We must *guard against* complacency.
identical with or to	Our floor plan is *identical with* (or *to*) yours.
independent of	Living alone, the young man was *independent of* his parents.
infer from	I *infer from* your comments that you are dissatisfied.
interest in	Jerry has a great *interest in* Web site design.
negligent of	Pat was *negligent of* the important duties of his position.

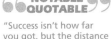

NOTABLE QUOTABLE

"Success isn't how far you got, but the distance you traveled from where you started."
—Peter Frame

SPOT THE BLOOPER

From the *Patriot-Ledger* [Quincy, MA]: "Clemens is able to come off the disabled list Sunday, but tests by Dr. Arthur Pappas led to the conclusion that Clemens' groin is still too weak to pitch in a game."

oblivious of or to	He is often *oblivious of* (or *to*) what goes on around him.
plan to (not <u>on</u>)	We *plan to* expand the marketing of our products.
prefer to	Do you *prefer to* work a four-day week?
reason with	We tried to *reason with* the unhappy customer.
reconcile with (match)	Our expenditures must be *reconciled with* our budget.
reconcile to (accept)	Martin has never become *reconciled to* our decision to discontinue the product line.
responsible for	William is *responsible for* locking the building.
retroactive to	The salary increase is *retroactive to* the first of this year.
sensitive to	Our employer is especially *sensitive to* the needs of employees.
similar to	Your proposal is *similar to* mine.
standing in (not <u>on</u>) line	How long have you been *standing in* line?
talk to (tell something)	Gene will *talk to* us about the reorganization plans.
talk with (exchange remarks)	Let's *talk with* Teresa about our mutual goals.

HOTLINE QUERIES

QUESTION Another employee and I are collaborating on a report. I wanted to write this: *Money was lost due to poor attendance.* She says the sentence should read: *Money was lost because of poor attendance.* My version is more concise. Which of us is right?

ANSWER Most language authorities agree with your coauthor. *Due to* is acceptable when it functions as an adjective, as in *Success was due to proper timing*. In this sense, *due to* is synonymous with *attributable to*. However, when *due to* functions as a preposition, as in your sentence, language experts find fault. Your friend is right; substitute *because of.*

QUESTION What's wrong with saying *Lisa graduated college last year*?

ANSWER The preposition *from* must be inserted for syntactical fluency. Two constructions are permissible: *Lisa graduated from college* or *Lisa was graduated from college.* The first version is more popular; the second is preferred by traditional grammarians.

QUESTION Should *sometime* be one or two words in the following sentence? *Can you come over (some time) soon?*

ANSWER In this sentence you should use the one-word form. *Sometime* means "an indefinite time" (*the convention is sometime in December*). The two-word combination means "a period of time" (*we have some time to spare*).

QUESTION I saw this printed recently: *Some of the personal functions that are being reviewed are job descriptions, job specifications, and job evaluation*. Is *personal* used correctly here?

ANSWER Indeed not! The word *personal* means "private" or "individual" (*your personal letters are being forwarded to you*). The word *personnel* refers to employees (*all company personnel are cordially invited*). The sentence you quote requires *personnel*.

QUESTION Is there any difference between *proved* and *proven*?

ANSWER As a past participle, the verb form *proved* is preferred (*he has proved his point*). However, the word *proven* is preferred as an adjective form (*that company has a proven record*). *Proven* is also commonly used in the expression *not proven*.

QUESTION We're writing a letter to our subscribers, and this sentence doesn't sound right to me: *Every one of our subscribers benefit. . .*

ANSWER As you probably suspected, the verb *benefit* does not agree with the subject *one*. The sentence should read as follows: *Every one of our subscribers benefits. . . .* Don't let intervening phrases obscure the true subject of a sentence.

QUESTION In my dictionary I found three ways to spell the same word: *life-style*, *lifestyle*, and *life style*. Which should I use?

ANSWER The first spelling shown is usually the preferred one. In your dictionary a second acceptable form may be introduced by the word *also*. If two spellings appear side by side (*ax*, *axe*), they are equally acceptable.

QUESTION How should I write *industry wide*? It's not in my dictionary.

ANSWER A word with the suffix *wide* is usually written solid: *industrywide*, *nationwide*, *countrywide*, *statewide*, *worldwide*.

NAME ______________________________

9 REINFORCEMENT EXERCISES

A. (Self-check) Select the correct word and write it in the space provided.

1. We (should of, should have) prepared harder for the presentation. ________________
2. Amy brought (to, too) few copies to give to all meeting participants. ________________
3. Everyone received the e-mail announcement but (I, me). ________________
4. Can you get a ride (off of, from) Stephanie to the seminar? ________________
5. With more experience, Kyle (could of, could have) gotten the position. ________________
6. Vending machines are located (inside, inside of) the cafeteria. ________________
7. It looks (like, as if) you will be our new managing editor. ________________
8. (Except, Accept) for the long hours, this is an excellent position. ________________
9. We divided the work evenly (between, among) Eric and Tom. ________________
10. The office suite (beside, besides) ours has been vacant for three months. ________________
11. Because she was negligent (in, of) her duties, she was given a poor performance review. ________________
12. Elizabeth is an expert (at, in) computer programming. ________________
13. How long do you plan (to stay, on staying) at the conference? ________________
14. Your work ethic is similar (with, to) mine. ________________
15. Are you angry (with, at) me for disagreeing with you at the meeting? ________________

Check your answers below.

B. Underline any errors you find in the following sentences. Write the correct forms in the spaces provided. Write *C* if the sentence is correct as written.

EXAMPLE: Employees like Hayley and she are valuable to this company. her

1. All the participants except he called the conference a success. ________________
2. Dawn told Joshua and I that she appreciated our efforts. ________________
3. It's never to early to start saving for retirement. ________________
4. Just between you and I, I hear the company is downsizing. ________________
5. Diana Abernathy told Andrew and me that we should of read the installation directions more carefully. ________________
6. Can you get their address off of the letter they sent last week? ________________
7. You can always count on coworkers like Lisa and she when you need help. ________________
8. Our warehouse complies to the new governmental safety regulations. ________________
9. His principal goals are quite different than mine. ________________

1. should have, 2. too, 3. me, 4. from, 5. could have, 6. inside, 7. as if, 8. Except, 9. between, 10. beside, 11. of, 12. in, 13. to stay, 14. to, 15. with.

10. Cary often finds it difficult to reconcile the company checkbook to the bank statement. ____________

11. I differ from you on only a few small points. ____________

12. Our raises are retroactive from the first of the fiscal year. ____________

13. Is your manager usually sensitive with your feelings? ____________

14. It was a pleasure talking to you yesterday during the interview. ____________

15. A firewall will help guard against unauthorized access to our intranet. ____________

16. Robert has a great interest with designing a Web site for the company. ____________

17. The light background on the Web page contrasts to the font color. ____________

18. Are you acquainted with our company's e-mail policy? ____________

19. Our competitor's product is similar with ours. ____________

20. The company plans on developing a new interactive Web site. ____________

C. In the following sentences, cross out unnecessary prepositions and insert necessary ones.

EXAMPLE: What type ^of wheel bearings are needed?

EXAMPLE: Where are you going ~~to~~?

1. Leah couldn't help from laughing when dropped his briefcase in the hallway.

2. Charles has great respect and interest in the stock market.

3. Where is your headquarters being moved to?

4. You must write up her performance appraisal before her raise can be approved.

5. Who can tell me where the meeting is scheduled at?

D. Select the correct word(s) and write them in the space provided.

1. Relief funds were divided (among, between) all earthquake victims. ____________

2. (As, Like) we were told last week, budget cuts are pending. ____________

3. Please try to complete the steps just (as, like) I do. ____________

4. It looks (like, as if) Moira will be our next vice president. ____________

5. Has anyone been (in to, into) see Kelsey since she returned from vacation? ____________

6. I cannot (accept, except) the terms of this contract. ____________

7. (Accept, Except) for Allison, no one is going to work on the holiday. ____________

8. (Beside, Besides) Manny and Alex, whom have you told about our plans? ____________

9. Put your business card (in, into) the basket for a free lunch. ____________

10. This program seems to be (to, too) difficult to learn. ____________

10 Conjunctions to Join Equals

OBJECTIVES When you have completed the materials in this chapter, you will be able to do the following:

- Distinguish between simple and compound sentences.
- Punctuate compound sentences joined by *and, or, nor,* and *but.*
- Punctuate compound sentences using conjunctive adverbs such as *therefore, however,* and *consequently.*
- Recognize correlative conjunctions such as *either . . . or, not only . . . but also,* and *neither . . . nor.*
- Use a parallel construction in composing sentences with correlative conjunctions.

Conjunctions are connecting words. They may be separated into two major groups: those that join grammatically equal words or word groups and those that join grammatically unequal words or word groups. This chapter focuses on those conjunctions that join equals. Recognizing conjunctions and understanding their patterns of usage will, among other things, enable you to use commas and semicolons more appropriately.

COORDINATING CONJUNCTIONS

NOTABLE QUOTABLE

"The quality, not the longevity, of one's life is what is important."
—Martin Luther King

Coordinating conjunctions connect words, phrases, and clauses of equal grammatical value or rank. The most common coordinating conjunctions are *and, or, but,* and *nor.* Notice in these sentences that coordinating conjunctions join grammatically equal elements.

> The qualities I admire most are *honesty, integrity,* and *reliability.* (Here the word *and* joins equal words.)
>
> Open your mind *to new challenges* and *to new ideas.* (Here *and* joins equal phrases.)
>
> *Mr. Catalano opens the mail,* but *Ms. Santana fills the orders.* (Here *but* joins equal clauses.)

Phrases and Clauses

STUDY TIP

Clauses have subjects and verbs. Phrases do not. Clauses may have phrases within them.

A group of related words without a subject and a verb is called a *phrase.* You are already familiar with verb phrases and prepositional phrases. It is not important that you be able to identify the other kinds of phrases (infinitive, gerund, participial), but it is very important that you be able to distinguish phrases from clauses.

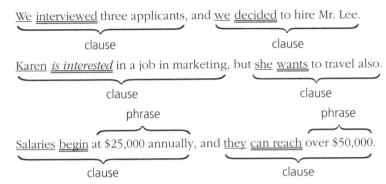

The alarm was coming from another part of the building.

phrase phrase phrase

A group of related words including a subject and a verb is a clause.

We interviewed three applicants, and we decided to hire Mr. Lee.

clause clause

Karen *is interested* in a job in marketing, but she wants to travel also.

clause clause

phrase phrase

Salaries begin at $25,000 annually, and they can reach over $50,000.

clause clause

SPOT THE BLOOPER

Advertisement published in the *Los Angeles Times*: "Brother Word Processor with Grammer Check and Word Spell"

Simple and Compound Sentences

A *simple sentence* has one independent clause, that is, a clause that can stand alone. A *compound sentence* has two or more independent clauses.

We agreed to lease the equipment. (Simple sentence.)

Our Travel Department planned the sales trip, but some salespeople also made private excursions. (Compound sentence.)

Punctuating Compound Sentences

When coordinating conjunctions join clauses in compound sentences, a comma precedes the conjunction unless the clauses are very short (four or fewer words in each clause).

We can ship the merchandise by air, *or* we can ship it by rail.

Ship by air *or* ship by rail. (Clauses are too short to require a comma.)

Do not use commas when coordinating conjunctions join compound verbs, objects, or phrases.

The bank will notify you of each transfer, or it will send you a monthly statement. (Comma used because *or* joins two independent clauses.)

The bank will notify you of each transfer or will send you a monthly statement. (No comma needed because *or* joins the compound verbs of a single independent clause.)

Our CEO said that employees should not have to choose between working overtime *and* spending time with their families. (No comma needed because *and* joins the compound objects of a prepositional phrase.)

Stockholders are expected to attend the meeting *or* to send their proxies. (No comma needed because *or* joins two infinitive phrases.)

Analyze all your possible property risks, *and* protect yourself with insurance. (Comma needed to join two independent clauses; the subject of each clause is understood to be *you*.)

SPOT THE BLOOPER

Headline in *The Orlando* [FL] *Sentinel*: "Women Are Likely to Eat More Than Men Under Stress"

CONJUNCTIVE ADVERBS

Conjunctive adverbs may also be used to connect equal sentence elements. Because conjunctive adverbs are used to effect a transition from one thought to another, and because they may consist of more than one word, they have also been called *transitional expressions.* The most common conjunctive adverbs follow.

STUDY TIP

Some authorities call the conjunctive adverb a "conjunctive joiner." Such a term may help you remember its function.

accordingly	in fact	on the other hand
consequently	in the meantime	that is
furthermore	moreover	then
hence	nevertheless	therefore
however	on the contrary	thus

In the following compound sentences, observe that conjunctive adverbs join clauses of equal grammatical value. Note that semicolons (*not* commas) are used before conjunctive adverbs that join independent clauses. Commas should immediately follow conjunctive adverbs of two or more syllables. Note also that the word following a semicolon is not capitalized—unless, of course, it is a proper noun.

Sarah did her best; *nevertheless,* she failed to pass the bar exam.
Some machines require separate outlets; *consequently,* new outlets were installed.
Equipment expenditures are great this quarter; *on the other hand,* new equipment will reduce labor costs.
Complex equipment requires operators who are specialists; *thus* we must train operators to become specialists.
Competition among computer manufacturers is intensive; *hence* prices may decrease sharply.

Generally, no comma is used after one-syllable conjunctive adverbs such as *hence, thus,* and *then* (unless a strong pause is desired).

DISTINGUISHING CONJUNCTIVE ADVERBS FROM PARENTHETICAL ADVERBS

STUDY TIP

Use a semicolon only when you are joining two complete sentences.

Many words that function as conjunctive adverbs may also serve as *parenthetical* (interrupting) *adverbs* that are employed to effect transition from one thought to another. Use semicolons *only* with conjunctive adverbs that join independent clauses. Use commas to set off parenthetical adverbs that interrupt the flow of a sentence.

The credit for our success, *however,* belongs to Rachel.
Robert deserves credit for our success; *however,* he will not accept it.
The Federal Reserve System, *moreover,* is a vital force in maintaining a sound banking system and a stable economy.
The Federal Reserve System is a vital force in maintaining a sound banking system; *moreover,* it is instrumental in creating a stable economy.
I am afraid, *on the other hand,* that we may lose money on our investment.
I am afraid that we may lose money on our investment; *on the other hand,* first-quarter sales were encouraging.

OTHER CONJUNCTIONS

We have studied thus far two kinds of conjunctions used to join grammatically equal sentence elements: coordinating conjunctions (used to join equal words, phrases, and clauses) and conjunctive adverbs (used to join grammatically equal clauses in compound sentences). *Correlative conjunctions* form the third and final group of conjunctions that join grammatically equal sentence elements.

Correlative Conjunctions

Correlative conjunctions are always paired: *both . . . and, not only . . . but (also), either . . . or,* and *neither . . . nor.* When greater emphasis is desired, these paired conjunctions are used instead of coordinating conjunctions.

> Your best chances for advancement are in the marketing department *or* in the sales department.
>
> Your best chances for advancement are *either* in the marketing department *or* in the sales department. (More emphatic.)

In using correlative conjunctions, place them so that the words, phrases, or clauses being joined are parallel in construction.

PARALLEL:	Molly was flying *either* to Seattle *or* to Portland.
NOT PARALLEL:	*Either* Molly was flying to Seattle *or* to Portland.
PARALLEL:	She was *not only* talented *but also* bright.
NOT PARALLEL:	She was *not only* talented, *but* she was *also* bright.
PARALLEL:	I have *neither* the time *nor* the energy for this.
NOT PARALLEL:	I *neither* have the time *nor* the energy for this.

Additional Coordinating Conjunctions

NOTABLE QUOTABLE

"Great minds have purposes; others have wishes."
—Washington Irving

To begin this chapter, we reviewed the four most commonly used coordinating conjunctions: *and, or, nor,* and *but.* Three other coordinating conjunctions should also be mentioned: *yet, for,* and *so.*

The words *yet* and *for* may function as coordinating conjunctions, although they are infrequently used as such.

> We have only two hours left, *yet* we hope to finish.
>
> The weary traveler was gaunt and ill, *for* his journey had been long and arduous.

The word *so* is sometimes informally used as a coordinating conjunction. In more formal contexts the conjunctive adverbs *therefore* and *consequently* should be substituted for the conjunction *so.*

INFORMAL:	The plane leaves at 2:15, *so* you still have time to pack.
FORMAL:	The plane leaves at 2:15; *therefore,* you still have time to pack.

HOTLINE QUERIES

QUESTION A friend of mine gets upset when I say something like, *I was so surprised by her remark.* She thinks I'm misusing *so.* Am I?

ANSWER Your friend is right, if we're talking about formal expression. The intensifier *so* requires a clause to complete its meaning. For example, *I was so surprised by her remark that I immediately protested.* It's like waiting for the other shoe to drop when one hears *so* as a modifier without a qualifying clause. *He was so funny.* So funny that what? *He was so funny that he became a stand-up comedian.*

QUESTION Please help me decide which *maybe* to use in this sentence: *He said that he (maybe, may be) able to help us.*

ANSWER Use the two-word *may be*, which is the verb form. *Maybe* is an adverb that means "perhaps" (*maybe she will call*).

QUESTION At the end of a printed line, is it acceptable to type part of an individual's name on one line and carry the rest to the next line?

ANSWER Full names may be divided between the first and last names or after the middle initial. For example, you could type *John R.* on one line and *Williamson* on the next line. Do not, however, separate a short title and a surname (such as *Mr./Williamson*), and do not divide a name (such as *William/son*). By the way, many computer programs make unacceptable line-ending decisions. Be sure to inspect your copy, either on the screen or on the printout, so that you can correct poor hyphenation and unacceptable word separations.

QUESTION What should the verb in this sentence be? *There (has, have) to be good reasons . . .*

ANSWER Use the plural verb *have*, which agrees with the subject *reasons*. In sentences that begin with the word *there*, look for the subject after the verb.

QUESTION Does *Ms.* have a period after it? Should I use this title for all women in business today?

ANSWER *Ms.* is probably a blend of *Miss* and *Mrs.* It is written with a period following it. Some women in business prefer to use *Ms.*, presumably because it is a title equal to *Mr.* Neither title reveals one's marital status. Many other women, however, prefer to use *Miss* or *Mrs.* as a title. It's always wise, if possible, to determine the preference of the individual.

QUESTION I just typed this sentence: *He was given a new title <u>in lieu of</u> a salary increase.* I went to my dictionary to check the spelling of *in lieu of*, but I can't find it. How is it spelled and what does it mean?

ANSWER The listing in the dictionary is under *lieu*, and it means "instead of." Many authorities today are recommending that such phrases be avoided. It's easier and clearer to say "instead of."

QUESTION Can you help me with the words *averse* and *adverse*? I've never been able to straighten them out in my mind.

ANSWER *Averse* is an adjective meaning "disinclined" and generally is used with the preposition *to* (*the little boy was averse to bathing*; *she is averse to statistical typing*). *Adverse* is also an adjective, but it means "hostile" or "unfavorable" (*adverse economic conditions halted the company's growth*; *the picnic was postponed because of adverse weather conditions*). In distinguishing between these two very similar words, it might help you to know that the word *averse* is usually used to describe animate (living) objects.

QUESTION What should I write: *You are our No. 1 account*, or *You are our number one account*? Should anything be hyphenated?

ANSWER Either is correct, but we prefer *No. 1* because it is more easily recognizable. No hyphen is required.

10 REINFORCEMENT EXERCISES

A. (Self-check) Indicate whether the following sentences are punctuated correctly (*C*) or incorrectly (*I*).

EXAMPLE: We completed most of the work, but left some for you. ___I___

1. The House passed the legislation, but the Senate rejected it. ______
2. Albert Einstein was four years old before he could speak, and seven years old before he could read. ______
3. I did not expect a profit, and did not fear a loss. ______
4. Word processing specialists must possess excellent English skills, and they must be skilled at keyboarding. ______
5. Look over the menu carefully, and place your order with the server. ______
6. The Human Resources Director will be interviewing applicants Monday and Tuesday, and will make a decision on the appointment by Friday. ______

In the following sentences, insert commas and semicolons. In the space provided, indicate the number of punctuation marks you added. Be prepared to explain your choices.

7. Mother Teresa was best known for her work in Calcutta however she also founded facilities for the poor in the United States. ______
8. We were late for the meeting thus we did not receive the handouts. ______
9. Lana is however still considered the best person for the job. ______
10. This position offers the higher salary on the other hand that one has better benefits. ______

Select the more effective version of each of the following pairs of sentences. Write its letter in the space provided.

11. **(a)** Either she took the train or the bus. ______
    (b) She took either the train or the bus.
12. **(a)** Ms. Lopez is not available to conduct the meeting, and neither is Mr. Stetson. ______
    (b) Neither Ms. Lopez nor Mr. Stetson is available to conduct the meeting.
13. **(a)** Our objectives are both to improve customer relations and to increase sales. ______
    (b) Our objectives are both to improve customer relations and increasing sales.
14. **(a)** Cheryl needed more time to devote to her family, so she asked for a part-time assignment. ______
    (b) Cheryl needed more time to devote to her family; therefore, she asked for a part-time assignment.
15. **(a)** My new computer is not only faster but also more efficient. ______
    (b) Not only is my new computer faster, but it is also more efficient.

Check your answers below.

1. C, 2. I, 3. I, 4. C, 5. C, 6. I, 7. 2, 8. 1, 9. 2, 10. 2, 11. b, 12. b, 13. a, 14. b, 15. a.

NAME ______________________________

B. A simple sentence has one independent clause. A compound sentence has two or more independent clauses. Indicate with a check mark whether the following sentences, all of which are punctuated correctly, are simple or compound. *Hint:* A sentence is not compound unless the words preceding and following a conjunction form independent clauses. If these groups of words could not stand alone as sentences, the sentence is not compound.

	Simple	Compound
1. Cecile Bendavid wrote a travel report, and she shared its information with other members of the staff.	________	________
2. Cecile Bendavid wrote a travel report and shared its information with other members of the staff.	________	________
3. The recently constructed corporate headquarters contained attractive executive offices, but the structure had few support facilities for employees.	________	________
4. Our compensation package includes many benefits for employees with families but provides little for single employees.	________	________
5. Our compensation package includes many benefits for employees with families, but it provides little for single employees.	________	________
6. Management trainees are sent to all our branch offices in this country and to some of the branch offices in South America and Europe.	________	________
7. Send in your order with a check for the full amount, and we will ship within three days.	________	________
8. Michael arrived early for the meeting, but he was unprepared for his presentation.	________	________
9. Send copies of the project report to me and to other management personnel in our three subsidiaries.	________	________
10. Supplies for three offices arrived today, but most of our order will not arrive until later.	________	________

C. Insert commas where appropriate in the following sentences. Then, in the space provided, indicate the number of commas you have added for each sentence. If no comma is needed, write ***0***.

EXAMPLE: Kevin came to work on Monday, but he was out sick on Tuesday. ___1___

1. Some employees think their e-mail should be confidential but courts generally uphold an employer's right to monitor it. _____

2. Kirk planned the presentation and delivered it himself. _____

3. Jack disagreed with the decision but he did not challenge it. _____

4. You may fax your application to our office or bring it with you to the interview. _____

5. Charles Goodyear failed to benefit from the rubber process he invented and he died in poverty. _____

6. Today's software can detect potentially troublesome words or identify high-pressure sales tactics in outgoing e-mail messages. _____

7. Listen carefully and follow directions. _____

8. Lauren is considering a career in finance but she is also interested in teaching. _____

9. Lyndon Johnson succeeded John F. Kennedy as president and was succeeded by Richard Nixon. _____

10. You may be interested in a career in this country or you may be interested in working abroad. _____

D. In the following sentences, insert commas and semicolons. In the space provided, indicate the number of punctuation marks you added. Be prepared to explain your choices.

EXAMPLE: Some loans must be secured; therefore, the borrower must supply collateral. 2

1. Cynthia had years of on-the-job experience however she returned to school to learn new technologies and to improve her communications skills. _____
2. Microwave relay stations have reduced telephone costs moreover cable and satellite circuits reduce costs even more. _____
3. Our company is faced nevertheless with unusually expensive communication costs. _____
4. We are drowning in information but starving for knowledge. _____
5. Insurance is controlled by the law of averages thus increased losses send the average cost of premiums upward. _____
6. The job candidate will however be required to provide us with transcripts. _____
7. New project assignments will be announced next month in the meantime continue working on your current project. _____
8. Gene offered to pay for the damage nevertheless I feel responsible. _____
9. Many of our employees moreover would like to take the advanced word processing class. _____
10. Please place your order immediately or you will not be eligible for the discount. _____

11 Conjunctions to Join Unequals

OBJECTIVES When you have completed the materials in this chapter, you will be able to do the following:

- Distinguish among phrases, dependent clauses, and independent clauses.
- Expand dependent clauses into complete sentences.
- Punctuate introductory and terminal dependent clauses.
- Punctuate parenthetical, essential, and nonessential dependent clauses.
- Recognize simple, compound, complex, and compound-complex sentences.
- Convert simple sentences into a variety of more complex patterns.

In Chapter 10 you learned about conjunctions that joined equal sentence elements such as words, phrases, and clauses. These equal sentence parts were joined by coordinate conjunctions (*and, or, nor, but*), conjunctive adverbs (such as *therefore, however, consequently*), and correlative conjunctions (such as *either . . . or*). Now let's look at a special group of conjunctions that join unequal sentence parts.

SUBORDINATING CONJUNCTIONS

SPOT THE BLOOPER

From *The San Francisco Chronicle*: "He [Burt Reynolds] describes himself growing up tough and brash as the part-Indian son of a Florida police chief and a football hero who thought he was destined for stardom until a knee injury sidelined him."

To join unequal sentence elements, such as independent and dependent clauses, use *subordinating conjunctions.* A list of the most common subordinating conjunctions follows.

after	because	since	when
although	before	so that	where
as	if	that	whether
as if	in order that	unless	while
as though	provided	until	

You should become familiar with this list of conjunctions, but do not feel that you must at all times be able to recall every subordinating conjunction. Generally, you can recognize a subordinating conjunction by the way it limits, or subordinates, the clause it introduces. In the clause *because he always paid with cash*, the subordinating conjunction *because* limits the meaning of the clause it introduces. The clause is incomplete and could not stand alone as a sentence.

INDEPENDENT AND DEPENDENT CLAUSES

Main clauses that can stand alone are said to be *independent.* They have subjects and verbs and make sense by themselves.

Business writing should be concise. (One main clause.)
Business writing should be concise, and it should be clear as well. (Two main clauses.)
Judy Foster writes many e-mail memos, but Bernice Dandridge writes more letters. (Two main clauses.)

STUDY TIP

Dependent clauses should never be written or punctuated as if they were complete sentences.

Clauses that cannot stand alone are said to be *dependent.* They have subjects and verbs, but they depend on other clauses for the completion of their meaning. Dependent clauses are often introduced by subordinating conjunctions.

When Mr. Goodleman wants a quick reply, he sends an e-mail message. (Dependent clause precedes the main clause.)
Since Ms. Young works with customers, she writes many letters. (Dependent clause precedes the main clause.)
Experience is required because this is a high-level position. (Dependent clause, *because this is a high-level position,* comes after the main clause.)

RELATIVE PRONOUNS

Although classified as pronouns, the words *who, whom, whose, which,* and *that* actually function as conjunctions when they introduce dependent clauses. *Who* and *whom* are used to refer to human antecedents. *Which* is used to refer to nonhuman antecedents, and *whose* and *that* may refer to either human or nonhuman antecedents.

Allan Lacayo is the person *who* can answer your questions.
The newest version of Quicken, *which* will help with our company finances, is due out soon.
The software *that* you requested will be installed next week.

PUNCTUATION OF SENTENCES WITH DEPENDENT CLAUSES

NOTABLE QUOTABLE

"You can have brilliant ideas, but if you can't get them across, your ideas won't get you anywhere."
—Lee Iacocca

Business writers are especially concerned with clarity and accuracy. A misplaced or omitted punctuation mark can confuse a reader by altering the meaning of a sentence. The following guidelines for using commas help ensure clarity and consistency in writing. Some professional writers, however, take liberties with accepted conventions of punctuation, particularly in regard to comma usage. These experienced writers may omit a comma when they feel that such an omission will not affect the reader's understanding of a sentence. Beginning writers, though, are well advised to first develop skill in punctuating sentences by following traditional guidelines.

Introductory Dependent Clauses

Use a comma after a dependent (subordinate) clause that precedes an independent clause.

Before they left the office, they finished the proposal.
Until I receive your records, I cannot complete your tax return.
When he gets here, we can start the meeting.

Use a comma after an introductory dependent clause even though the subject and verb may not be stated.

As [it is] expected, the opening is delayed.
If [it is] possible, send your application today.
When [they are] printed, your brochures will be distributed.

SPOT THE BLOOPER

From classified ads in local newspapers: "LAWN-MORE SHOP" and a house for sale with "walking closets."

Terminal Dependent Clauses

Generally, a dependent clause introduced by a subordinating conjunction does not require a comma when the dependent clause falls at the end of a sentence.

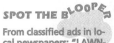

> We must finish the research *before* we write the report.
> They cannot leave *until* the manager returns.
> Be prepared to distribute brochures and annual reports *when* the clients arrive.

If, however, the dependent clause at the end of a sentence interrupts the flow of the sentence and sounds as if it were an afterthought, a comma should be used.

> I am sure I paid the bill, *although* I cannot find my receipt.
> We will begin immediately, *if* the materials are available.

Parenthetical Clauses

Within a sentence, dependent clauses that interrupt the flow of a sentence and are unnecessary for the grammatical completeness of the sentence are set off by commas.

> The motion, *unless* you want further discussion, will be tabled until our next meeting.
> At our next meeting, *provided* we have a quorum, the motion will be reconsidered.

STUDY TIP

Careful writers use the word *that* for essential clauses and the word *which* for nonessential clauses. Dependent clauses introduced by *which* require commas.

Relative Clauses

Dependent clauses introduced by relative pronouns such as *who*, *that*, and *which* may be essential (restrictive) or nonessential (nonrestrictive).

An *essential clause* is needed to identify the noun to which it refers; therefore, no commas should separate this clause from its antecedent.

> All employees *who have been here for more than five years* are eligible for the program. (Dependent clause needed to identify which employees are eligible for the program.)
> Parking permits *that were issued last year* must be validated for this year. (Dependent clause needed to identify which permits must be validated.)

A *nonessential clause* supplies additional information that is not needed to identify its antecedent; therefore, commas are used to separate the nonessential information from the rest of the sentence. Notice that *two* commas are used to set off internal nonessential dependent clauses.

> James Awbrey, *who has been here more than five years*, is eligible for the program. (Dependent clause: the antecedent of the clause, James Awbrey, is clearly identified.)
> Lot C parking permits, *which were issued last year*, must be validated for this year. (Dependent clause: the antecedent of the clause is clearly identified.)

Punctuation Review

Let's briefly review three common sentence patterns and their proper punctuation.

Independent clause, +	and or nor but	+	Independent clause.	(Comma used when a coordinating conjunction joins independent clauses.)

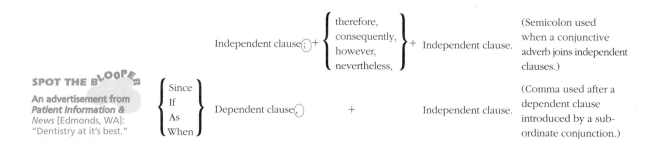

Independent clause ; +	{ therefore, / consequently, / however, / nevertheless, } +	Independent clause.	(Semicolon used when a conjunctive adverb joins independent clauses.)
{ Since / If / As / When } Dependent clause ,	+	Independent clause.	(Comma used after a dependent clause introduced by a subordinate conjunction.)

SPOT THE BLOOPER

An advertisement from *Patient Information & News* [Edmonds, WA]: "Dentistry at it's best."

HOTLINE QUERIES

QUESTION Can the word *that* be omitted from sentences? For example, *She said [that] she would come.*

ANSWER The relative pronoun *that* is frequently omitted in conversation and casual writing. For absolute clarity, however, skilled writers include it.

QUESTION Is there some rule about putting periods in organization names that are abbreviated? For example, does *IBM* have periods?

ANSWER When the names of well-known business, educational, governmental, labor, and other organizations or agencies are abbreviated, periods are normally not used to separate the letters. Thus, no periods would appear in IBM, ITT, UCLA, AFL-CIO, YWCA, and AMA. The names of radio and television stations and networks are also written without periods: Station WJR, KNX-FM, PBS, WABC-TV. Geographical abbreviations, however, generally do require periods: U.S.A., U.S.S.R., S.A. The two-letter state abbreviations recommended by the U.S. Postal Service require no periods: NY, OH, CA, MI, NJ, OR, MA, and so on.

QUESTION As a command, which is correct: *lay down* or *lie down*?

ANSWER Commands are given in the present tense. You would never tell someone to *Closed the door*, because commands are not given in the past tense. To say *Lay down* (which is the past tense form of *lie*) is the same as saying *Closed the door.* Therefore, use the present tense: *Lie down.*

QUESTION In this sentence which word should I use? *Your order will be sent to you in the (later or latter) part of the week.*

ANSWER Use *latter.* The word *latter* designates the second of two persons or things. In addition, *latter* can be used to mean "further advanced in time or sequence," or *latter* can be used to contrast with *former.* In your sentence, the *latter* part of the week contrasts with the *former* part of the week.

QUESTION We're having a sale on *nonChristmas* items. Should a hyphen follow *non*? In my dictionary the prefix *non* is not hyphenated when it is joined to other words.

ANSWER A hyphen is not used when a prefix is joined to most words: *nonessential, prewar, unwelcome, anticlimax.* A hyphen is used, however, when a prefix is joined to a proper (capitalized) noun: *non-Christmas, pre-Columbian, un-Christian, anti-American.*

QUESTION I have a lot of trouble with verbs in sentences like this: *He is one of the 8 million Americans who (has or have) a drinking problem.*

ANSWER You're not alone. Make your verb agree with its antecedent (*Americans*). One easy way to work with sentences like this is to concentrate on the clause that contains the verb. *Of the 8 million Americans who have a drinking problem, he is one.*

QUESTION It seems to me that the meaning of the word *impact* has changed. I thought it meant "an effect." But now I hear this use: *How does this policy impact on the Middle East?*

ANSWER In our language nouns often become verbs (to *bridge* the gap, to *corner* the market, to *e-mail* a friend). Whether a noun-turned-verb is assimilated into the language seems to depend on its utility, its efficiency, and the status of the individuals who use it. Skilled writers, for example, avoid the word *prioritize* because it is inefficient and sounds bureaucratic. Transformation of the noun *impact* into a verb would appear to be unnecessary, since the word *affect* clearly suffices in most constructions (*How does this program affect the Middle East?*). Although we hear *impact* used frequently today, some language specialists find it offensive.

QUESTION Why does *Martha's Vineyard* have an apostrophe while *Harpers Ferry* doesn't?

ANSWER The federal government maintains a Board on Geographic Names in the U.S. This board has a policy that "geographic names in the U.S. should not show ownership of a feature." British maps, says board secretary Roger Payne, are "littered with apostrophes." To avoid such clutter, the board allows no possessive on any federal maps or documents, unless previously dispensated. Only four geographic names have dispensations: *Martha's Vineyard* (Massachusetts), *Carlos Elmer's Joshua View* (Arizona), *Ike's Point* (New Jersey), and *John E.'s Pond* (Rhode Island).

NAME ______________________________

11 REINFORCEMENT EXERCISES

A. (Self-check) Indicate whether the following word groups are phrases (*P*), independent clauses (*I*), or dependent clauses (*D*). (Remember that phrases do not have both subjects and verbs.)

EXAMPLE: in the spring of this year ____P____

1. when you account for cultural differences ______
2. paralegals and administrative assistants worked together ______
3. on the last day of the week ______
4. as we explained in our brochure ______
5. she answered immediately ______
6. earlier they agreed to a settlement ______
7. because they had no source of financing ______
8. during the middle of the four-year fiscal period from 1995 through 1999 ______

Where appropriate, insert commas in the following sentences. In the space provided after each sentence, indicate the number of commas you have added to that sentence. Do not add any commas that you cannot justify.

EXAMPLE: Before we make the investment, we want to do some research. ____1____

9. Procter and Gamble which made a fortune with Ivory soap discovered the formula by accident. ______
10. As predicted interest rates will climb during any period of inflation. ______
11. Money for the child-care program which included salaries for five teachers and three assistants came from the federal government. ______
12. A memo that explains the facts of the reorganization was distributed Monday. ______
13. Edward Casala who was the first salesperson to reach the quota earned a $5,000 bonus. ______
14. Anyone who wants the product should order immediately. ______
15. If possible send the report that shows your current sales figures compared with last year's. ______

Check your answers below.

B. Indicate whether the following word groups are phrases (*P*), independent clauses (*I*), or dependent clauses (*D*). For the clauses, underline the subjects once and the verbs twice.

EXAMPLE: until we are able to make a decision ____D____

1. as you walk into the conference room ______
2. so that everyone will be included ______
3. our offices are located in Charlotte ______
4. on the first page of the Web site ______
5. after he opened his own firm ______
6. he designed the Web site professionally ______

1. D, 2. I, 3. P, 4. D, 5. I, 6. I, 7. D, 8. P, 9. 2, 10. 1, 11. 2, 12. 0, 13. 2, 14. 0, 15. 1.

7. might have been considered ____

8. before Samir finished his presentation ____

9. Division Manager Kelsey analyzed the data ____

10. during our lunch hour last week ____

C. After each sentence write the correct word in the space provided.

1. We're shopping for software (which, that) we can use without customizing. ____________

2. Are you the one (who, that) organized the company picnic? ____________

3. The IRS, (who, which) audits only 2 percent of all income tax returns, is choked with paperwork. ____________

4. REI is known as a company (who, that) makes quality outdoor products. ____________

5. The CEO has a dog (who, that) lies under the desk all day. ____________

D. Where appropriate, insert commas in the following sentences. In the space provided after each sentence, indicate the number of commas that you added. Be prepared to discuss the reasons for the commas you use.

1. Philip Knight who is CEO of Nike was tattooed with the company's "swoosh" logo. ____

2. Employees who are tattooed with a company logo may regret it one day. ____

3. If you have any further budget questions please e-mail them to Roberta McKee. ____

4. We were notified that the computer server would be down for six hours although we were not told why. ____

5. We can schedule the meeting for 5 p.m. if that time is convenient for you. ____

6. When completed the newly created Web site will enable customers to track shipments. ____

7. All the information on my personal résumé which I prepared myself fills just one page. ____

8. Although we requested a new printer we don't believe we will get it. ____

9. The warranty that you refer to in your letter covers only merchandise brought to our shop for repair. ____

10. Justin Edwards who works in the Traffic Department received last month's merit award. ____

11. An administrative assistant who joined our staff only two months ago received this month's merit award. ____

12. Zone Improvement Program codes which are better known as ZIP codes were designed to expedite the sorting and delivery of mail. ____

13. I would like to give your suggestion more thought when I am not quite so preoccupied. ____

14. The president will surely when she delivers her speech discuss these personnel issues. ____

15. Before you make a decision consider carefully our strained financial condition. ____

16. No additional tax increases can be made if I understand the legislation correctly. ____

17. Because we need the hard drive space everyone must delete all unnecessary files. ____

18. In the coming fiscal year provided enough funds are available we hope to expand our employee fitness program. ____

19. The programmer who designed the code will answer your questions. ____

20. Marketers that develop advertising targeted at heavy users are attempting to build brand loyalty. ____

NAME ______________________________

UNIT 3 REVIEW ■ Chapters 8–11 (Self-Check)

Begin your review by rereading Chapters 8–11. Then test your comprehension of those chapters by completing the exercises that follow. Compare your responses with those at the end of the review.

In the blank provided, write the letter of the word or phrase that correctly completes each of the following sentences.

1. Enclosed is (a) a, (b) an example of a typical report. _____

2. It's (a) to, (b) too hot to go running during our lunch hour. _____

3. Colleagues like Thomas and (a) he, (b) him are hard to find. _____

4. Our company is seeking a recent graduate (a) whom, (b) which we can train. _____

5. The group of words *when you find it* is a(n) (a) phrase, (b) independent clause, (c) dependent clause. _____

Insert appropriate commas and semicolons in the following sentences. In the space provided, indicate the number of punctuation marks you added. Write *0* if you add none.

6. Rich accepted the position in May but took a leave of absence in July. _____

7. Hai Nguyen might be assigned to work in our legal office or he might be assigned to our administrative headquarters. _____

8. Use proper posture and take adequate breaks. _____

9. Kristin wrote a chronological résumé but Cameron preferred a functional strategy for his résumé. _____

10. Charlie was our trainer for the session and we followed his instructions carefully. _____

Write the letter of the word or phrase that correctly completes each sentence.

11. Let's not discuss this matter any (a) further, (b) farther until the mediator arrives. _____

12. Microsoft's employee search was launched (a) coast-to-coast, (b) coast to coast. _____

13. If we have (a) less, (b) fewer than ten agenda items, we can probably finish the meeting in one hour. _____

14. Because he was personally involved, Robert read the report (a) cynical, (b) cynically. _____

15. Power in our government is balanced (a) among, (b) between its three branches. _____

Insert appropriate commas and semicolons in the following sentences. In the space provided, indicate the number of marks you added.

16. Ms. Daily's accounting service was an immediate success consequently she is considering opening a second office. _____

17. Before she agreed to serve on the committee Sheila asked for a list of responsibilities. _____

18. Direct your questions to Mr. Ceglia who is responsible for quality control. _____

19. As expected sales have declined this quarter. _____

20. We believe however that we are entitled to a refund. _____

NAME ______________________________

Write the letter of the word or phrase that correctly completes each sentence.

21. New York is larger than (a) any other city, (b) any city in the United States. _____

22. Examine carefully the (a) 50 first, (b) first 50 pages of the booklet. _____

23. She worked only part-time, yet she remained independent (a) of, (b) from her parents. _____

24. Although our backgrounds are quite different, your values are not very different (a) than, (b) from mine. _____

25. Will our salary increases be retroactive (a) to, (b) from January 1? _____

Insert appropriate commas and semicolons in the following sentences. In the space provided, indicate the number of marks you added.

26. If you want to create a good impression be sure to write a thank-you letter after a job interview. _____

27. When you offered your resignation last week I did not think you were serious. _____

28. I did not think you were serious when you offered your resignation last week. _____

29. Sales in your district have really increased moreover requests for service have decreased. _____

30. Although he had no use for bodyguards Elvis Presley is said to have had a very special use for two highly trained CPAs. _____

Hotline Review

31. She has (a) all ready, (b) already completed over half of her recommendation report. _____

32. After two years, every employee is entitled to a (a) two-week, (b) two weeks vacation. _____

33. When you attend the conference, be sure to spend (a) sometime, (b) some time talking to vendors. _____

34. All (a) personnel, (b) personal matters are now handled in human resources. _____

35. Roger Allen (a) maybe, (b) may be transferring to our Indiana branch. _____

1. b, 2. b, 3. b, 4. a, 5. c, 6. 0, 7. 1, 8. 0, 9. 1, 10. 1, 11. a, 12. b, 13. b, 14. b, 15. a, 16. 2, 17. 1, 18. 1, 19. 1, 20. 2, 21. a, 22. b, 23. a, 24. b, 25. a, 26. 1, 27. 1, 28. 0, 29. 2, 30. 1, 31. b, 32. a, 33. b, 34. a, 35. b.

UNIT

4 Punctuating Sentences

12 Commas

OBJECTIVES When you have completed the materials in this chapter, you will be able to do the following:

- Correctly place commas in series, direct address, and parenthetical expressions.
- Use commas correctly in punctuating dates, addresses, geographical items, and appositives.
- Place commas correctly in punctuating independent adjectives, verbal phrases, and prepositional phrases.
- Use commas correctly in punctuating independent, introductory, terminal, and nonessential clauses.
- Use commas correctly in punctuating degrees, abbreviations, and numerals.
- Use commas to indicate omitted words, contrasting statements, clarity, and short quotations.

DID YOU KNOW

Some writers in other languages envy English. Our systematic use of commas and other punctuation makes it easy to signal pauses, to emphasize ideas, and to enhance readability.

When you talk with a friend, you are probably unaware of the "invisible" commas, periods, and other punctuation marks that you are using. In conversation your pauses and voice inflections punctuate your thoughts and clarify your meaning. In writing, however, you must use a conventional set of symbols, punctuation marks, to help your reader understand your meaning.

Over the years we have gradually developed a standardized pattern of usage for all punctuation marks. This usage has been codified (set down) in rules that are observed by writers who wish to make their writing as precise as possible. As noted earlier, some professional writers may deviate from conventional punctuation practices. In addition, some organizations, particularly newspapers and publishing houses, maintain their own style manuals to establish a consistent "in-house" style.

The punctuation guidelines presented in this book represent a consensus of punctuation styles that are acceptable in business writing. Following these guidelines will enable you to write with clarity, consistency, and accuracy.

BASIC GUIDELINES FOR USING COMMAS

The most used and misused punctuation mark, the comma, indicates a pause in the flow of a sentence. *Not all sentence pauses, however, require commas.* It is important for you to learn the standard rules for the use of commas so that you will not be tempted to clutter your sentences with needless, distracting commas. Here are the guidelines for basic comma usage.

STUDY TIP

As you begin to learn about commas, try to name a rule or guideline for every comma you insert. For example, *comma/series*, *comma/parenthetical*, and so forth.

SPOT THE BLOOPER

Poster for a university departmental event: "Door prizes will include lab equipment, books written by members of the biology department and a fruitcake."

SPOT THE BLOOPER

An article in the *Enterprise* [Brockton, MA] referred to "the Massachusetts Society for the Prevention of Animals."

STUDY TIP

Phrases are essential (no commas) when they answer the questions *when? where? why?* or *how?*

Series

Commas are used to separate three or more equally ranked (coordinate) elements (words, phrases, or short clauses) in a series. A comma before the conjunction ensures separation of the last two items. No commas are used when conjunctions join all the items in a series.

Only in June, July, and August are discounts offered. (Series of words. Notice that a comma precedes *and*, but no comma follows the last item, *August.*)
Kevin Twohy conducted the research, organized the data, and wrote the first draft of the engineering report. (Series of phrases.)
Mr. Horton is the owner, Ms. Travis is the marketing manager, and Ms. Savala is the executive assistant. (Series of clauses.)
Cathi Sasek asked that all proper nouns and numbers and formulas be verified. (No commas needed when conjunctions are repeated.)

Direct Address

Words and phrases of direct address are set off with commas.

I do believe, *Daphne*, that you have outdone yourself.
I respectfully request, *sir*, that I be transferred.

Parenthetical Expressions

Parenthetical words, phrases, and clauses may be used to create transitions between thoughts. These expressions interrupt the flow of a sentence and are unessential to its grammatical completeness. These commonly used expressions, some of which are listed below, are considered unessential because they do not answer specifically questions such as *when? where? why?* or *how?* Set off these expressions with commas.

accordingly	hence	namely
all things considered	however	needless to say
as a matter of fact	in addition	nevertheless
as a result	incidentally	no doubt
as a rule	in fact	of course
at the same time	in my opinion	on the contrary
by the way	in other words	on the other hand
consequently	in the first place	otherwise
for example	in the meantime	therefore
furthermore	moreover	under the circumstances

In addition, your computer skills are excellent. (At beginning of sentence.)
This report is not, *however*, one that must be classified. (Inside sentence.)
You have checked with other suppliers, *no doubt*. (At end of sentence.)

The words in question are set off by commas only when they are used parenthetically and actually interrupt the flow of a sentence.

However the vote goes, we will abide by the result. (No comma needed after *however.*)
We have *no doubt* that our marketing program must be revamped. (No commas needed to set off *no doubt.*)

Don't confuse short introductory essential prepositional phrases for parenthetical expressions. Notice that the following phrases are essential and, therefore, require no commas.

In the spring more rental units become available. (No comma is needed because the short prepositional phrase answers the question *when?*)

At the seminar we will discuss goals and objectives. (No comma is needed because the short prepositional phrase answers the question *where?*)

For this reason we must be at the meeting. (No comma is needed because the short prepositional phrase answers the question *why?*)

With your help our production team can meet its goal. (No comma is needed because the short prepositional phrase answers the question *how?*)

Dates, Addresses, and Geographical Items

STUDY TIP

In separating cities and states and dates and years, many writers remember the initial comma but forget the final one (*my friend from Albany, New York, called*).

When dates, addresses, and geographical items contain more than one element, the second and succeeding elements are normally set off by commas. Study the following illustrations.

■ ***Dates***

On January 3 we opened for business. (No comma needed for one element.)

On January 3, 2000, we opened for business. (Two commas set off second element.)

On Monday, January 3, 2000, we opened for business. (Commas set off second and third elements.)

In June, 1999, the reorganization was effected. (Commas set off second element.)

Note: In June 1999 the reorganization was effected. (This alternate style is acceptable in writing the month and year only.)

■ ***Addresses***

Please send the application to Ms. Barbara Briggs, 1913 Piazza Court, Baton Rouge, Louisiana 70817, as soon as possible. (Commas are used between all elements except the state and zip code, which are in this special instance to be considered a single unit.)

SPOT THE BLOOPER

From *The Union-Leader* [Manchester, NH]: "Prince Louis Ferdinand of Prussia, a grandson of Germany's last emperor who worked in a Detroit auto plant in the 1930s and later opposed Nazi dictator Adolf Hitler, has died at age 86." [Could a comma help clarify who worked in the auto plant? Would the idea be better expressed in two sentences?]

■ ***Geographical items***

He moved from Nashville, Tennessee, to Chicago, Illinois. (Two commas set off the state unless it appears at the end of the sentence.)

Appositives

You will recall that appositives rename or explain preceding nouns or pronouns. An appositive that provides information not essential to the identification of its antecedent should be set off by commas.

Marti Martin, *the Datamax sales representative*, is here. (The appositive adds nonessential information; commas set it off.)

The sales representative *Marti Martin* is here to see you. (The appositive is needed to identify which sales representative has arrived; therefore, no commas are used.)

One-word appositives do not require commas.

My supervisor *Doug* sometimes uses my computer.

NOTABLE QUOTABLE

"When one door of opportunity closes, another opens; however, we often look so long at the closed door that we do not see the one that has been opened for us."
—Helen Keller

SPECIAL GUIDELINES FOR USING COMMAS

Independent Adjectives

Separate two or more adjectives that equally modify a noun (see Chapter 8).

An *industrious, ambitious* employee came to see me.

Introductory Verbal Phrases

Verbal phrases (see Chapter 7) that precede main clauses should be followed by commas.

> *To qualify for the position*, you must have two years' experience.
> *Working steadily*, we completed the project by the end of the week.

Prepositional Phrases

One or more introductory prepositional phrases totaling five or more words should be followed by a comma.

> *On the third Tuesday of each month*, we hold a steering committee meeting.
> *In a company of this size*, standards and procedures are necessary.

Introductory prepositional phrases of fewer than five words require *no* commas.

> *In August* that stock reached its highest price.
> *In this case* I believe we can waive the filing fee.

Prepositional phrases in other positions do not require commas when they are essential and do not interrupt the flow of the sentence.

> She has included *in her monthly report* a summary of her findings. (No commas are needed around the prepositional phrase because it answers the question *where?* and does not interrupt the flow of the sentence.)
> You may *at your convenience* stop by to pick up your check. (No commas are needed because the prepositional phrase answers the question *when?* and does not interrupt the flow of the sentence.)

Independent Clauses

When a coordinating conjunction (see Chapter 10) joins independent clauses, use a comma before the coordinating conjunction, unless the clauses are very short.

> We may have Barbara Sawyer work on that project, *or* we may ask Laurie Lema.

Introductory Clauses

Dependent clauses that precede independent clauses are followed by commas.

> *When you have finished*, please return the style manual.
> *If you need help*, please call me in the afternoon.
> *Since I am the project leader*, I will attend all meetings.

STUDY TIP

The comma after an introductory clause is probably the most frequently missed comma in student writing. Be sure to insert a comma after a clause beginning with *If*, *When*, *As*, *Since*, and so forth.

Terminal Dependent Clauses

Use a comma before a dependent clause at the end of a sentence only if the dependent clause is an afterthought.

> Please return the style manual *when you have finished*. (No comma needed.)
> I plan to leave at 3:30, *if that meets with your approval*. (Dependent clause added as an afterthought.)

SPOT THE BLOOPER

From a sports column in *The Atlanta Journal-Constitution*: [The teams] "were tied, thanks to Smith, who had spent Saturday night at the hospital witnessing the birth of his daughter, who on Sunday had lofted a pinch-hit home run."

Nonessential Clauses

Use commas to set off clauses that are used parenthetically or that supply information unneeded for the grammatical completeness of a sentence.

> An increase in employee benefits, *as you can well understand*, must be postponed until profits improve.

We received a reply from Senator Moore, *who will be visiting our firm next week.*

Do *not* use commas to set off clauses that contain essential information.

An executive assistant *who is preparing proposals* certainly needs an up-to-date reference manual. (No commas are necessary because the italicized clause is essential; it tells what student needs an up-to-date dictionary.)

ADDITIONAL GUIDELINES FOR USING COMMAS

Degrees and Abbreviations

Except for *Jr.* and *Sr.*, degrees, personal titles, and professional designations following individuals' names are set off by commas.

John T. O'Dell Jr. is frequently confused with John T. O'Dell Sr.
Ratha Ramoo, M.D., has a flourishing practice in Tempe, Arizona.
Yukie Tokuyama, Ph.D., discussed degree requirements with the college president.
We have retained Craig Bjurstrom, Esq., to represent us.

The abbreviations *Inc.* and *Ltd.* are set off by commas if the company's legal name includes the commas.

Blackstone & Smythe, Inc., exports goods worldwide. (Company's legal name includes comma.)
Shoes Inc. operates at three locations in Tampa. (Legal name does not include comma before *Inc.*)

Numerals

Unrelated figures appearing side by side should be separated by commas.

A total of 150, 1999 graduates attended the reception.

Numbers of more than three digits require commas.

1,760 47,950 6,500,000

However, calendar years and zip codes are written without commas within the numerals.

NOTABLE QUOTABLE

"Both tears and sweat are salty, but they render a different result. Tears will get you sympathy; sweat will get you change."
—Jesse Jackson

CALENDAR YEARS:	1776	1999	2001
ZIP CODES:	02116	45327	90265

Telephone numbers, house numbers, decimals, page numbers, serial numbers, and contract numbers are also written without commas within the numerals.

TELEPHONE NUMBER:	(212) 555-4432
HOUSE NUMBER:	20586 Victory Avenue
DECIMAL NUMBER:	.98651, .0050
PAGE NUMBER:	Page 3561
SERIAL NUMBER:	36-5710-1693285763
CONTRACT NUMBER:	No. 359063420

Omitted Words

A comma is used to show the omission of words that are understood.

Last summer we hired 12 employees; this summer, only 3 employees. (Comma shows omission of *we hired* after *summer.*)

Contrasting Statements

SPOT THE BLOOPER

From *The Boston Globe*: "Then her hair caught fire while sitting in a front seat during a fireworks display."

Commas are used to set off contrasting or opposing expressions. These expressions are often introduced by such words as *not, never, but,* and *yet.*

We chose Tomasso's, not Luigi's, to cater our reception. (Two commas set off contrasting statement that appears in the middle of a sentence.)

Our earnings this year have been lower, yet quite adequate. (One comma sets off a contrasting statement that appears at the end of a sentence.)

The more he protests, the less we believe. (One comma sets off contrasting statement that appears at the end of a sentence.)

Clarity

Commas are used to separate words repeated for emphasis and words that may be misread if not separated.

Mr. Long said it was a very, very complex contract.
Whoever goes, goes at his own expense.
No matter what, you know you have our support.
In business, time is money.

Short Quotations

STUDY TIP

Here's a good rule to follow in relation to the comma: *When in doubt, leave it out!*

A comma is used to separate a short quotation from the rest of a sentence. If the quotation is divided into two parts, two commas are used.

Ms. Lara said, "The deadline for the McBride contract is June 6."
"The deadline for the McBride contract," said Ms. Lara, "is June 6."

HOTLINE QUERIES

QUESTION My boss always leaves out the comma before the word *and* when it precedes the final word in a series of words. Should the comma be used?

ANSWER Although some writers omit that comma, present practice favors its use so that the last two items in the series cannot be misread as one item. For example, *The departments participating are Engineering, Accounting, Personnel, and Human Resources.* Without that final comma, the last two items might be confused as one item.

QUESTION Should I use a comma after the year in this sentence: *In 1995 we began operations?*

ANSWER No. Commas are not required after short introductory prepositional phrases unless confusion might result without them. If two numbers, for example, appear consecutively, a comma would be necessary to prevent confusion: *In 1995, 156 companies used our services.*

QUESTION Are these three words interchangeable: *assure, ensure,* and *insure?*

ANSWER Although all three words mean "to make secure or certain," they are not interchangeable. *Assure* refers to persons and may suggest setting someone's mind at rest (*let me assure you that we are making every effort to locate it*). *Ensure* and *insure* both mean "to make secure from loss," but only *insure* is now used in the sense of protecting or indemnifying against loss (*the building and its contents are insured*).

QUESTION It seems to me that the word *explanation* should be spelled as *explain* is spelled. Isn't this unusual?

ANSWER Many words derived from root words change their grammatical form and spelling. Consider these: *maintain, maintenance*; *repeat, repetition*; *despair, desperate, desperation*; *pronounce, pronunciation.*

QUESTION Is *appraise* used correctly in this sentence? *We will appraise stockholders of the potential loss.*

ANSWER No. Your sentence requires *apprise*, which means "to inform or notify." The word *appraise* means "to estimate" (*he will appraise your home before you set its selling price*).

QUESTION Is an apostrophe needed in this sentence: *The supervisor('s) leaving early on Thursday prevented us from finishing the job by Friday?*

ANSWER The apostrophe is needed: *the supervisor's leaving* . . . The word *leaving* is a verbal noun (a gerund), and its modifier must be possessive. Other examples are: *the boy's whistling, the lion's roaring, my friend's driving.*

QUESTION Which word is correct in this sentence? *The officer (cited, sited, sighted) me for speeding.*

ANSWER Your sentence requires *cited*, which means "to summon" or "to quote." *Site* means "a location," as in *a building site. Sight* means "a view" or "to take aim," as in *the building was in sight.*

NAME ______________________________

12 REINFORCEMENT EXERCISES

A. (Self-check) Insert necessary commas. In the space provided, indicate briefly the reason for the comma (for example, *series, parenthetical, direct address, date, address, essential appositive, independent adjectives, introductory verbal phrases, independent clauses*, and so forth). Write *C* if the sentence is correct.

EXAMPLE: He stated, on the contrary, that he would decline the offer. ___parenthetical___

1. Saturday June 3 2000 is the date of our company picnic. ____________

2. Hong Kong is on the other hand one of the most densely populated areas in the world. ____________

3. Seminars will be held in Detroit Michigan and Chicago Illinois. ____________

4. Your client Troy Adkins called this morning. ____________

5. Clarence Darrow the famous trial lawyer defended John Scopes in the evolution trial. ____________

6. At the end of each fiscal year we prepare a progress report. ____________

7. Only college graduates will be considered and only those with technical skills will be hired. ____________

8. When our company first began we had only five employees. ____________

9. We are ready to sign the contract if that meets with your approval. ____________

10. Your testimony Ms. Murphy is essential to the prosecution's case. ____________

Check your answers below.

B. Insert necessary commas. In the space provided, indicate briefly the reason for the comma (for example, *series, parenthetical, direct address, date, address, essential appositive, independent adjectives, introductory verbal phrase, introductory clause*, and so forth). Write *C* if the sentence is correct.

1. Forward the package to Patricia Douglas 546 Fairmont Drive Miami Florida 30021 as soon as possible. ____________

2. Nancy Stewart our former office manager is now a CEO in the Southwest. ____________

3. We will of course provide you with any necessary information. ____________

4. In 1998 we asked employees to offer compliments criticism and suggestions as feedback to management. ____________

5. We feel however that a job transfer would be appropriate. ____________

6. It is a pleasure to announce that interest on your investment account at this bank will now be credited every three months. ____________

7. For you Ms. Estrada we have a three months' subscription to *Forbes.* ____________

1. Saturday, June 3, 2000, (date), 2. Hong Kong, hand, (parenthetical), 3. Detroit, Michigan, Chicago, (geographical items), 4. C, 5. Darrow, lawyer, (nonessential appositive), 6. year, (long intro. prep. phrase), 7. considered, (independent clauses), 8. began, (intro. clause), 9. contract, (dependent clause, afterthought), 10. testimony, Ms. Murphy, (direct address).

8. Horst Werner joined the staff in April 1999. ________

9. It is necessary consequently for you to pay the return postage. ________

10. Under these circumstances I believe you deserve a second chance. ________

11. Agreeing to serve as our leader Frances Sheppard made a great contribution to the committee. ________

12. If I were you I would look for openings in the technical writing department. ________

13. Our first article was published in 1999 and our second is scheduled for publication this summer. ________

14. Whenever you need my help just give me a call. ________

15. The firm has been in business 11 years and its principal offices are in Ashland. ________

16. Any increase in salaries as you might have expected is presently impossible because of declining profits. ________

17. For a period of at least six months I will not be able to take any time off. ________

18. In six months I may be able to take some time off. ________

19. Clearing the papers from his desk he finally located the contract. ________

20. We are hoping to find a talented dependable paralegal for our firm. ________

C. Insert necessary commas. For each sentence write, in the space provided, the number of commas that you inserted. If the sentence is correct, write *C*. Be prepared to explain each comma.

1. I hope Mark that you will accept the position in Hannibal Missouri as soon as possible. ____

2. My colleague Brandon will arrive Monday July 17 from Dayton Ohio. ____

3. Vickie calculated employee benefits Jennifer managed the payroll and Todd processed all accounts receivable and payable. ____

4. Alice Wells the first policewoman became a member of the Los Angeles Police Department in 1910. ____

5. We hope to hold our grand opening on Saturday April 2. ____

6. Send your application to Shannon McCarthy 160 E. Tolman Drive Philadelphia Pennsylvania 19106 before August 4. ____

7. For that reason we believe that they must of course be given first consideration. ____

8. In the meantime my plan is to gather information organize the data and prepare a report. ____

9. I have no doubt about his competency and integrity. ____

10. I noticed on our company Web site by the way that your friend Charles was promoted. ____

11. If we could change the date to Friday April 9 more people would be able to participate. ____

12. Jeff's chances in view of the newly approved rules are not good. ____

13. Starting as a bookkeeper I moved to Accounts Payable as an accountant. ____

14. Last spring our office which is located in Virginia City Nevada was destroyed by fire. ____

15. Although our staff is small we are well equipped to handle your needs. ____

16. We do not at this time see any way to incorporate this powerful versatile software. ____

17. I believe that it's time for our company to consider e-commerce and that we should work on a plan immediately. ____

18. Craig was looking for new health insurance but he did not know where to get adequate economical coverage. ____

19. At our last sales meeting we decided to focus on areas with dense populations. ____

20. In the past we have offered discounts to our customers who pay their bills promptly. ____

D. Insert necessary commas. In the space provided, indicate briefly the reason for the comma (for example, *omitted words*, *contrasting statement*, *clarity*, *short quotation*, and so forth. Write *C* if the sentence is correct.

1. On January 1 your Policy No. 8695959 will expire. ____________

2. John Ashland CPA will be preparing our tax returns. ____________

3. In reality checks in our business seldom bounce. ____________

4. The faster we do this work the sooner we can go home. ____________

5. Major responsibility for the loan lies with the signer; secondary responsibility with the cosigner. ____________

6. In short employees must be more considerate of others. ____________

7. Patricia Wille Ph.D. and Dominic Corloni M.D. spoke at the opening session. ____________

8. Cooperation not competition is what is needed at this time. ____________

9. What the problem was was a lack of communication. ____________

10. Half of the payment is due on delivery; the balance in 30 days. ____________

11. Although unhappy employees decided to ratify the contract. ____________

12. Albert Camus said "What doesn't kill me makes me stronger." ____________

13. In Room 201 32 computers and 16 printers are operating. ____________

14. "Frankly" said Brian "I don't really understand his motivation." ____________

15. Our yearly budget was over $2000000 for equipment alone. ____________

13 Semicolons and Colons

OBJECTIVES When you have completed the materials in this chapter, you will be able to do the following:

- Use semicolons correctly in punctuating compound sentences.
- Use semicolons when necessary to separate items in a series.
- Distinguish between the proper and improper use of colons to introduce listed items.
- Correctly use colons to introduce quotations and explanatory sentences.
- Distinguish between the use of commas and semicolons preceding expressions such as *namely, that is,* and *for instance.*
- Understand why semicolons are sometimes necessary to separate independent clauses joined by *and, or, nor,* or *but.*
- Use colons appropriately and be able to capitalize words following colons when necessary.

Skilled writers use semicolons and colons to signal readers about the ideas that will follow. Semicolons tell readers that two closely related ideas should be thought of together. The semicolon is a stronger punctuation mark than a comma, which signifies a pause; but the semicolon is not as strong as a period, which signifies a complete stop. Understanding the use of semicolons will help you avoid fundamental writing errors, such as the *comma splice* and the *run-on sentence.* This chapter presents basic uses and advanced applications of semicolons and colons.

BASIC USES OF THE SEMICOLON

Independent Clauses Separated by Conjunctive Adverbs

STUDY TIP

Remember that a comma is used only after a two-syllable conjunctive adverb. And don't capitalize the word following a semicolon unless it's a proper noun.

Semicolons are used primarily when two independent clauses are separated by a conjunctive adverb or a transitional expression. You studied this basic semicolon use in Chapter 10. Here are some review examples.

> Companies make no profits until they recover costs; *therefore,* most companies use a cost approach in pricing. (Semicolon separates two independent clauses joined by the conjunctive adverb *therefore.*)
>
> Wendy Spangler worked for the company for over 20 years; *thus* she had witnessed many changes. (Semicolon separates two independent clauses joined by the conjunctive adverb *thus.*)

In addition to the application shown here, semicolons may be used in other constructions, as we'll discuss next.

Independent Clauses Without a Coordinating Conjunction or a Conjunctive Adverb

SPOT THE BLOOPER

Advertisement for a car wash: "We do not scratch your paint finish with machinery; we do it by hand."

Two or more closely related independent clauses not separated by a conjunctive adverb or a coordinating conjunction (*and, or, nor, but*) require a semicolon.

> The contract was delivered on Monday; it was not signed until Thursday.
> Jake provided the business experience; Sue provided the capital.

A serious punctuation error results when separate independent clauses are joined by only a comma (a comma splice) or without any punctuation whatever (a run-on sentence).

COMMA SPLICE:	Jake provided the business experience, Sue provided the capital.
RUN-ON SENTENCE:	Jake provided the business experience Sue provided the capital.

Series Containing Internal Commas or Complete Thoughts

SPOT THE BLOOPER

Sign in a craft shop in Buxton, MA: "Her's and Mine."

Semicolons are used to separate items in a series when one or more of the items contain internal commas.

> Our company has branches in Austin, Texas; San Jose, California; and São Paulo, Brazil.
> Attending the conference were Richard Royka, executive vice president, Cabrillo Industries; Toni Cannizzaro, president, Santa Rosa Software; and Dawn Freeman, program director, Club Mediterranean.

Semicolons are used to separate three or more serial independent clauses.

> The first step consists of surveying all available information related to the company objective so that an understanding of all problems can be reached; the second step involves interviewing consumers, wholesalers, and retailers; and the third step consists of developing a research design in which the actual methods and procedures to be used are indicated.

A series of short independent clauses, however, may be separated by commas.

> The monitor size is satisfactory, the keyboard action is excellent, and the processing speed is more than adequate for our needs.

BASIC USES OF THE COLON

Formally Listed Items

NOTABLE QUOTABLE

"There are but two powers in the world: the sword and the mind. In the long run the sword is always beaten by the mind."
—Napoleon

Use a colon after an independent clause that introduces one item, two items, or a formal list. A list may be shown vertically or horizontally and is usually introduced by such words as *the following, as follows, these,* or *thus.* A colon is also used when words like these are implied but not stated.

> Creating a company Web site offered the following advantage: improved customer service. (Independent clause introduces single item.)
> Some of the most commonly used manufacturers' discounts are *the following*: trade, cash, quantity, and seasonal. (Formal list with introductory expression stated.)
> Our company uses several delivery services for our important packages: UPS, FedEx, and Airborne. (Formal list with introductory expression only implied.)

SPOT THE BLOOPER

From a student paper: "The three kinds of blood vessels are: arteries, vanes, and caterpillars." [Check spelling, word use, and punctuation.]

These are just a few of the services our advertising agency will provide for you:

1. Developing long-term advertising strategies and budgets
2. Designing memorable and effective ads
3. Analyzing sales to determine the value of the campaign

Do not use a colon unless the list is introduced by an independent clause. Lists often function as sentence complements or objects. When this is the case and the statement introducing the list is incomplete, no colon should be used. It might be easiest to remember that lists introduced by verbs or prepositions require no colons (because the introductory statement is incomplete).

SPOT THE BLOOPER

From *The Milwaukee Sentinel* in an article describing a restaurant called Twins Cafe: "There are two bathrooms and two sets of silverware at most tables."

Three requirements for this position are a master's degree, computer knowledge, and five years' experience in accounting. (No colon is used because the introductory statement is not complete; the list is introduced by a *to be* verb and functions as a complement to the sentence.)

Awards were given to the accounts payable, human resources, and sales departments for increased productivity. (No colon is used because the introductory statement is not an independent clause; the list functions as an object of the preposition *to*.)

Do not use a colon when an intervening sentence falls between the introductory statement and the list.

The following cities have been chosen as potential convention sites. A final decision will be made May 1.

New Orleans	San Francisco
Chicago	Orlando

(No colon appears after *sites* because an intervening sentence comes between the introductory statement and the list.)

Quotations

Use a colon to introduce long one-sentence quotations and quotations of two or more sentences.

Consumer advocate Lorraine Fairfield said: "Historically, in our private-enterprise economy, consumers determine what and how much is to be produced through their purchases in the marketplace; hence the needs of consumers are carefully monitored by producers."

Incomplete quotations not interrupting the flow of a sentence require no colon, no comma, and no initial capital letter.

I took her seriously when she said to "be on time."

Explanatory Sentences

Use a colon to separate two independent clauses if the second clause explains, illustrates, or supplements the first.

We were faced with a difficult problem: we could continue to fund the program in the hopes it would become self-supporting, or we could redirect the funds to a program that showed more promise.

One of the traits of highly successful people is this: they never give up on themselves.

SPECIAL CONSIDERATIONS IN USING SEMICOLONS AND COLONS

Introductory Expressions Such As *namely, for instance,* and *that is*

STUDY TIP

Notice that a comma follows *namely, for instance, that is,* and *for example* when these words are used as introductory expressions.

When introductory expressions (such as *namely, for instance, that is,* and *for example*) are used immediately following independent clauses, they may be preceded by either commas or semicolons. Generally, if the words following the introductory expression appear at the end of the sentence and form a series or an independent clause, use a semicolon before the introductory expression. If not, use a comma.

Numerous fringe benefits are available to employees; *namely,* injury compensation, life insurance, health insurance, dental care, and vision care. (A semicolon is used because *namely* introduces a series at the end of the sentence.)

Several books give additional information you may find useful when opening your own business; *for example,* Steve Mariotti's *The Young Entrepreneur's Guide to Starting and Running a Business* is an excellent resource. (A semicolon is used because *for example* introduces an independent clause.)

We are proposing many new additions to the health care package, *for example,* vision and dental benefits. (A comma is used because *for example* introduces neither a series nor an independent clause.)

SPOT THE BLOOPER

From a column in *The Chicago Tribune*: "[A] letter from her mother, written in Polish, for example, has the date (for we dummies in the audience) written in English."

These same introductory expressions may introduce parenthetical words within sentences. Usually, commas punctuate parenthetical words within sentences. If the parenthetical words thus introduced are punctuated by internal commas, however, use dashes or parentheses. (Dashes and parentheses will be treated in detail in Chapter 14.)

The biggest health problems facing workers, *namely,* drug abuse and alcoholism, cost American industry over $10 billion a year. (Commas are used because the parenthetical words contain only two items joined by *and.*)

The pursuit of basic job issues—*for instance,* wages, job security, and working conditions—has been the main concern of American workers. (Dashes are used because the parenthetical words are punctuated with commas.)

Independent Clauses With Coordinating Conjunctions

Normally, a comma precedes a coordinating conjunction (*and, or, nor, but*) when it joins two independent clauses. If either of the independent clauses contains an additional comma, however, the reader might be confused as to where the second independent clause begins. For this reason many writers prefer to use a semicolon, instead of the normally expected comma, to separate independent clauses when either independent clause contains a comma.

We have forwarded your suggestions to our product manager, and he will consider them in future product-design decisions. (Comma precedes coordinating conjunction because no additional punctuation appears within either clause.)

At the recommendation of our Customer Service Department, we have forwarded your suggestions to our product manager; and he will consider them in future product-design decisions. (Semicolon precedes coordinating conjunction because a comma appears within one of the independent clauses.)

Other Uses of the Colon

SPOT THE BLOOPER

Headline in *Parade* magazine: "What Our Children Need Is Adults Who Care."

- After the salutation of a business letter.

  Dear Mr. Tarson: Dear Human Resources Manager: Dear Felicia:

- In expressions of time to separate hours from minutes.

  10:15 a.m. 9:45 p.m.

- Between titles and subtitles.

  High Tech Start Up: The Complete Handbook for Creating Successful New High Tech Companies

- Between place of publication and name of publisher.

  Guffey, Mary Ellen, and Carolyn M. Seefer. *Essentials of College English*, 2d ed. Cincinnati: South-Western Publishing, 2001.

Capitalization Following Colons

STUDY TIP

Generally, no punctuation follows incomplete statements listed vertically.

Do not capitalize the initial letter of words or of phrases listed following a colon unless the words so listed are proper nouns or appear as a vertical array.

> The qualities we are looking for in a manager are the following: experience, demonstrated management ability, product knowledge, and good communication skills.
>
> These cities will receive heavy promotional advertising: Omaha, Lincoln, Sioux City, and Council Bluffs.
>
> To be legally enforceable, a contract must include at least four elements:
> 1. Mutual assent of all parties
> 2. Parties who are competent
> 3. A consideration
> 4. A lawful purpose

Do not capitalize the first letter of an independent clause following a colon if that clause explains or supplements the first one (unless, of course, the first word is a proper noun).

> We have chosen your bid for one reason: it encompasses all our needs for half the cost of the next lowest bidder.

Capitalize the first letter of an independent clause following a colon if that clause states a formal rule or principle.

> In business the Golden Rule is often stated in the following way: He with the gold rules.

For a quotation following a colon, capitalize the initial letter of each complete sentence.

> In their book *Clicks and Mortar*, David S. Pottruck and Terry Pierce say: "To distinguish one business from others, the people in the company have to be personally dedicated to the culture of the company. Their dedication needs to be such that they will automatically take the actions that make the company's culture live."

SPOT THE BLOOPER

From a Hewlett-Packard contest form: "If you would like the name of the winner . . . send a elf-addressed stamped envelope."

A FINAL WORD

Semicolons are excellent punctuation marks when used carefully and knowingly. After reading this chapter, though, some business communicators are guilty of semicolon overkill. They begin to string together two—and sometimes even three—independent clauses with semicolons. Remember to use semicolons in compound sentences *only* when two ideas are better presented together. Forget about joining three independent clauses with semicolons—too unconventional and too difficult to read. In most instances, independent clauses should end with periods.

HOTLINE QUERIES

QUESTION Here's a sentence we need help with: *We plan to present the contract to whoever makes the lowest bid.* My supervisor recommends *whoever* and I suggest *whomever.* Which of us is right?

ANSWER Your supervisor. The preposition *to* has as its object the entire clause (*whoever makes the lowest bid*). Within that clause *whoever* functions as the subject of the verb *makes*; therefore, the nominative case form *whoever* should be used.

QUESTION When I list items vertically, should I use a comma or a semicolon after each item? Should a period be used after the final item? For example,

Please inspect the following rooms and equipment:
1. The control room
2. The power transformer and its standby
3. The auxiliary switchover equipment

ANSWER Do not use commas or semicolons after items listed vertically, and do not use a period after the last item in such a list. However, if the listed items are complete sentences or if they are long phrases that complete the meaning of the introductory comment, periods may be used after each item.

QUESTION Is there a plural form of *plus and minus*?

ANSWER The plural form is *pluses* (or *plusses*) *and minuses* (*consider all the pluses and minuses before you make a decision*).

QUESTION I'm setting up advertising copy, and this sentence doesn't look right to me: *This line of fishing reels are now priced . . .*

ANSWER Your suspicion is correct. The subject of the verb in this sentence is *line*; it requires the singular verb *is.*

QUESTION I wonder if the possessive is correctly expressed in this sentence that I'm transcribing: *I appreciate the candor of both you and Neil in our conversation.* Shouldn't both *you* and *Neil* be made possessive?

ANSWER No. It would be very awkward to say *your and Neil's candor.* It's much better to use the *of* construction, thus avoiding the awkward double possessive.

QUESTION Is this a double negative: *We can't schedule the meeting because we have no room available?*

ANSWER No, this is not regarded as a double negative. In grammar a double negative is created when two negative adverbs modify a verb, such as *can't hardly, won't barely,* or *can't help but.* Avoid such constructions.

NAME ____________________

13 REINFORCEMENT EXERCISES

A. (Self-check) For each of the following sentences, underline any errors in punctuation. Then in the space provided, write the correct punctuation mark plus the word preceding it. Write *C* if the sentence is correct.

EXAMPLE: Elliot invested wisely, consequently, he was able to retire early. ___wisely;___

1. Many people sell items on eBay it is the most widely used Internet auction site. ________
2. The price of our stock has been steadily increasing therefore, I will make quite a profit when I sell. ________
3. Jeff Bezos worked for years to build Amazon.com, the company has just begun to make a profit. ________
4. Our equipment costs have tripled in the last five years personnel expenses have grown even faster. ________
5. E-commerce is a risky undertaking, .com companies disappear as quickly as they appear. ________

For each of the following sentences, underline any errors in punctuation. If a colon should be omitted, write *Omit colon* in the space provided. Write *C* if the sentence is correct.

EXAMPLE: Seats were reserved for: the president, the vice president, and the treasurer. ___Omit colon___

6. We need sales reports for the following months. They must be submitted before this afternoon's meeting: ________

   February May
   August October

7. Shane proposed a solution to our day-care problem: open a home office and share childcare duties. ________
8. The computer virus was called: "the Love Bug." ________
9. We have requests for information from three local companies: Sterling Laboratories, Putnam Brothers, and Data Control. ________
10. We sent the report by fax to: the CEO, the CFO, and the COO. ________

Insert necessary punctuation. In the space provided, write the number of punctuation marks that you inserted. Write *C* if the sentence is correct.

11. Four employees have been recognized for achievement awards; namely, Michael Taylor, Corrine Chan, Todd Wilde, and Katie Freeman. ____
12. Many banks now offer automated transfers from savings to checking accounts that is money may be kept in an interest-bearing savings account until needed. ____
13. All executive assistants are urged to observe the following rule: When in doubt, consult the company style manual. ____
14. She used many visual aids during her presentation for example, slides, overheads, and handouts. ____
15. You may repay your loan according to one of the following plans: the annual plan, the semiannual plan, the quarterly plan, or the weekly plan. ____

Check your answers below.

1. eBay; 2. increasing; 3. Amazon.com; 4. years; 5. undertaking; 6. Omit colon 7. C 8. Omit colon 9. C 10. Omit colon 11. C 12. (2) accounts; that is, 13. C 14. (1) presentation; 15. C.

NAME ________________________________

B. Add any necessary commas or semicolons to the following sentences. (Do not add periods.) In the spaces provided, write the number of punctuation marks you inserted. Write *C* if a sentence is correct as written.

EXAMPLE: New equipment was ordered eight weeks ago; delivery is expected within two weeks. ___1___

1. Thu Tran is self-employed therefore she makes quarterly tax payments. ______
2. The Islands of Langerhans cannot be found on a map they are really cells found in the human pancreas. ______
3. Serving on the panel of experts are Pam Rippin marketing director Santa Rosa Associates Evelyn Katusak sales supervisor Broome Products and Timothy Miank market analyst Lansing Enterprises. ______
4. The global economy is shifting toward services and knowledge-based work consequently the kinds of careers and jobs available are changing. ______
5. Cindy is a talented artist hence she was able to help our company design its Web site. ______
6. Change can be painful resisting change is even more painful. ______
7. His retirement party is next week and I hope you will be able to attend. ______
8. Microsoft hired over 2,000 new employees last year it plans to hire even more next year. ______
9. Computer hackers can easily decode short passwords thus passwords should be at least eight characters long and be a mix of letters and numerals. ______
10. Smart companies assume their computer networks will be broken into consequently they develop computer-use policies to limit the damage. ______

C. For the following sentences, add any necessary but missing punctuation marks. For each sentence indicate in the space provided the number of additions you have made. Mark *C* if the sentence is correct as it stands.

EXAMPLE: Brochures will be sent to our offices in Dallas, Cleveland, and St. Louis. ___2___

1. Japan faces a serious economic threat its dependence on oil imports endangers its future economic growth. ______
2. Commenting on the astounding advance of computer technology, Randall Tobias said "If we had similar progress in automotive technology, today you could buy a Lexus for about $2. It would travel at the speed of sound and go about 600 miles on a thimble of gas." ______
3. I will serve on the committee on one condition: it must not require more than two hours per week. ______
4. The following four reference books will be required for this project dictionary thesaurus book of quotations and atlas. ______
5. Additional costs in selling the house are title examination, title insurance, transfer tax, preparation of documents, and closing fee. ______
6. Marilyn solved her problem with repetitive motion she purchased an ergonomic keyboard. ______
7. In addition to providing product information, a good Web site will also tell you how to purchase the product, how to return the product, and how to contact the company. ______
8. I sent articles to three top magazines: *Forbes*, *The Economist*, and *Newsweek*. ______
9. The law of supply and demand can function only under the following condition producers must know what consumers want. ______

10. Of all the discoveries and inventions in human history, the four greatest are said to be these speech, fire, agriculture, and the wheel. _____

11. Because of her computer expertise Allison was chosen as our network administrator and because of his people skills Gordon was chosen as trainer. _____

12. Have you read the book *The Next New Thing A Silicon Valley Story*? _____

13. We offer a semiannual salary review that is your salary will be reviewed once every six months and adjusted if necessary. _____

14. Les enjoyed living in Ohio very much but when he received a job offer in San Francisco he found it hard to decline. _____

15. Stories circulated about Henry Ford founder Ford Motor Company Lee Iacocca former CEO Chrysler Motor Company and Shoichiro Toyoda chief Toyota Motor Company. _____

14 Other Punctuation

OBJECTIVES When you have completed the materials in this chapter, you will be able to do the following:

- Use periods to correctly punctuate statements, commands, indirect questions, and polite requests.
- Use periods to correctly punctuate abbreviations, initials, and numerals.
- Use question marks and exclamation points correctly.
- Recognize acceptable applications of the dash.
- Use parentheses to de-emphasize material.
- Explain when to use commas, dashes, or parentheses to set off nonessential material.
- Correctly punctuate and capitalize material set off by parentheses and dashes.
- Correctly use double and single quotation marks.
- Correctly place other punctuation marks in relation to quotation marks.
- Use brackets, underscores, and italics appropriately.

This chapter teaches you how to use periods, question marks, and exclamation points correctly. It also includes suggestions for punctuating with dashes, parentheses, single quotation marks, double quotation marks, brackets, and underscores (italics).

USES FOR THE PERIOD

To Punctuate Sentences

NOTABLE QUOTABLE

"There's not so much to be said about the period except that most people don't reach it soon enough."
—William Zinsser, writing expert

Use a period at the end of a statement, a command, an indirect question, or a polite request. Although it may have the same structure as a question, a polite request ends with a period.

> Annette Jenkins was promoted to a position with increased salary and responsibilities. (Statement.)
> Send an e-mail message to all employees immediately. (Command.)
> Tracey asked whether we had sent the price list. (Indirect question.)
> Would you please send me a copy of your latest brochure. (Polite request.)

To Punctuate Abbreviations

Because of their inconsistencies, abbreviations present problems to writers. The following suggestions will help you organize certain groups of abbreviations and provide many models. In studying these models, note the spacing, capitalization, and use of periods. Always consult a good dictionary or style manual when in doubt.

Use periods after many abbreviations beginning with lowercase letters.

a.m. (ante meridiem)	i.e. (that is)
e.g. (for example)	ft. (foot or feet)

Exceptions: mph (miles per hour), wpm (words per minute), mm (millimeter), and kg (kilogram).

Use periods for most abbreviations containing capital and lowercase letters.

Dr. (Doctor)	Mr. (Mister)
Esq. (Esquire)	No. (number)
Ms. (blend of Miss and Mrs.)	Sat. (Saturday)

Use periods with abbreviations that represent academic degrees, geographical expressions, and initials of a person's first and middle names.

B.A. (bachelor of arts)	S.A. (South America)
M.B.A. (master of business administration)	U.K. (United Kingdom)
M.D. (doctor of medicine)	U.S.A. (United States of America)
Ph.D. (doctor of philosophy)	Mr. J. A. Jones (initials of name)

Do *not* use periods for most capitalized abbreviations.

STUDY TIP

Most abbreviations fall in this group. Note capitalized letters, lack of periods, and tight spacing.

CEO (chief executive officer)	IBM (International Business Machines)
CFO (chief financial officer)	ID (identification)
CPA (certified public accountant)	RAM (random-access memory)
CPU (central processing unit)	SASE (self-addressed, stamped envelope)
EPA (Environmental Protection Agency)	SEC (Securities and Exchange Commission)
EST (Eastern Standard Time)	SOP (standard operating procedure)
FYI (for your information)	URL (Universal Resource Locator)
GDP (gross domestic product)	WWW (World Wide Web)

Some abbreviations have two forms.

c.o.d., COD (collect on delivery)	f.o.b., FOB (free on board)
d.b.a., DBA (doing business as)	p.o.e., POE (port of entry)

To Punctuate Numerals

For a monetary sum use a period (decimal point) to separate dollars from cents.

> The two items in question, $13.92 and $98, were both charged in the month of October.

Use a period (decimal point) to mark a decimal fraction.

> Only 35.3 percent of eligible voters are registered in this precinct.

USES FOR THE QUESTION MARK

To Punctuate Direct Questions

Use a question mark at the end of a direct question.

> When is your manager scheduled to return?
> Have you received a response from the software company?

STUDY TIP

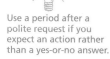

Use a period after a polite request if you expect an action rather than a yes-or-no answer.

Do not punctuate polite requests as questions. These are considered to be commands or "please do" statements. A polite request asks the reader to perform a specific action and is usually answered by an action rather than a verbal response.

Will you please take a moment to complete this survey.

To Punctuate Questions Appended to Statements

Place a question mark after a question that is appended to a statement. Use a comma to separate the statement from the question.

They have already established a Web site, haven't they?
This human resources announcement should be sent by e-mail, don't you think?

To Indicate Doubt

A question mark within parentheses may be used to indicate a degree of doubt about some aspect of a statement.

Each application should be accompanied by two (?) letters of recommendation.
A starting salary of $3,500 (?) per month is expected.

SPOT THE BLOOPER

Ad for an electronics store published in the *Journal-News* [Rockland, NY]: "Bring in any competitor's ad and we will beat the price plus 10% of the difference in price or it's your's free!"

USES FOR THE EXCLAMATION POINT

To Express Strong Emotion

After a word, phrase, or clause expressing strong emotion, use an exclamation point. In business writing, however, exclamation points should be used sparingly.

Ridiculous! I will never be able to meet such a tight deadline.
Unbelievable! Have you seen these sales figures?
It is amazing that the copier has not broken down after all this abuse!

Do not use an exclamation point after mild interjections, such as *oh* and *well.*

Well, I was expecting something like this.

USES FOR THE DASH

The dash is a legitimate and effective mark of punctuation when used according to accepted conventions. As an emphatic punctuation mark, however, the dash loses effectiveness when it is overused. In typewritten or simple word processing-generated material, a dash is formed by typing two hyphens with no space before, between, or after the hyphens. In printed or desktop publishing-generated material, a dash appears as a solid line (an *em* dash). (Note: Most current word processors will automatically convert two hyphens to an *em* dash.) Study the following suggestions for and illustrations of appropriate uses of the dash.

NOTABLE QUOTABLE

"In the Information Age, flexibility is the critical foundation for success. Future generations will need more than just mastery of subject matter. They will need mastery of learning."
—Morris Weeks

To Set Off Parenthetical Elements

Within a sentence parenthetical elements are usually set off by commas. If, however, the parenthetical element itself contains internal commas, use dashes (or parentheses) to set it off.

Sources of raw materials—farming, mining, fishing, and forestry—are all dependent on energy.
Four administrative assistants—Priscilla Alvarez, Sonia Vargas, Yoshiki Ono, and Edward Botsko—received cash bonuses for outstanding performance in their departments.

To Indicate an Interruption

An interruption or abrupt change of thought may be separated from the rest of a sentence by a dash.

> We will refund your money—you have my guarantee—if you are not satisfied.
> You can submit your report on Friday—no, we must have it by Thursday at the latest.

Sentences with abrupt changes of thought or with appended afterthoughts can usually be improved through rewriting.

To Set Off a Summarizing Statement

Use a dash (not a colon) to separate an introductory list from a summarizing statement.

> Experience, communication skills, patience—these are the qualities I appreciate most in a manager.
> Cal Bears, Georgia Bulldogs, Michigan State Spartans—those are Chip's favorite college football teams.

To Attribute a Quotation

Place a dash between a quotation and its source.

> "Live as if you were to die tomorrow. Learn as if you were to live forever."
> —Gandhi
> "The future belongs to those who believe in the beauty of their dreams."
> —Eleanor Roosevelt

USES FOR PARENTHESES

To Set Off Nonessential Sentence Elements

Generally, nonessential sentence elements may be punctuated as follows: (a) with commas, to make the lightest possible break in the normal flow of a sentence; (b) with dashes, to emphasize the enclosed material; and (c) with parentheses, to de-emphasize the enclosed material.

> Figure 17, which appears on page 9, clearly illustrates the process involved. (Normal punctuation.)
> Figure 17—which appears on page 9—clearly illustrates the process involved. (Dashes emphasize enclosed material.)
> Figure 17 (which appears on page 9) clearly illustrates the process involved. (Parentheses de-emphasize enclosed material.)

Explanations, references, and directions are often enclosed in parentheses.

> The bank's current business hours (10 a.m. to 3 p.m.) will be extended in the near future (to 6 p.m.).
> I recommend that we direct more funds (see the budget on p. 14) to research and development.

Additional Considerations

If the material enclosed by parentheses is embedded within another sentence, a question mark or exclamation point may be used where normally expected. Do not, however, use a period after a statement embedded within another sentence.

I visited the new business travel Web site (have you seen it?) last night. (A question mark concludes a question enclosed by parentheses and embedded in another sentence.)

We held a special meeting (but no one attended it!) to discuss these policy issues. (An exclamation mark concludes an exclamation enclosed by parentheses and embedded in another sentence.)

The program's AutoCorrect feature (this will be described in a later chapter) corrects misspelled words as soon as you type them. (A period is not used at the end of a statement that is enclosed by parentheses and embedded in another sentence.)

If the material enclosed by parentheses is not embedded in another sentence, use whatever punctuation is required.

SPOT THE BLOOPER

From an ad for PageMaker, a computer program: "It is still the most easiest program to learn yet the most powerful."

Our proposal is to hire eight new employees immediately to keep the project on track. (See Appendix A for job descriptions and associated costs.)

An estimated two-thirds of U.S. employees work in the services sector. (Does anyone remember when most jobs were in manufacturing?)

In sentences involving expressions within parentheses, a comma, semicolon, or colon that would normally occupy the position occupied by the second parenthesis is then placed after that parenthesis.

SPOT THE BLOOPER

From *The Press* [Atlantic City, NJ]: "John Merrill of Dorchester in Cumberland County called to say he'd seen an immature [rattlesnake] crossing a dirt road while out running for exercise."

When we deliver the product (in late June), we can begin testing on site. (Comma follows parenthesis.)

Your tax return was received before the deadline (April 15); however, you did not include a payment. (Semicolon follows parenthesis.)

USES FOR QUOTATION MARKS

To Enclose Direct Quotations

Double quotation marks are used to enclose direct quotations. Unless the exact words of a writer or speaker are being repeated, however, quotation marks are not employed.

SPOT THE BLOOPER

From *The Journal-American* [Bellevue, WA]: "Youths caught breaking the law or their parents could face a $250 fine or community service."

"Never trust a computer you can't throw out a window," said Apple Computer Corporation cofounder Steve Wozniak. (Direct quotation enclosed.)

Abraham Lincoln said that we cannot escape tomorrow's responsibility by evading it today. (Indirect quotation requires no quotation marks.)

Capitalize only the first word of a direct quotation.

"The human race has one really effective weapon," said Mark Twain, "and that is laughter." (Do not capitalize *and.*)

SPOT THE BLOOPER

From *The Times & Record News* [Wichita Falls, TX]: "Do not sweep an area where there have been rodents with a broom."

To Enclose Quotations Within Quotations

Single quotation marks (apostrophes on most keyboards) are used to enclose quoted passages cited within quoted passages.

My boss said, "I agree with Woody Allen, who said, 'Eighty percent of success is showing up.'" (Single quotation marks within double quotation marks.)

To Enclose Short Expressions

Slang, words used in a special sense, and words following *stamped* or *marked* are often enclosed within quotation marks.

Cheryl feared that her presentation would "bomb." (Slang.)

Computer criminals are often called "hackers." (Words used in a special sense.)

In computer terminology a "bit" is the smallest unit of measure. (Word used in a special sense.)

The package was stamped "Handle with Care." (Words following *stamped.*)

To Enclose Definitions

Quotation marks are used to enclose definitions of words or expressions. The word or expression being defined should be underscored or set in italics.

The French term *fait accompli* means "an accomplished deed or fact."

Business owners use the term *working capital* to indicate an "excess of current assets over current debts."

To Enclose Titles

Quotation marks are used to enclose the titles of subdivisions of literary and artistic works, such as magazine and newspaper articles, chapters of books, episodes of television shows, poems, lectures, and songs. However, italics (or underscores) are used to enclose the titles of complete works, such as the names of books, magazines, pamphlets, movies, television series, albums, and newspapers.

One source of information for your proposal might be the magazine article "Networking at the Speed of Light," which appeared in *Business Week* recently.

Job seekers find the section entitled "The Impatient Job-Hunter" from *What Color Is Your Parachute?* very helpful.

The episode "Requiem," in which Dana Scully announced her pregnancy, ended the season for the *X Files* TV series.

To Kill a Mockingbird has always been one of her favorite films.

Additional Punctuation Considerations

DID YOU KNOW

Keeping periods and commas inside quotation marks is an American style that stems from the days of hot type. Periods and commas tended to break off at the ends of lines. Printers set them inside to make sturdier lines. Once established, this practice continued in America—but not in Britain.

Periods and commas are always placed inside closing quotation marks, whether single or double. Semicolons and colons are, on the other hand, always placed outside quotation marks.

Angie said, "I'm sure the package was stamped 'First Class.'"

The article is entitled "Corporate Espionage," but I don't have a copy.

Our contract stipulated that "both parties must accept arbitration as binding"; therefore, the decision reached by the arbitrators is final.

Three dates have been scheduled for the seminar called "Success on the Internet": April 1, May 3, and June 5.

Question marks and exclamation points may go inside or outside closing quotation marks, as determined by the form of the quotation.

SPOT THE BLOOPER

From an invitation to a dinner honoring newly elected Board of Education members [Scarborough, MA]: "Your Invited."

Kalonji Watts said, "How may I apply for that position?" (Quotation is a question.)

"If your cell phone rings again," fumed Ms. Henshaw, "we will ask you to leave!" (Quotation is an exclamation.)

Do you know who it was who said, "Hold fast to dreams, for if dreams die, life is a broken winged bird that cannot fly"? (Incorporating sentence asks question; quotation does not.)

I can't believe the package was marked "Fragile"! (Incorporating sentence is an exclamation; quotation is not.)

SPOT THE BLOOPER

Sign on I-75 in Florida: "Speed Limit Strickly Enforced"

When did the manager say, "Who wants to reserve a summer vacation?" (Both incorporating sentence and quotation are questions. Use only one question mark inside the quotation marks.)

USES FOR BRACKETS

Within quotations, brackets are used by writers to enclose their own inserted remarks. Such remarks may be corrective, illustrative, or explanatory. Brackets are also used within quotations to enclose the word *sic*, which means "thus" or "so." This Latin form is used to emphasize the fact that an error obvious to all actually appears *thus* in the quoted material.

"A British imperial gallon," reported Ms. Sohoori, "is equal to 1.2 U.S. gallons [4.54 liters]."

"The company's reorganization program," wrote President Todd Holt, "will have its greatest affect [*sic*] on our immediate sales."

USES FOR THE UNDERSCORE AND ITALICS

STUDY TIP

With today's sophisticated software programs and printers, you can, like professional printers, use italics instead of underscoring for titles and special words.

The underscore or italics are normally used for titles of books, magazines, newspapers, movies, and other complete works published separately. In addition, words under discussion in the sentence and used as nouns are italicized or underscored.

No Such Thing As a Bad Day, the latest book by author Hamilton Jordan, was favorably reviewed in *The Wall Street Journal.*

Two of the most frequently misused words are *affect* and *effect.* (Words used as nouns.)

They saw *Star Wars Episode I: The Phantom Menace* on opening night.

HOTLINE QUERIES

QUESTION We can't decide whether the period should go inside quotation marks or outside. At the end of a sentence, I have typed the title "Positive Vs. Negative Values." The author of the document that I'm typing wants the period outside because she says the title does not have a period in it.

ANSWER In the U.S., typists and printers have adopted a uniform style: when a period or comma falls at the same place quotation marks would normally fall, the period or comma is always placed inside the quotation marks—regardless of the content of the quotation. In Britain a different style is observed.

QUESTION I'm not sure where to place the question mark in this sentence: *His topic will be "What Is a Good Health Plan (?)"* Does the question mark go inside the quotation marks? Too, should a comma precede the title of the talk?

ANSWER First, a question mark goes inside the quotation mark because the quoted material is in the form of a question. Be sure that you do not use another end punctuation mark after the quotation mark. Second, do not use a comma preceding the title of the topic because the sentence follows normal subject-verb-complement order. No comma is needed to separate the verb and the complement.

QUESTION Is it correct to say *Brad and myself were chosen . . .*?

ANSWER No. Use the nominative case pronoun *I* instead of *myself.*

QUESTION What salutation should I use when addressing a letter to Sister Mary Elizabeth?

ANSWER The salutation of your letter should be *Dear Sister Mary Elizabeth.* For more information on forms of address, consult a good dictionary or reference manual.

QUESTION Is anything wrong with saying *someone else's car*?

ANSWER Although it sounds somewhat awkward, the possessive form is acceptable. The apostrophe is correctly placed in *else's.*

QUESTION I've looked in the dictionary, but I'm still unsure about whether to hyphenate *copilot.*

ANSWER The hyphen is no longer used in most words beginning with the prefix *co* (*coauthor, cocounsel, codesign, cofeature, cohead, copilot, costar, cowrite*). Only a few words retain the hyphen (*co-anchor, co-edition, co-official*). Check your dictionary for usage. In reading your dictionary, notice that centered periods are used to indicate syllables (*co•work•er*); hyphens are used to show hyphenated syllables (*co-own*).

QUESTION Can you tell me what sounds strange in this sentence and why? *The building looks like it was redesigned.*

ANSWER The word *like* should not be used as a conjunction, as has been done in your sentence. Substitute *as if* (*the building looks as if it was redesigned*).

NAME ______________________________

14 REINFORCEMENT EXERCISES

A. (Self-check) Write the letter of the correctly punctuated sentence in the space provided.

1. (a) He scored a perfect 800 (can you believe it) on the GMAT. ____
(b) He scored a perfect 800 (can you believe it?) on the GMAT.
(c) He scored a perfect 800 (can you believe it) on the GMAT?

2. (Emphasize parenthetical element.)
(a) Currently our basic operating costs: rent, utilities, and wages, are 10 percent higher than last year. ____
(b) Currently our basic operating costs (rent, utilities, and wages) are 10 percent higher than last year.
(c) Currently our basic operating costs—rent, utilities, and wages—are 10 percent higher than last year.

3. (a) Removing the back panel (see the warning on page 1) should be done only by authorized repair staff. ____
(b) Removing the back panel, see the warning on page 1, should be done only by authorized repair staff.
(c) Removing the back panel: see the warning on page 1, should be done only by authorized repair staff.

4. (a) Last week you ordered disks (250MB Zip disks); however, you did not state a quantity. ____
(b) Last week you ordered disks; (250MB Zip disks) however, you did not state a quantity.
(c) Last week you ordered disks (250MB Zip disks;) however, you did not state a quantity.

5. (a) Sales, sales, and more sales: that's what we need to succeed.
(b) Sales, sales, and more sales—that's what we need to succeed.
(c) Sales, sales, and more sales; that's what we need to succeed. ____

Indicate whether the following statements are true (*T*) or false (*F*).

6. Quotation marks are used to enclose the exact words of a writer or speaker. ____

7. The names of books, magazines, pamphlets, and newspapers may be underscored or enclosed in quotation marks. ____

8. Periods and commas are always placed inside closing quotation marks. ____

9. Parentheses are used by writers to enclose their own remarks inserted into a quotation. ____

10. A quotation within a quotation is shown with single quotation marks. ____

11. Semicolons and colons are always placed inside closing quotation marks. ____

12. The underscore is used to emphasize words that would be italicized in printed copy. ____

13. If both a quotation and its introductory sentence are questions, use a question mark before the closing quotation marks. ____

14. The word *sic* is used to show that a quotation is free of errors. ____

15. A single quotation mark is typed by using the apostrophe key. ____

Check your answers below.

1. b, 2. c, 3. a, 4. a, 5. b, 6. T, 7. F, 8. T, 9. F, 10. T, 11. F, 12. T, 13. T, 14. F, 15. T.

B. In the following sentences all punctuation has been omitted. Insert commas, periods, question marks, colons, and exclamation points. Use a caret (^) to indicate each insertion. Periods and commas may be placed inside the caret. In the space at the right, indicate the number of punctuation marks you inserted. Consult a reference manual or a dictionary for abbreviation style if necessary.

EXAMPLE: Will you please send a copy to Mr^L^R^Smith Jr^at this address^ ___5___

1. Abbreviations such as misc and attn are generally not used in business correspondence ______
2. She arrived at 8 a m and was unable to leave until 10 p m ______
3. Dr Angela Morris was just named CFO at MileHigh Enterprises ______
4. You are planning to speak at the meeting aren't you ______
5. It was Robert not Julie who expected a cod shipment ______
6. We couldn't have completed our tax returns without the help of our CPA ______
7. Please install this CPU in Dr Ryan's office before 3 pm ______
8. Did you order from IBM or Apple ______
9. Dr R J Michaels has been hired as a benefits consultant to the AFL - CIO ______
10. I asked whether the New York office is open until 5 pm EST ______
11. The following speakers will address our participants Dr Joyce Brothers Mr Dan Rather and Ms Barbara Walters ______
12. Are you sure your PC has enough RAM to run this software ______
13. You did check the URL for that Web site, didn't you ______
14. Gail Sanchez MD and Timothy Johnston RN are coordinating the health fair ______
15. It is SOP in our office to use ZIP codes on every letter ______

C. Write the letter of the correctly punctuated sentence.

1. **(a)** I wonder whether I could return Mr. Lee's call as early as 8 am. ______
   (b) I wonder whether I could return Mr. Lee's call as early as 8 a.m.?
   (c) I wonder whether I could return Mr. Lee's call as early as 8 a.m.
2. **(a)** Did our CEO interview Ms. E. W. Rasheen for the CPA position? ______
   (b) Did our C.E.O. interview Ms. E. W. Rasheen for the C.P.A. position?
   (c) Did our CEO interview Ms E. W. Rasheen for the CPA position?
3. **(a)** Isabelle asked whether jobs from the U.K. or S.A. were listed online. ______
   (b) Isabelle asked whether jobs from the UK or SA were listed online.
   (c) Isabelle asked whether jobs from the U.K. or S.A. were listed online?
4. **(a)** Tell Mr. Willett to submit his proposal immediately to InfoWorld, Inc.. ______
   (b) Tell Mr. Willett to submit his proposal immediately to InfoWorld, Inc.
   (c) Tell Mr Willett to submit his proposal immediately to InfoWorld, Inc.
5. **(a)** The No 1 official at the EPA has a B.A. from Ohio State. ______
   (b) The No. 1 official at the E.P.A. has a BA from Ohio State.
   (c) The No. 1 official at the EPA has a B.A. from Ohio State.

D. Insert dashes or parentheses in the following sentences. In the space provided after each sentence, write the number of punctuation marks you inserted. Count each parenthesis and each dash as a single mark.

EXAMPLE: (Emphasize.) Three of the biggest problems with e-mail—privacy, overuse, and etiquette—will be discussed. ___2___

1. (De-emphasize.) A classic version of Goethe's *Faust* have you read it? will be playing here in May. ____

2. (Emphasize.) Four great desert regions the Great Sandy, the Outback, the Gibson, and the Great Victoria are in Australia. ____

3. "We must use time wisely and forever realize that the time is always ripe to do right." Nelson Mandela ____

4. (Emphasize.) Three branch assistant managers Courtney Young, Ramon Lopez, and Samantha Johnson will be promoted this month. ____

5. (De-emphasize.) Three branch assistant managers Courtney Young, Ramon Lopez, and Samantha Johnson will be promoted this month. ____

6. (De-emphasize.) As soon as your forms are complete try to submit them by June 30 , we will process your claim. ____

7. Quality copies, low cost, ease of operation, speedy output what more could a customer want in an economical office copy machine? ____

8. Project reviews will be held on the following dates see the attached calendar: January 15, April 11, and July 31. ____

9. (De-emphasize.) Although clubs are also located elsewhere Detroit, Lansing, and Ann Arbor, the largest membership is in Battle Creek. ____

10. The warranty period for this DVD player is limited to sixty 60 days. ____

NAME ______________________________

UNIT 4 REVIEW ■ Chapters 12–14 (Self-Check)

First, review Chapters 12–14. Then test your comprehension of those chapters by completing the exercises that follow. Compare your responses with those at the end of the review.

Insert necessary punctuation in the following sentences. In the space provided write the number of punctuation marks you inserted. Write *C* if the sentence is correct.

1. Because of your many years of service Ms. Welch, we are presenting you with this plaque. ____

2. However the matter is resolved, the goodwill of the customer is paramount. ____

3. Our Human Resources Department is concerned with recruiting hiring and training new employees. ____

4. A sales rep who brings in new accounts will receive a bonus at the end of the month. ____

5. I feel on the other hand that I must do some independent research. ____

6. The field technician Janice Maxwell knows the equipment thoroughly. ____

Select (a), (b), or (c) to indicate the correctly punctuated sentence.

7. **(a)** Reports have arrived from our offices in Bonn, Switzerland, Munich, Germany, and Vienna, Austria. ____
(b) Reports have arrived from our offices in Bonn, Switzerland; Munich, Germany; and Vienna, Austria.
(c) Reports have arrived from our offices in: Bonn, Switzerland; Munich, Germany; and Vienna, Austria.

8. **(a)** Most of your order was shipped Thursday the rest will be shipped today. ____
(b) Most of your order was shipped Thursday, the rest will be shipped today.
(c) Most of your order was shipped Thursday; the rest will be shipped today.

9. **(a)** His proposal arrived after the deadline; therefore, we could not consider it. ____
(b) His proposal arrived after the deadline, therefore, we could not consider it.
(c) His proposal arrived after the deadline; therefore we could not consider it.

10. **(a)** Would you please send the shipment COD. ____
(b) Would you please send the shipment c.o.d.?
(c) Would you please send the shipment COD?

Select (a), (b), or (c) to indicate the correctly punctuated sentence.

11. **(a)** Molly holds both BS and MS degrees doesn't she? ____
(b) Molly holds both B.S. and M.S. degrees, doesn't she?
(c) Molly holds both BS and MS degrees, doesn't she?

12. **(a)** Wow, sales increased by over 15 point five percent. ____
(b) Wow! Sales increased by over 15.5 percent!
(c) Wow, Sales increased by over 15.5%.

13. **(a)** We're looking for three qualities in employees; honesty, intelligence, and experience. ____
(b) We're looking for three qualities in employees, honesty, intelligence, and experience.
(c) We're looking for three qualities in employees: honesty, intelligence, and experience.

14. **(a)** Thus far, we have received brochures from Gateway, IBM, and Dell. ____
(b) Thus far, we have received brochures from, Gateway, IBM, and Dell.
(c) Thus far, we have received brochures from: Gateway, IBM, and Dell.

15. **(a)** Tom said, "This is not my area of responsibility."
(b) Tom said: "This is not my area of responsibility."
(c) Tom said; "This is not my area of responsibility."

16. **(a)** Three of the most populous states: Illinois, New York, and California, will receive extra federal funding. _____
(b) Three of the most populous states—Illinois, New York, and California—will receive extra federal funding.
(c) Three of the most populous states, Illinois, New York, and California, will receive extra federal funding.

17. **(a)** October, November, and December—these are our busiest months. _____
(b) October, November, and December: these are our busiest months.
(c) October, November, and December, these are our busiest months.

18. (Emphasize.)
(a) In only three months, October, November, and December, our store does 80 percent of its yearly business. _____
(b) In only three months: October, November, and December, our store does 80 percent of its yearly business.
(c) In only three months—October, November, and December—our store does 80 percent of its yearly business.

19. **(a)** The three Alaskan towns selected are Nome, Anchorage, and Juneau. _____
(b) The three Alaskan towns selected are: Nome, Anchorage, and Juneau.
(c) The three Alaskan towns selected are—Nome, Anchorage, and Juneau.

20. (De-emphasize.)
(a) Recent statistics—refer to page 4 of this study—show an increase in Internet usage. _____
(b) Recent statistics, refer to page 4 of this study, show an increase in Internet usage.
(c) Recent statistics (refer to page 4 of this study) show an increase in Internet usage.

Select (a), (b), or (c) to indicate the correctly punctuated sentence.

21. **(a)** In summary reports of a hostile takeover are exaggerated. _____
(b) In summary—reports of a hostile takeover are exaggerated.
(c) In summary, reports of a hostile takeover are exaggerated.

22. **(a)** Our goal is to encourage, not hamper, good communication. _____
(b) Our goal is to encourage—not hamper, good communication.
(c) Our goal is to encourage, not hamper good communication.

23. **(a)** Only one source can be used to format reports, namely our company style guide. _____
(b) Only one source can be used to format reports, namely, our company style guide.
(c) Only one source can be used to format reports: namely, our company style guide.

24. **(a)** The location of the convention has been narrowed to three sites, namely, Phoenix, Atlanta, and San Francisco. _____
(b) The location of the convention has been narrowed to three sites; namely, Phoenix, Atlanta, and San Francisco.
(c) The location of the convention has been narrowed to three sites; namely Phoenix, Atlanta, and San Francisco.

25. **(a)** The output we received was "garbage," that is, the printout showed only indecipherable characters. _____
(b) The output we received was "garbage"; that is, the printout showed only indecipherable characters.
(c) The output we received was "garbage;" that is, the printout showed only indecipherable characters.

26. (a) Netiquette is defined as "the rules of etiquette on the Internet." ____
(b) "Netiquette" is defined as 'the rules of etiquette on the Internet.'
(c) *Netiquette* is defined as "the rules of etiquette on the Internet."

27. (a) Fast Company, a monthly magazine for businesspeople in the Internet age, featured an article called "The Art of Getting Things Done." ____
(b) *Fast Company,* a monthly magazine for businesspeople in the Internet age, featured an article called "The Art of Getting Things Done."
(c) "Fast Company," a monthly magazine for businesspeople in the Internet age, featured an article called <u>The Art of Getting Things Done</u>.

28. (a) "Our strategy," said Mark Nichols, "is to take the competition by surprise." ____
(b) "Our strategy," said Mark Nichols, "Is to take the competition by surprise."
(c) "Our strategy, said Mark Nichols, "is to take the competition by surprise."

29. (a) Do you know who said, "Nothing great was ever achieved without enthusiasm."? ____
(b) Do you know who said, "Nothing great was ever achieved without enthusiasm?"
(c) Do you know who said, "Nothing great was ever achieved without enthusiasm"?

30. (a) Did the office manager really say, "Stamp this package 'Fragile?'" ____
(b) Did the office manager really say, "Stamp this package 'Fragile'"?
(c) Did the office manager really say, "Stamp this package "Fragile"?

Hotline Review

Write the letter of the word or phrase that correctly completes each sentence.

31. Following directions carefully will (a) insure, (b) ensure a smooth installation. ____

32. Has the value of your home been (a) appraised, (b) apprised in the last five years? ____

33. Direct your inquiries to the manager or (a) I, (b) me, (c) myself. ____

34. The restaurant was (a) cited, (b) sited, (c) sighted for health code violations last year. ____

35. We give our Web address to (a) whomever, (b) whoever requests it. ____

1. 1, 2. C, 3. 2, 4. C, 5. 2, 6. C, 7. b, 8. c, 9. a, 10. a, 11. b, 12. b, 13. c, 14. a, 15. a, 16. b, 17. a, 18. c, 19. a, 20. c, 21. c, 22. a, 23. b, 24. b, 25. b, 26. c, 27. b, 28. a, 29. c, 30. b, 31. b, 32. a, 33. b, 34. a, 35. b.

UNIT

5

Writing With Style

15 Capitalization

OBJECTIVES When you have completed the materials in this chapter, you will be able to do the following:

- Understand when to capitalize personal titles, numbered items, and points of the compass.
- Correctly capitalize departments, divisions, committees, government terms, product names, and literary titles.
- Capitalize beginning words, celestial bodies, and ethnic references.
- Apply special rules in capitalizing personal titles and terms.

Rules governing capitalization reflect conventional practices; that is, they have been established by custom and usage. By following these conventions, a writer tells a reader, among other things, what words are important. In earlier times writers capitalized most nouns and many adjectives at will; few conventions of capitalization or punctuation were then consistently observed. Today most capitalization follows definite rules that are fully accepted and practiced at all times. Dictionaries are helpful in determining capitalization practices, but they do not show all capitalized words. To develop skill in controlling capitals, study the rules and examples shown in this chapter.

BASIC RULES OF CAPITALIZATION

Proper Nouns

NOTABLE QUOTABLE

"Find a job you love, and you'll never have to work a day in your life."
—Anonymous

Capitalize proper nouns, including the *specific* names of persons, places, schools, streets, parks, buildings, religions, holidays, months, nicknames, agreements, and so forth. Do *not* capitalize common nouns that make *general* reference.

Proper Nouns	Common Nouns
Nathan Jackson	a young man on the staff
Alaska, Hawaii	two states in the U.S.
Foothill College, University of Georgia	a community college and a university
Pac Bell Park	a baseball park
Episcopalian, Methodist	representatives of two religions
Sycamore Room, Fairmont Hotel	a room in the hotel
Labor Day, Thanksgiving	two holidays
Golden Gate Bridge	a bridge over the bay
Empire State Building	the building in the city
Supreme Court, Congress	components of government
October, November, December	last three months of the year
the Windy City, the Big Apple	nicknames of cities
North American Free Trade Agreement	an agreement between countries

STUDY TIP

Most proper nouns retain their capital letters when they become adjectives—for example, French toast, Russian roulette, Persian cat, Spanish moss, Italian marble, and Swedish massage.

Proper Adjectives

Capitalize most adjectives that are derived from proper nouns.

Renaissance art	Socratic method
Danish pastry	Belgian waffle
Freudian slip	Roman numeral
Heimlich maneuver	Greek symbols

Do not capitalize those adjectives originally derived from proper nouns that have become common adjectives (without capitals) through usage. Consult your dictionary when in doubt.

venetian blinds	epicurean feast
plaster of paris	french fries
india ink	diesel engine
manila folder	china dishes

Beginning of Sentence

Capitalize the first letter of a word beginning a sentence.

Inventory and sales data are transmitted electronically.

Geographic Locations

Capitalize the names of *specific* places such as states, cities, mountains, valleys, lakes, rivers, oceans, and geographic regions. Capitalize *county* and *state* when they follow the proper nouns.

Maine, New Hampshire, Vermont	Columbia River, Mississippi River
Kansas City, San Francisco	Atlantic Ocean, Arctic Ocean
Death Valley	Pacific Northwest, Texas Panhandle
Lake Ontario, Dead Sea	European Community (EC)
Dade County, Montgomery County (*but* the city of Miami, the county of Dade, the state of Missouri)	New York State

Organization Names

Capitalize the principal words in the names of all business, civic, educational, governmental, labor, military, philanthropic, political, professional, religious, and social organizations.

NOTABLE QUOTABLE

"A genius is a talented person who does his homework."
—Thomas Edison

United States Air Force	American Heart Association
Society for Technical Communication	San Francisco Unified School District
Habitat for Humanity	Microsoft Corporation
Securities and Exchange Commission	Federal Reserve Board
Screen Actors Guild	The Boeing Company*

Generally, do *not* capitalize *company, association, board,* and other shortened name forms when they are used to replace full organization names. If these

*Capitalize *the* only when it is part of an organization's official name (as it would appear on the organization's stationery).

shortened names, however, are preceded by the word *the* and are used in formal or legal documents (contracts, bylaws, minutes, etc.), they may be capitalized.

The *company* is moving its headquarters to Carbondale, Illinois. (Informal document.)

The Treasurer of the *Association* is herein authorized to disburse funds. (Formal document.)

Academic Courses and Degrees

STUDY TIP

Course titles with numbers are usually capitalized (*Marketing 101*). Those without numbers usually are not capitalized (*marketing*).

Capitalize the names of numbered courses and specific course titles. Do not capitalize the names of academic subject areas unless they contain a proper noun.

Shaun plans to take keyboarding, Spanish, and Accounting 28 next semester.

Anna excelled in business management, Japanese, and computer programming.

All accounting majors must take business English and business law.

Capitalize abbreviations of academic degrees whether they stand alone or follow individuals' names. Do not capitalize general references to degrees.

Wendy Spangler earned B.S., M.S., and Ph.D. degrees before her thirtieth birthday. (Bachelor of Science, Master of Science, and Doctor of Philosophy degrees.)

Paul hopes to earn bachelor's and master's degrees in business administration. (General reference to degrees.)

Annette Jenkins, M.S., manages my department.

New employees include Marialice Kern, Ph.D., and Dave Parrisher, B.S.

Seasons

SPOT THE BLOOPER

Headline in *The Washington Times*: "Threat of espionage hinder Paris air show."

Do not capitalize seasons unless they are personified (spoken of as if alive).

Our annual sales meeting is held each spring.

"Come, Winter, with thine angry howl . . ."—Burns

SPECIAL RULES OF CAPITALIZATION

Titles of People

Capitalize courtesy titles (such as *Mr.*, *Mrs.*, *Ms.*, *Miss*, and *Dr.*) when they precede names. Also capitalize titles representing a person's profession, company position, military rank, religious station, political office, family relationship, or nobility when the title precedes the name and replaces a courtesy title.

The staff greeted *Ms.* Susan Smith and *Mr.* Paul Bernhardt. (Courtesy titles.)

Speakers included *Professor* Martha Laham and *Dr.* Jackie Harless-Chang. (Professional titles.)

Sales figures were submitted by *Budget Director* Magee and *Vice President* Anderson. (Company titles.)

Will *Major General* Donald M. Franklin assume command? (Military title.)

Appearing together were *Rabbi* David Cohen, *Archbishop* Sean McKee, and *Reverend* Thomas White. (Religious titles.)

We expect *President* Clinton to offer support for *Senator* Dianne Feinstein and *Mayor* Willie Brown in the next campaign. (Political titles.)

Only *Aunt* Brenda and *Uncle* Skip had been to Alaska. (Family relationship.)

Onlookers waited for *Prince* Charles and *Queen* Elizabeth to arrive. (Nobility.)

Do not capitalize a person's title—professional, business, military, religious, political, family, or one related to nobility—when the title is followed by an appositive. You will recall that appositives rename or explain previously mentioned nouns or pronouns.

> Only one *professor*, Ruth Sison, favored a tuition hike.
> Democratic candidates asked their *president*, Bill Clinton, to help raise funds.
> Reva Hillman discovered that her *uncle*, Paul Royka, had named her as his heir.

Do not capitalize titles or offices following names.

> Leon Jones, *president* of Allied Chemical, met with Cecille Stone, *director* of Human Resources.
> After repeated requests, Rose Valenzuela, *supervisor*, Document Services, announced extended hours.
> Bill Clinton, *president* of the U.S., confronted Robert Hollingsworth, *senator* from Wyoming.
> Alexander M. Berquist, *chief justice* of the Supreme Court, promised a ruling in June.

Generally, do not capitalize a title or office that replaces a person's name.

> Neither the *president* of the company nor the *executive vice president* could be reached for comment.
> An ambitious five-year plan was developed by the *director of marketing* and the *sales manager*.
> The *president* conferred with the *joint chiefs of staff* and the *secretary of defense*.
> At the reception the *mayor* of New York spoke with the *governor* of New Jersey.

STUDY TIP

Capitalize only the first word in a salutation (*My dear Ms. Jones*) or in a complimentary close (*Very truly yours*).

Capitalize titles in addresses and closing lines.

Ms. Carol A. Straka	Very sincerely yours,
Executive Vice President, Planning	
Energy Systems Technology, Inc.	
8907 Canoga Avenue	Lisa W. Greenway
Canoga Park, CA 91371	Marketing Manager

SPOT THE BLOOPER

From a Wendy's International poster: "Be Cool in School! Good Grades Has Its Rewards!" [See any problem with subject–verb agreement? How about pronoun–antecedent agreement?]

Do not capitalize family titles used with possessive pronouns.

my mother	our aunt
his father	your cousin

But do capitalize titles of close relatives when they are used without pronouns.

> Please call Father immediately.

Numbered and Lettered Items

Capitalize nouns followed by numbers or letters except in page, paragraph, line, size, and verse references.

Gate 15, Flight 1679	IRS Form 1040	Building A-31
Invoice No. 1314	Volume I, Appendix B	Medicare Form 23B
page 4, line 10	Interstate 85	Supplement No. 2

STUDY TIP

A clue to the capitalization of a region is the use of *the* preceding it: *the East Coast, the West, the Pacific Northwest.*

SPOT THE BLOOPER

From *The San Francisco Chronicle*: "Keenan has just awoken from a nap."

To learn more about trademarks, visit the U.S. Patent and Trademark Office's Web site (http://www.uspto.gov/web/menu/tm.html).

DID YOU KNOW

One of the most widely publicized legal battles over trademark protection involved Parker Brothers. It threatened to sue an economics professor at San Francisco State University for naming his new board game "Anti-Monopoly." After nine years of litigation, courts stripped "Monopoly" of trademark protection, thus making the name generic.

DID YOU KNOW

The words *corn flakes*, *escalator*, and *raisin bran* all were once trademarks but have slipped into common use. The Coca-Cola Company reportedly employs eight full-time attorneys who do nothing but watch over its trademark. Why such protection? Companies have huge marketing investments in their trademarks.

Points of the Compass

Capitalize *north, south, east, west,* and their derivatives (*northeast, southwest,* etc.) when they represent *specific* regions. Do not capitalize the points of the compass when they are used in directions or in general references.

the Middle East, the Far East	turn east on Guadalupe Parkway
the Midwest, the Pacific Northwest	to the west of town
the East Coast, the West Coast	eastern Washington, western Wyoming
Easterners, Southerners	southern Georgia
Northern Hemisphere	in the northern Rockies

Departments, Divisions, and Committees

Capitalize the names of departments, divisions, or committees within your own organization. Outside your organization capitalize only *specific* department, division, or committee names.

Contact our Client Support Department for more information.
He works with the International Division of Apple.
Address your request to their public relations department.
You have been appointed to the Process Improvement Committee.
A steering committee has not yet been named.

Governmental Terms

Do not capitalize the words *federal, government, nation,* or *state* unless they are part of a specific title.

Neither the state government nor the federal government would fund the proposal.
The Federal Communications Commission regulates broadcasting in all the states.

Product Names

Capitalize product names only when they represent trademarked items. Except in advertising, common names following manufacturers' names are not capitalized.

Coca-Cola	DuPont Teflon	Kodak camera
Kleenex tissues	Xerox copier	NordicTrack Walkfit
Magic Marker	Maytag washer	Styrofoam cup
Amana Radarange	IBM computer	Jeep Cherokee
Q-Tip	Frigidaire refrigerator	Formica counter

Literary Titles

Capitalize the principal words in the titles of books, magazines, newspapers, articles, movies, plays, songs, poems, and reports. Do *not* capitalize articles (*a, an, the*), conjunctions (*and, but, or, nor*), and prepositions with three or fewer letters (*in, to, by, for,* etc.) unless they begin or end the title.

By the way, remember that the titles of published works that contain subdivisions (such as books, magazines, pamphlets, newspapers, TV series, movies, plays, and musicals) are italicized or underscored. Titles of literary or artistic works without subdivisions (such as newspaper articles, magazine articles, poems, and episodes in a TV series) are placed in quotation marks.

Amir Hartman's *Net Ready: Strategies for Success in the E-conomy* (Book.)
Roger Fisher's *Getting to Yes: Negotiating Agreement Without Giving In* (Book with preposition at end of title.)
The Simpsons (TV series.)
The Sound of Music (Movie.)
"Can Online Investing Work for You?" (Magazine article.)
Robert Frost's "Stopping by Woods on a Snowy Evening" (Poem.)

ADDITIONAL RULES OF CAPITALIZATION

Beginning Words

In addition to capitalizing the first word of a complete sentence, capitalize the first words in quoted sentences, independent phrases, enumerated items, and formal rules or principles following colons.

Benjamin Jowett said, "The way to get things done is not to mind who gets the credit for doing them."(Quoted sentence.)
No, not at the present time. (Independent phrase.)
Big utilities formed an alliance to sell the following:

1. Electricity
2. Natural gas
3. Energy management services

Our office manager responded with his favorite rule: Follow the company stylebook for correct capitalization. (Rule following colon.)

Celestial Bodies

Capitalize the names of celestial bodies such as Jupiter, Saturn, and Neptune. Do not capitalize the terms *earth*, *sun*, or *moon* unless they appear in a context with other celestial bodies.

Where on earth did you find that ancient typewriter?
The planets closest to the Sun are Mercury, Mars, and Earth.

Ethnic References

Terms that relate to a particular culture, language, or race are capitalized.

In Hawaii, Asian and Western cultures merge.
Both English and Hebrew are spoken by Jews in Israel.

Words Following *marked* and *stamped*

Capitalize words that follow the words *marked* and *stamped.*

My check came back marked "Insufficient Funds."
Please make sure the package is stamped "First Class."

NOTABLE QUOTABLE

"Most of the things worth doing in the world had been declared impossible before they were done."
—Louis D. Brandeis

Special Uses of Personal Titles and Terms

Generally, titles are capitalized according to the specifications set forth earlier. However, when a title of an official appears in that organization's minutes, bylaws, or other official document, it may be capitalized.

The Controller will have authority over departmental budgets. (Title appearing in bylaws.)
By vote of the stockholders, the President is empowered to implement a stock split. (Title appearing in annual report.)

When the terms *ex, elect, late,* and *former* are used with capitalized titles, they are not capitalized.

> We went to hear ex-President Carter speak at the symposium.
> Mayor-elect Cortazzo proposed a city council meeting for next week.
> I have just learned that former Secretary of Transportation Dole will attend our conference.

Titles other than *sir, ladies,* and *gentlemen* are capitalized when used in direct address.

> I hope, Doctor, that you will be able to see me today.
> Welcome, ladies and gentlemen, to our grand opening.

HOTLINE QUERIES

QUESTION I don't know how to describe the copies made from our copy machine. Should I call them *Xerox* copies or something else?

ANSWER They are *Xerox* copies only if made on a Xerox copier. Copies made on other machines may be called *xerographic* copies, *machine* copies, or *photocopies.*

QUESTION In the doctor's office where I work, I see the word *medicine* capitalized, as in *the field of Medicine.* Is this correct?

ANSWER No. General references should not be capitalized. If it were part of a title, as in the Northwestern College of *Medicine*, it would be capitalized.

QUESTION I work for the National Therapy Association. When I talk about *the association* in a letter, should I capitalize it?

ANSWER No. When a shortened form of an organization name is used alone, it is generally not capitalized. In formal or legal documents (contracts, bylaws, printed announcements), it may be capitalized.

QUESTION I work for a state agency, and I'm not sure what to capitalize or hyphenate in this sentence: *State agencies must make forms available to <u>non-English speaking</u> applicants.*

ANSWER Words with the prefix *non* are usually not hyphenated (*nonexistent, nontoxic*). But when *non* is joined to a word that must be capitalized, it is followed by a hyphen. Because the word *speaking* combines with *English* to form a single-unit adjective, it should be hyphenated. Thus, the expression should be typed *non-English-speaking applicants.*

QUESTION When we use a person's title, such as *business manager,* in place of a person's name, shouldn't the title always be capitalized?

ANSWER No. Business titles are capitalized only when they precede an individual's name, as in *Business Manager Smith.* Do not capitalize titles when they replace an individual's name: *Our business manager will direct the transaction.*

QUESTION How do you spell *marshal,* as used in *the Grand Marshal of the Rose Parade?*

Answer The preferred spelling is with a single *l*: *marshal.* In addition to describing an individual who directs a ceremony, the noun *marshal* refers to a high military officer or a city law officer who carries out court orders (*the marshal served papers on the defendant*). As a verb, *marshal* means "to bring together" or "to order in an effective way" (*the attorney marshaled convincing arguments*). The similar-sounding word *martial* is an adjective and means "warlike" or "military" (*martial law was declared after the riot*).

Question My colleague and I can't agree on something. If two people own a business together, say a graphic design firm, how should we refer to the business? Would it be *Charlie and Tianna's graphic design firm*? Or would it be *Charlie's and Tianna's graphic design firm*?

Answer When two people own something together, we refer to it as joint ownership or combined ownership. With combined ownership, only the second name has the *'s*. In your example you would use *Charlie and Tianna's graphic design firm.*

Question The following three sentences appeared in an assignment my son received from his fifth grade teacher. *It's going to be interesting! For each state list it's geographic region. On your map identify each state and note its' capital.* I always have trouble myself with *its* and *it's*, but it seems as if something is wrong here.

Answer You're absolutely right! And you and your son's teacher are not alone in having trouble with *its* and *it's.* In the first sentence *it's* has been used correctly. *It's* is a contraction that stands for *it is.* The teacher is, therefore, saying *It is going to be interesting!* In the second sentence the teacher should have used the possessive form of *it*, which is *its*, to show that the geographic region belongs to the state. The teacher should also have used *its* in the third sentence to show that the capital belongs to the state. In fact, the word *its'* does not exist. Now your only decision is whether you should point this out to your son's teacher!

Question Should the words *Internet* and *World Wide Web* be capitalized?

Answer The *Internet* and the *World Wide Web* are currently proper nouns because these words represent specific places. They should, therefore, be capitalized. Likewise, the word *Web* should be capitalized when you are using it to refer specifically to the *World Wide Web.* We may see this change as more internets and webs are developed. For example, many companies have their own *intranets.* The word *intranet* is, therefore, not capitalized because it is considered a common noun.

NAME ____________________

15 REINFORCEMENT EXERCISES

A. (Self-check) Use standard proofreading marks to correct errors you find in capitalization. Indicate at the right the total number of changes you make.

EXAMPLE: Project manager James Willis was promoted to Vice President. 3

1. Nicole Scott, a member of our marketing research department, will be our new Far East representative. ____
2. Additional information on the features of this program is available on Page 41 in appendix B. ____
3. Personnel director Rosenburg will head the new steering committee. ____
4. Our human resources department and computer sales division are sponsoring a conference on recruiting strategies. ____
5. Address your inquiries to Mr. David Martin, manager, customer services, Atlas Fitness Equipment, 213 Summit Drive, Spokane, Washington 99201. ____
6. Because the package was marked "fragile," we handled it carefully. ____
7. The guiding principle of capitalization is this: capitalize *specific* names and references, but do not capitalize *general* references. ____
8. You, Sir, may be held in contempt of court. ____
9. My manager said, "you must submit your timecards by Friday afternoon." ____
10. Only Ex-President Clinton and Mayor-Elect Brown have responded to our invitations. ____

Check your answers below.

B. Use proofreading marks to correct errors in the following sentences. Indicate the number of changes you make for each sentence.

1. Jasmine Lee, President of Manning Corporation, offered the position of Budget Director to Jim Reynolds. ____
2. Our research and development division is moving to Houston, Texas. ____
3. The Sales Manager will be arriving on Southwest Airlines flight 341 at gate 12B. ____
4. I have just read a magazine article entitled "The 100 best companies to work for." ____
5. Memorial Day is a Federal holiday; therefore, banks will be closed. ____
6. Our Advertising Agency operates according to this rule: you must spend money to make money. ____
7. Most Brazilians speak portugese, most Surinamese speak dutch, and most Guyanese speak english. In all other South American countries, the official language is spanish. ____
8. Please take this fax marked "confidential" to our human resources department. ____
9. She said she would move Heaven and Earth to meet her deadline. ____
10. Mexico's Ex-President Salinas met with the President-Elect. ____
11. I am planning a trip to southern California to meet with potential clients. ____

1. (3) Marketing Research Department, 2. (2) page Appendix, 3. (1) Director, 4. (6) Human Resources Department Computer Sales Division, 5. (3) Manager Customer Services, 6. (1) Fragile, 7. (1) Capitalize, 8. (1) sir, 9. (1) You, 10. (2) ex-President Mayor-elect.

12. When the president met with the secretary of agriculture, they discussed crop subsidies for the midwest. _____

13. Turn to volume 2, page 16 for detailed installation instruction. _____

14. For lunch Ahmal ordered a big mac, French fries, and a coca-cola. _____

15. The Vice President and Marketing Director were called to the President's office for a conference. _____

16. Did you meet marketing director evans at the company meeting? _____

17. She suggested that I read *The Seven Habits Of Highly Successful People.* _____

18. The Northern part of the state is subject to extreme temperatures in the Winter. _____

19. Applicants must have a Master's degree to be considered for the position. _____

20. His case, first tried in the State of New York, will now be sent to the Supreme court. _____

16

Numbers

OBJECTIVES When you have completed the materials in this chapter, you will be able to do the following:

- Correctly choose between figure and word forms to express general numbers, money, and numbers beginning sentences.
- Express dates, clock time, addresses, and telephone numbers appropriately.
- Use the correct form in writing related numbers, consecutive numbers, periods of time, and ages.
- Use the correct form in expressing numbers in conventional phrases, with abbreviations and symbols, and as round numbers.
- Express correctly weights, measures, and fractions.
- Use the correct form in expressing percentages, decimals, and ordinals.

Just as capitalization is governed by convention, so is the expression of numbers. Usage and custom determine whether numbers are to be expressed in the form of a figure (for example, *5*) or in the form of a word (for example, *five*). Numbers expressed as figures are shorter and more easily comprehended, yet numbers used as words are necessary in certain instances. The following guidelines are observed in expressing numbers that appear in written *sentences.* Numbers that appear in business documents such as invoices, statements, and purchase orders are always expressed as figures.

BASIC GUIDELINES FOR EXPRESSING NUMBERS

General Rules

STUDY TIP

To remember it better, some people call this the "Rule of Ten": Words for one through ten; figures for 11 and above.

The numbers *one* through *ten* are generally written as words. Numbers above *ten* are written as figures.

> The committee consisted of *nine* regular members and *one* chair.
> Gift taxes are imposed by *49* states.

Numbers that begin sentences are written as words. If a number involves more than two words, however, the sentence should be rewritten so that the number no longer falls at the beginning.

> *Thirty-four* people applied for the Web designer position.
> A total of *320* distributors agreed to market the product. (Not *Three hundred twenty* distributors agreed to market the product.)

Money

Sums of money $1 or greater are expressed as figures. If a sum is a whole dollar amount, most business writers omit the decimal and zeros (even if the amount appears with fractional dollar amounts).

> Although she budgeted only *$200*, Martha spent *$234.50* for the scanner.
> Our monthly statement showed purchases of *$7.13*, *$10*, *$43.50*, *$90*, and *$262.78*.

Sums less than $1 are written as figures that are followed by the word *cents*. If they are part of sums greater than $1, use a dollar sign and a decimal instead of the word *cents*.

> Jack said he had only *65 cents* with him.
> Supplies for the project were listed at $1.35, *$.99*, $2.80, $1, and *$.40*.

Dates

In dates, numbers that appear after the name of the month are written in cardinal figures (*1*, *2*, *3*, etc.). Those that stand alone or appear before the name of a month are written in ordinal figures (*1st*, *2d*, *3d*, etc.*).

> The meeting is scheduled for *October 5* in our office.
> On the *3d* Thursday of each month, we hold a team project meeting.

Most American business communicators express dates in the following form: month, day, year. An alternative form, used primarily in military and international correspondence, begins with the day of the month. Some business organizations prefer the international date style for its clarity, since it separates the numerical date of the month from the year.

> By *October 1, 2003*, all construction on the annex must be completed. (General date format.)
> Our lease expires on *31 July 2004*. (Military and international format.)

Clock Time

Figures are used when clock time is expressed with *a.m.* or *p.m.* Omit the colon and zeros with whole hours. When exact clock time is expressed with *o'clock*, either figures or words may be used. Note that phrases such as "in the afternoon" or "in the morning" may follow clock time expressed with *o'clock* but not with time expressed with *a.m.* and *p.m.*

> The first shift starts at *8 a.m.*, and the second begins at *3:30 p.m.*
> Department mail is usually distributed at *four* (or *4*) *o'clock*.

Addresses and Telephone/Fax Numbers

SPOT THE BLOOPER

From *The Suburban & Wayne Times* [Chester County, PA]: "Cases of Lyme disease, which is transmitted by deer-carrying ticks, are on the rise." [What unintended meaning resulted from the unneeded hyphen?]

Except for the number *One*, house numbers are expressed as figures.

805 Sierra Drive	27321 Van Ness Avenue
One Wilshire Plaza	1762 Peachtree Street

Street names that involve the number *ten* or a lower number are written entirely as words. In street names involving numbers greater than *ten*, the numeral portion is written in figures. If no compass direction (*North*, *South*, *East*, *West*)

*Many writers today are using the more efficient *2d* and *3d* instead of *2nd* and *3rd*.

separates a house number from a street number, the street number is expressed in ordinal form (*-st, -d, -th*).

201 Third Street
958 Eighth Avenue
201 West 53 Street
3261 South 105 Avenue
901 34th Avenue (Use *th* when no compass direction separates house number and numerical portion of street name.)

Telephone and fax numbers are expressed with figures. When used, the area code is placed in parentheses preceding the telephone number. As an alternate form, you may separate the area code from the telephone number with a hyphen. A format that is emerging is to separate the parts of the number with periods.

Please call us at *555-1101* for further information.
You may reach me at *(801) 643-3267, Ext. 244*, after 9:30 a.m.
Orders faxed to us at *(415) 392-2194* will be processed immediately.
Call our toll-free number at *800-340-3281* for the latest sports updates.
You can place an order by calling us at *800.937.5594*.

SPECIAL GUIDELINES FOR EXPRESSING NUMBERS

Related Numbers

Numbers used similarly in the same document are considered related and should be expressed as the largest number is expressed. Thus, if the largest number is greater than *ten*, all the numbers should be expressed as figures.

SPOT THE BLOOPER

Classified advertisement: "For Sale. 8 puppies from a German Shepherd and an Alaskan Hussy."

In March *four* orders were placed, in April *eight* orders were placed, and in May an additional *nine* orders were placed.
Only *3* companies out of *147* failed to return the survey form.
Of the *46* jobs in the print queue, only *4* reports and *3* letters printed.
Nearly *20* employees will be expected to share the *15* computers, *8* printers, and *3* fax machines. (Note that items appearing in a series are always considered to be related.)

Unrelated numbers within the same reference are written as words or figures according to the general guidelines presented earlier in this chapter.

Two proposals covered *22* employees working in *three* branch offices.
During the *four* peak traffic hours, *three* bridges carry at least *20,000* cars.

Consecutive Numbers

STUDY TIP

With consecutive numbers, remember that the second number is ALWAYS a figure. The first number is usually a word, unless it requires three or more words (*120 5-year-old* children.)

When two numbers appear consecutively and both modify a following noun (such as *ten 33-cent* stamps), generally express the first number in words and the second in figures. If, however, the first number cannot be expressed in *one or two words*, place it in figures also (*120 33-cent* stamps). Do not use commas to separate the figures.

Historians divided the era into *four 25-year* periods. (Use word form for the first number and figure form for the second.)
We ordered *ten 30-page* color brochures. (Use word form for the first number and figure form for the second.)
Did you request *twenty 100-watt* bulbs?. (Use word form for the first number and figure form for the second.)

We'll need at least *150 100-watt* bulbs. (Use figure form for the first number since it requires more than two words.)

Periods of Time

NOTABLE QUOTABLE

"Everyone must row with the oars he or she has."
—English proverb

Periods of time that can be expressed in one or two words are usually written in word form when used in a general way. Periods of time that cannot be expressed in one or two words are written in figure form.

Congress has regulated minimum wages for over *sixty-five years.* (Use word form for periods of time that can be expressed in one or two words.)
We agreed to keep the video for only *fifteen days.*
After a *183-day* strike, workers returned to their jobs. (Use figure form for a period of time that cannot be expressed in one or two words.)

Figures may be used to achieve special emphasis in expressing business concepts such as discount rates, interest rates, warranty periods, credit terms, loan periods, and payment terms.

You earn a *2 percent* discount if your bill is paid within *10 days* of purchase.
High interest rates are offered even on *6-* and *9-month* certificates of deposit.
Your loan must be repaid within *60 days* in accordance with its terms.

Ages and Anniversaries

SPOT THE BLOOPER

From *The Times Union* [Albany, NY], featuring an advertisement with the following 2-inch headline: "On Thursday morning, I found the car of my dreams in my pajamas."

Ages and anniversaries that can be expressed in one or two words are generally written in word form. Those that require more than two words are written in figures. Figures are also used when an age (a) appears immediately after a name, (b) is expressed in exact years and months, or (c) is used in a legal or technical sense.

When he was *forty-one,* Gordon Young became the company's president. (Use word form for age expressed in two or fewer words.)
This year marks the *thirty-fifth* anniversary of the company's founding. (Use word form for anniversary expressed in two or fewer words.)
Lisa Gores, *63,* plans to retire in two years. (Use figure form for age appearing immediately after name.)
The child was adopted when he was *3 years* and *8 months* old. (Use figure form for age expressed in terms of exact years and months.)
Although the legal voting age is *18,* young people must be *21* to purchase alcohol. (Use figure form for age used in a legal sense.)

Numbers Used in Conventional Phrases, With Abbreviations, and With Symbols

Numbers used in conventional phrases are expressed as figures.

page 6	Policy 651040	Area Code 925
Room 232	Volume 7	Section 8
Option 2	Form 1040	Assembly Bill 109

Numbers used with abbreviations are expressed as figures.

Apt. 19	Serial No. 2198675	Nos. 203 and 301
Ext. 167	Account No. 08166-05741	Social Security No. 250-93-6749

Notice that the word *number* is capitalized and abbreviated when it precedes a number. Notice, too, that no commas are used in serial, account, and policy numbers.

Symbols (such as #, %, ¢) are usually avoided in contextual business writing (sentences). In other business documents where space is limited, however, symbols are frequently used. Numbers appearing with symbols are expressed as figures.

50%   34¢   #2 can   2/10, n/60

Round Numbers

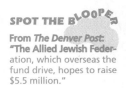

SPOT THE BLOOPER

From *The Denver Post*: "The Allied Jewish Federation, which overseas the fund drive, hopes to raise $5.5 million."

Round numbers are approximations. They may be expressed in word or figure form, although figure form is shorter and easier to comprehend.

> Almost *400* (or *four hundred*) employees signed the petition.
> At last count we had received about *20* (or *twenty*) reservations.

For ease of reading, round numbers in the millions or billions should be expressed with a combination of figures and words.*

> The president asked for a budget cut of *$8 billion.*
> The world population has reached *6 billion.*
> Nearly *1.5 million* imported cars were sold this year.

ADDITIONAL GUIDELINES FOR EXPRESSING NUMBERS

Weights and Measurements

Weights and measurements are expressed as figures.

> A typical index card measures *3 by 5 inches.*
> Our specifications show the weight of the laptop to be *7 pounds 9 ounces.*
> The truck required *21 gallons* of gasoline and *2 quarts* of oil to travel *150 miles per hour.*

In sentences the nouns following weights and measurements should be spelled out (for example, *21 gallons* instead of *21 gal.*). In business forms or in statistical presentations, however, such nouns may be abbreviated.

5″ × 17″   #10   16 oz.   20 sq. yds.   4 lb.   3 qt.

Fractions

STUDY TIP

A fraction immediately followed by an *of* phrase usually functions as a noun (*one third of the cars*). Therefore, it is not hyphenated.

Simple fractions are expressed as words. If a fraction functions as a noun, no hyphen is used. If it functions as an adjective, a hyphen separates its parts.

> Over *three fourths* of the employees attended the seminar. (Fraction used as a noun.)
> A *two-thirds* majority is needed to carry the measure. (Fraction used as an adjective.)

Complex fractions appearing in sentences may be written either as figures or as a combination of figures and words.

> The computer will execute a command in *1 millionth* of a second. (Combination of words and figures is easier to comprehend.)
> Flight records revealed that the emergency system was activated *13/200* of a second after the pilot was notified. (Figure form is easier to comprehend.)

Mixed fractions (whole numbers with fractions) are always expressed by figures. Use the extended character set of your word processing program to insert fractions that are written in figures. Fractions written in figures that are not found

*Note that only when *one million* is used as an approximation is it generally written in word form; otherwise, it is written *1 million.*

NOTABLE QUOTABLE

"Patience is the greatest of all shock absorbers. The only thing you can get in a hurry is trouble."
—Lord Thomas R. Dewar

in extended character sets of word processing programs are formed by using the diagonal to separate the two parts. When fractions that are constructed with diagonals appear with key fractions, be consistent by using the diagonal construction for all the fractions involved.

> Office desks are expected to be *35¼* inches long, not *35½* inches. (Notice that no space follows a whole number and a key fraction.)
>
> The shelves were ordered to be *36 5/8* inches wide, not *36 1/2* inches. (Notice that fractions that must be constructed with slashes are separated from their related whole numbers.)

Percentages and Decimals

Percentages are expressed with figures followed by the word *percent.* The percent sign (%) is used only on business forms or in statistical presentations.

> Interest rates have been as low as *5½ percent* and as high as *19 percent.*
>
> Union leaders report that *52 percent* of all workers joined the union.

SPOT THE BLOOPER

From a newspaper ad for an attorney in Winter Park, FL: "For your family's protection . . . and piece of mind."

Decimals are expressed with figures. If a decimal does not contain a whole number (an integer) and does not begin with a zero, a zero should be placed before the decimal.

> Daryl Thomas set a record when he ran the race in *9.86* seconds. (Contains a whole number.)
>
> Close examination revealed the settings to be *.005* inch off. (Begins with a zero.)
>
> Less than *0.1* percent of the costs will be passed on to consumers. (Zero placed before decimal that neither contains a whole number nor begins with a zero.)

Ordinals

Although ordinal numbers are generally expressed in word form (*first, second, third,* etc.), three exceptions should be noted: (a) figure form is used for dates appearing before a month or appearing alone, (b) figure form is used for street names involving numbers greater than *ten,* and (c) figure form is used when the ordinal would require more than two words.

- ***Most ordinals***

> The company is celebrating its *fortieth anniversary.*
>
> Before the *twentieth century,* child labor laws were almost nonexistent.
>
> Of 237 sales representatives, Joanna ranked *second* in total sales.
>
> Paul Guerrero represents the *Twenty-ninth Congressional District.*

- ***Dates***

> Your payment must be received by the *30th* to qualify for the cash discount.
>
> On the *2d of June* we will begin construction.

- ***Streets***

> Traffic lights installed on *Second Street* have improved pedestrian safety.
>
> Our Customer Service Division has moved to *35th Street.*

- ***Larger ordinals***

> First Federal Bank ranks *103d* in terms of capital investments.

HOTLINE QUERIES

QUESTION I recently saw the following format used by a business to publish its telephone number on its stationery and business cards: 512.582.0903. Is it now an option to use periods in telephone numbers?

ANSWER Using periods in telephone numbers is an emerging format, particularly in graphics design and Web design. It seems to be a stylistic affectation, perhaps reflecting European influences. To some, the style is upscale and chic; to others, it's just confusing. Telephone numbers written in the traditional formats are most readily recognized. That's why it's safe to stick with hyphens or parentheses: 512-582-0903 or (513) 582-0903.

QUESTION I'm never sure when to hyphenate numbers, such as *thirty-one.* Is there some rule to follow?

ANSWER When written in word form, the numbers *twenty-one* through *ninety-nine* are hyphenated. Numbers are also hyphenated when they form compound adjectives and precede nouns (*ten-year-old* child, *16-story* building, *four-year* term, *30-day* lease).

QUESTION I've always been confused by *imply* and *infer.* Which is correct in this sentence: *We (imply* or *infer) from your letter that the goods are lost.*

ANSWER In your sentence use *infer. Imply* means "to state indirectly." *Infer* means "to draw a conclusion" or "to make a deduction based on facts." A listener or reader *infers.* A speaker or writer *implies.*

QUESTION When fractions are written as words, why are they hyphenated sometimes and not hyphenated other times?

ANSWER Most writers do not hyphenate a fraction when it functions as a noun (*one fourth of the letters*). When a fraction functions as an adjective, it is hyphenated (*a one-third gain in profits*).

QUESTION Should I put quotation marks around figures to emphasize them? For example, *Your account has a balance of "$2,136.18."*

ANSWER Certainly not! Quotation marks are properly used to indicate an exact quotation, or they may be used to enclose the definition of a word. They should not be used as a mechanical device for added emphasis.

QUESTION I'm an engineer, and we have just had a discussion in our office concerning spelling. I have checked the dictionary, and it shows *usage.* Isn't this word ever spelled *useage?*

ANSWER No. The only spelling of *usage* is without the internal *e.* You are probably thinking of the word *usable,* which does have a variant spelling—*useable.* Both forms are correct, but *usable* is recommended for its simplicity. Incidentally, if the word *usage* can be replaced by the word *use,* the latter is preferred (*the use* [not *usage*] *of ink pens is declining*).

QUESTION How should I spell the word *lose* in this sentence: *The employee tripped over a (lose* or *loose) cord?*

ANSWER In your sentence use the adjective *loose*, which means "not fastened," "not tight," or "having freedom of movement." Perhaps you can remember it by thinking of the common expression *loose change*, which suggests unattached, free coins jingling in your pocket. If you *lose* (*mislay*) some of those coins, you have less money and fewer *o's*.

QUESTION I'm sending a letter of application to a company, and I don't know the name of the person in charge of hiring. What salutation should I use? One person in our office suggested *Ladies and Gentlemen*. Is this being used? It sounds too formal to me.

ANSWER The salutation *Ladies and Gentlemen* is appropriate for any organization in which your reader may be a man or a woman. Businesses and individuals can avoid sexism in language without using stilted constructions. Salutations such as *Dear Sir* and *Gentlemen* are no longer used automatically. Today we are more sensitive to women as employees, managers, and executives. You should avoid using *To Whom It May Concern* as a salutation. If you think *Ladies and Gentlemen* sounds too formal, you should consider using the AMS (American Management Society) simplified letter style. It substitutes a subject line for the salutation. You can find this letter format in any office reference manual. Your best bet, however, is to try to find the name of the person before sending your letter. You can try calling the human resources department to find this information. A letter of application addressed to an individual is more likely to be read.

QUESTION What is the plural of *mouse*, as in a computer mouse?

ANSWER According to experts in the computer field, the plural of a computer *mouse* is *mice*.

NAME ____________________

16 REINFORCEMENT EXERCISES

A. (Self-check) Select (a) or (b) to complete each of the following sentences.

1. The documentation group has prepared (a) four 20-page, (b) 4 twenty-page reports. ______
2. We do not plan to move for at least (a) 15, (b) fifteen years. ______
3. A seminar on investing is being held in (a) Room Two, (b) Room 2. ______
4. Of the 650 envelopes sent, (a) nine, (b) 9 were returned. ______
5. Although she is over (a) 65, (b) sixty-five, Jill Roberson has no plans to retire. ______
6. Judge Boni reduced the jury's award to (a) $2 million, (b) $2,000,000. ______
7. Have you completed your IRS Form (a) Ten Forty, (b) 1040? ______
8. About (a) 750, (b) seven hundred fifty orders were processing in our warehouse this week. ______
9. For a discount, your payment must be received within (a) 60, (b) sixty days. ______
10. You must tell the representative that our model number is (a) 45,678,901, (b) 45678901. ______
11. This copier can make copies up to (a) 11" x 17", (b) 11 by 17 inches. ______
12. Next year marks my (a) 15th, (b) fifteenth anniversary with this company. ______
13. Payroll accounts for almost (a) two thirds, (b) two-thirds of our entire budget. ______
14. This year's office expenses are up by only (a) 0.5, (b) .5 percent over last year's. ______
15. Did you know that many buildings have no (a) 13th, (b) thirteenth floor? ______

Check your answers below.

B. For the following sentences underscore any numbers or words that are expressed inappropriately, and write the correct forms in the spaces provided. If a sentence is correct as written, write *C*.

EXAMPLE: Only <u>2</u> 33-cent stamps are required for that letter. ______two______

1. Our board of directors is composed of 15 members, of whom three are doctors, four are nurses, and eight are other health-care professionals. ______________
2. We plan to print one thousand four-page brochures. ______________
3. After a period of sixteen years, ownership reverts to the state. ______________
4. These policy Nos. are affected by the change in coverage: No. 12434-12575. ______________
5. Serial No. 1,245,679 is registered to Pon Electronics. ______________
6. A revolutionary new light bulb will reduce the demand for electricity by 8,000,000,000 kilowatt-hours per year. ______________
7. Of the 65 typed pages, nine pages require minor revisions and six pages demand heavy revision. ______________
8. Peter Dillon, thirty-three, and Barbara Marney, thirty-five, have recently been chosen for the management training program. ______________

1. a, 2. b, 3. b, 4. b, 5. b, 6. a, 7. b, 8. a, 9. a (preferred), 10. b, 11. b, 12. b, 13. a, 14. a, 15. b.

9. On page twenty-two of Volume two, the total sales are listed at nearly $22 million. ______________

10. The warranties on our new monitors are limited to ninety days. ______________

11. About fifty people will be laid off from our Atlanta office. ______________

12. The square mileage of Washington, DC, is 67; and its population is about 650,000. ______________

13. When the child was two years six months old, his parents established a trust fund for $1.6 million. ______________

14. Bill Gates's mansion on Lake Washington features a wall of twenty-four video screens, parking for twenty cars, and a reception hall for one hundred people. ______________

15. The Pacific Ocean covers about 70,000,000 square miles. ______________

C. Assume that the following phrases appear in business correspondence. Write the preferred forms in the spaces provided. If a phrase is correct as shown, write *C*.

1. three disks with eleven directories and nineteen files ______________
2. nine sixty-five page reports ______________
3. loan periods of thirty days ______________
4. Joan Haitz, fifty-eight, and Frank Brault, sixty-one ______________
5. Account No. 362,486,012 ______________
6. five point one million dollars ______________
7. about three hundred requests ______________
8. Section six point one ______________
9. twenty-five four-bedroom homes ______________
10. page nineteen of Volume Four ______________

17 Effective Sentences

OBJECTIVES When you have completed the materials in this chapter, you will be able to do the following:

- Eliminate wordy phrases and redundant words.
- Use the active voice in writing efficient sentences.
- Compose unified sentences by avoiding excessive detail and extraneous ideas.
- Write clear sentences using parallel construction for similar ideas.
- Place words, phrases, and clauses close to the words they modify.
- Avoid ambiguous pronoun references such as *this*, *that*, and *which*.

Business and professional people value efficient, economical writing that is meaningful and coherent. Wordy communication wastes the reader's time; unclear messages confuse the reader and are counterproductive. In the business world, where time is valuable, efficient writing is demanded. You can improve your writing skills by emulating the practices of good writers. Most good writers begin with a rough draft that they revise to produce a final version. This chapter shows you how to revise your rough draft sentences to make them more efficient, clear, emphatic, and coherent.

WRITING EFFICIENT SENTENCES

Revising Wordy Phrases

NOTABLE QUOTABLE

"I write as I walk because I want to get somewhere; and I write as straight as I can, just as I walk as straight as I can, because that is the best way to get there."
—H. G. Wells

Sentences are efficient when they convey a thought directly and economically—that is, in the fewest possible words. Good writers excise all useless verbiage from their writing. Some of the most common and comfortable phrases are actually full of "word fat"; when examined carefully, these phrases can be pared down considerably.

Wordy Phrases	Concise Substitutes
as per your suggestion	as you suggested
at the present time	now
at this point in time	now
due to the fact that	because
for the purpose of	to
give consideration to	consider
in addition to the above	also
in all probability	probably
in connection with	for
in spite of the fact that	even though

SPOT THE BLOOPER

From a company newsletter: "Our next issue will present an article that will allow you to understand the elements necessary to a better comprehension."

Wordy Phrases	Concise Substitutes
in the amount of	for
in the event that	if
in the near future	soon
in the neighborhood of	about
in view of the fact that	since
it is recommended that	we suggest that
under date of	on, dated
until such time as	until
with regard to	about

Notice that the revised versions of the following wordy sentences are more efficient:

WORDY: *As per your suggestion*, we will change the meeting.
MORE EFFICIENT: *As you suggested*, we will change the meeting.
WORDY: *Until such time as* we receive the contract, we cannot proceed.
MORE EFFICIENT: *When* we receive the contract, we can proceed.
WORDY: Bob Eustes will *in all probability* run for reelection.
MORE EFFICIENT: Bob Eustes will *probably* run for reelection.

SPOT THE BLOOPER

Announcer's voice on a TV ad for Ford: "What is it about Ford cars that makes it the best-selling car in America?"

Eliminating Redundant Words

Words that are needlessly repetitive are said to be "redundant." Business writers can achieve greater efficiency (and thus more effective sentences) by eliminating redundant words or phrases, such as the following:

advance warning	exactly identical	perfectly clear
alter or change	few in number	personal opinion
assemble together	free and clear	potential opportunity
basic fundamentals	grateful thanks	positively certain
collect together	great majority	proposed plan
consensus of opinion	integral part	serious interest
contributing factor	last and final	refer back
dollar amount	midway between	true facts
each and every	new changes	very unique
end result	past history	visible to the eye

REDUNDANT: Have you *assembled together* all the pages?
MORE EFFICIENT: Have you *assembled* all the pages?
REDUNDANT: This paragraph is *exactly identical* to that one.
MORE EFFICIENT: This paragraph is *identical* to that one.
REDUNDANT: *First and foremost*, we must balance the budget.
MORE EFFICIENT: *First*, we must balance the budget.
REDUNDANT: *The examples shown in Figure 3* illustrate truck bodies.
MORE EFFICIENT: *Figure 3* illustrates truck bodies.

Using Active Voice

Sentences that use active verbs are more economical—and, of course, more direct—than those using passive verbs.

PASSIVE: A discrepancy in the bank balance *was detected by auditors*.
ACTIVE: *Auditors detected* a discrepancy in the bank balance.

SPOT THE BLOOPER

From *The Northern Star*, student newspaper of Northern Illinois University: "Never pet, play with, or give commands to a person using a guide dog without permission."

PASSIVE:	In the April issue your article *will be published by us.*
ACTIVE:	In the April issue *we will publish* your article.
PASSIVE:	The CEO *was informed by the vice president* that the merger fell through.
MORE EFFICIENT:	The *vice president informed* the CEO that the merger fell through.

Writing Unified Sentences

A sentence is unified if it contains only closely related ideas. When extraneous or unrelated ideas appear in a sentence, they confuse the reader. Sentences lacking unity can be improved by excising the extraneous ideas or by shifting the unrelated ideas to separate sentences.

LACKS UNITY:	I am appreciative of the time you spent interviewing me last week, and I plan to enroll in a computer application course immediately.
IMPROVED:	I appreciate the time you spent with me last week. Because of our interview, I plan to enroll in a computer application course immediately.
LACKS UNITY:	It is easy for you to do your holiday shopping, and we offer three unique catalogs.
IMPROVED:	Because we offer three unique catalogs, it is easy for you to do your holiday shopping.
LACKS UNITY:	Last spring the Treasury Department asked Americans to circulate pennies, and many people toss these coins in a junk drawer or hoard them in mayonnaise jars, creating a shortage, and some people just throw them away.
IMPROVED:	Last spring the Treasury Department asked Americans to circulate pennies. Many people toss these coins in junk drawers or hoard them in mayonnaise jars. Some people even throw them away, thus creating a shortage.

NOTABLE QUOTABLE

"I have never thought of myself as a good writer. Anyone who wants reassurance of this should read one of my first drafts. But I'm one of the world's greatest rewriters."
—James Michener

The inclusion of excessive detail can also damage sentence unity. If many details are necessary for overall clarity, put them in additional sentences.

EXCESSIVE DETAIL:	Germany is preparing to auction 20 castles that formerly belonged to the Communist government, although hundreds of bidders have submitted offers and price is not the determining factor because the government is looking for responsible investors who can protect the cultural values of the monuments as well as preserve their structures.
IMPROVED:	Germany will auction 20 castles that formerly belonged to the Communist government. Price is not as important as finding responsible investors who can protect and preserve the monuments.
EXCESSIVE DETAIL:	A report can be important, but it may not be effective or be read because it is too long and bulky, which will also make it more difficult to distribute, to store, and to handle, as well as increasing its overall cost.
IMPROVED:	An important report may be ineffective because it is too long. Its bulk may increase its costs and make it difficult to read, handle, distribute, and store.

WRITING CLEAR SENTENCES

DID YOU KNOW

The language of the Information Age is English. More than 80 percent of the information stored in the more than 100 million computers around the world is stored in English. And 85 percent of international telephone conversations are conducted in English.

Clear sentences are those that immediately convey their central thought. Good writers achieve sentence clarity by the use of parallel construction, the avoidance of misplaced modifiers, and the use of unambiguous pronoun references.

Developing Parallel Construction

Sentence clarity can be improved by expressing similar ideas with similar grammatical structures. For example, if you are listing three ideas, do not use *ing* words for two of the ideas and a *to* verb for the third idea: *buying, trading,* and *selling* (not *to sell*). Use nouns with nouns, verbs with verbs, phrases with phrases, and clauses with clauses. In the following list, use all verbs: *the machine sorted, stamped,* and *counted* (not *and had a counter*). For phrases, the wording for all parts of the list should be matched: *Stopping distances were checked on concrete pavement, over winding roads, and on wet surfaces* (not *when it rains*).

FAULTY:	Improving the stability of the car resulted in less passenger comfort, reduced visibility, and the car weighed more.
IMPROVED:	Improving the stability of the car resulted in less passenger comfort, reduced visibility, and added weight. (Matches nouns.)
FAULTY:	The new laser printer helped us improve quality, save money, and we got our work done faster.
IMPROVED:	The new laser printer helped us improve quality, save money, and work faster. (Matches verb–noun construction.)
FAULTY:	Collecting, organizing, and documentation—these are important steps in researching a problem.
IMPROVED:	Collecting, organizing, and documenting—these are important steps in researching a problem. (Matches *ing* nouns.)

Avoiding Misplaced Modifiers

SPOT THE BLOOPER

From *The Daily Camera* [Boulder, CO]: "A dog bit a man in the face, who walked into the dog's residence on Pheasant Run on August 15."

SPOT THE BLOOPER

From *The Florida Times-Union* [Jacksonville]: "The club was closed in 1947 after A.L. Lewis died and was eventually sold."

As you will recall, modifiers are words, phrases, or clauses that limit or restrict other words, phrases, or clauses. To be clear, modifiers must be placed carefully so that the words modified by them are obvious. When a modifier is placed so that it does not appear to be modifying the word or words intended to be modified, that modifier is said to be *misplaced*. In Chapter 7 introductory verbal modifiers were discussed. An introductory verbal modifier is sometimes misplaced simply by being at the beginning of the sentence. Consider how the introductory verbal modifier makes the following sentence nonsensical: *While pumping gas, an unoccupied car rolled into mine.* After all, the unoccupied car is not pumping gas. In positions other than the beginning of the sentence, misplaced modifiers may also damage sentence clarity.

FAULTY:	Please take time to examine the brochure *that is enclosed with your family.*
IMPROVED:	Please take time to examine *with your family* the enclosed brochure.
FAULTY:	We provide a map for all *visitors reduced to a one-inch scale.*
IMPROVED:	For all visitors we provide a *map reduced to a one-inch scale.*
FAULTY:	A 30-year-old St. Petersburg man *was found murdered by his parents* in his home late Tuesday.
IMPROVED:	Murdered in his home, a 30-year-old St. Petersburg man *was found by his parents* late Tuesday.

Improving Pronoun References

SPOT THE BLOOPER

From *The Murray* [KY] *Ledger & Times*: "The car was reported stolen by the police."

Sentence confusion results from the use of pronouns without clear antecedents. Be particularly careful with the pronouns *this*, *that*, *which*, and *it*. Confusion often results when these pronouns have as their antecedents an entire clause. Such confusion can usually be avoided by substituting a noun for the pronoun or by following the pronoun with a clarifying noun (or nouns).

FAULTY: Bucket seats in the car were large and luxurious, with a multitude of power-operated adjustments. *They* provided comfort for occupants of all sizes and shapes.

IMPROVED: Bucket seats in the car were large and luxurious, with a multitude of power-operated adjustments. *These power adjustments* provided comfort for occupants of all sizes and shapes.

FAULTY: We have a policy of responding to customer inquiries and orders on the day they are received. *That* keeps us busy and keeps our customers satisfied.

IMPROVED: We have a policy of responding to customer inquiries and orders on the day they are received. *That policy* keeps us busy and keeps our customers satisfied.

FAULTY: Our government contracts require work on hundreds of projects that demand constant updating and access to technical data, supplies, and references, *which* explains why an open office design allowing team interaction is necessary.

IMPROVED: Our government contracts require work on hundreds of projects that demand constant updating and access to technical data, supplies, and references. *These needs* explain why an open office design allowing team interaction is essential.

SPOT THE BLOOPER

From a local newspaper: "The driver had a narrow escape as a broken board penetrated his cabin and just missed his head. This had to be removed before he could be released."

HOTLINE QUERIES

QUESTION I just typed this sentence: *You will see in our manual where multiple bids must be obtained.* Somewhere from my distant past I seem to recall that *where* should not be used in this way. Can you help me?

ANSWER You're right. *Where* should not be substituted for the relative pronoun *that.* In your sentence, use *that.* A similar faulty construction to be avoided is the use of *while* for *although* (*although* [not *while*] *I agree with his position, I disagree with his procedures*).

QUESTION When the company name *Halperin, Inc.*, appears in the middle of a sentence, is there a comma following *Inc.*?

ANSWER Current authorities recommend the following practice in punctuating *Inc.*: If the legal company name includes a comma preceding *Inc.*, then a comma should follow *Inc.* if it is used in the middle of a sentence. (*We received from Kent, Inc., its latest catalog.*)

QUESTION Where should the word *sic* be placed when it is used?

ANSWER *Sic* means "thus" or "so stated," and it is properly placed immediately following the word or phrase to which it refers. For example, *The kidnappers placed a* *newspaper advertisement that read "Call Monna [sic] Lisa." Sic* is used within a quotation to indicate that a quoted word or phrase, though inaccurately spelled or used, appeared thus in the original. *Sic* is italicized and placed within brackets.

QUESTION Which is correct: *I feel* (*bad* or *badly*)?

ANSWER *Bad* is an adjective meaning "not good" or "ill." *Badly* is an adverb meaning "harmfully," "wickedly," or "poorly." Your sentence appears to require *bad* (I *feel ill*), unless you mean that your sense of touch is impaired (I *feel poorly*).

QUESTION Should I capitalize *oriental* rug?

ANSWER Yes. Adjectives derived from proper nouns are capitalized (*French* dressing, *German* shepherd, *Danish* furniture). Very well-known adjectives, however, are not capitalized (*pasteurized* milk, *venetian* blinds, *french* fries, *china* plates).

QUESTION In a business report is it acceptable to write the following: *Most everyone agrees . . .*?

ANSWER In this construction *most* is a shortened form of *almost.* Although such constructions are heard in informal speech, they should not appear in business writing. Instead, use the longer form: *Almost everyone agrees. . . .*

NAME ____________________

17 REINFORCEMENT EXERCISES

A. (Self-check) In the following sentences, inefficient phrases have been underlined. In the space provided after each sentence, suggest a more efficient substitute for each underlined phrase.

EXAMPLE: We are at the present time ready to sign the contract. ____now____

1. Due in large part to a reduction in costs, we are able to lower prices on some models. ____________
2. In spite of the fact that you have not responded to our letters, we are offering you one more chance to avoid ruining your credit. ____________
3. If the estimate is in the neighborhood of $200 or less, the repair can be made immediately. ____________
4. Your contract will be effective under date of September 15. ____________
5. Our principal concern is that you give consideration to upgrading equipment. ____________
6. The United States will in all probability eliminate the use of pennies. ____________
7. Please send your check in the amount of $55. ____________
8. In the event that your credit cards are lost, you may call this number. ____________
9. Until such time as we have your proxy, we cannot act. ____________
10. It is recommended that you finish your degree before taking a full-time job. ____________

In the sentences below, the underlined words illustrate the following: (a) faulty parallel construction, (b) faulty phrase placement, and (c) faulty pronoun reference. After each sentence, write the letter that best indicates the sentence fault.

EXAMPLE: Aluminum construction is lightest, wood is cheapest, and the strongest is steel. __a__

11. People at work and at home are using computers less as stand-alone machines and more as computers linked to networks that enable them to exchange messages, documents, and pictures. This is the future of computing. ____
12. The CEO's goals are to increase production, reduce costs, and improving the quality of customer service. ____
13. Please complete the enclosed survey being sent to representative employees questioning Internet usage. ____
14. Computerized billing now totals all balances, provides weekly summaries, and it also automatically prints customer statements. ____
15. About two years ago a wart appeared on my left hand, which I want removed. ____
16. Automatic cash transfers can be made only on the written authority of the customer from a checking account. ____
17. Collecting, organizing, and analysis—these are the tasks of a researcher. ____
18. Police said Allen's 1995 Toyota traveled down the shoulder for almost 1,000 feet and then hit a utility pole going about 45 miles per hour. ____
19. Three basic elements of a computer are input, processor, and output units, which can be configured to your specifications. ____

20. President Wall's objectives were to make the stock profitable, to operate efficiently, and good employee relations should also be developed. _____

Check your answers below.

1. Because of, 2. Although, 3. about, 4. on, 5. consider, 6. probably, 7. for, 8. If, 9. Until, 10. We recommend, 11. c, 12. a, 13. b, 14. a, 15. b, 16. b, 17. a, 18. b, 19. c, 20. a.

NAME ______________________________

UNIT 5 REVIEW ■ Chapters 15–17 (Self-Check)

First, review Chapters 15–17. Then test your comprehension of those chapters by completing the exercises that follow. Compare your responses with those shown at the end of the review.

Select (a) or (b) to describe the group of words that is more acceptably expressed.

1.	**(a)** courses in Business Law, Spanish, and Accounting	**(b)** courses in business law, Spanish, and accounting	_____
2.	**(a)** living in Contra Costa county	**(b)** living in Contra Costa County	_____
3.	**(a)** the State of Georgia	**(b)** the state of Georgia	_____
4.	**(a)** during summer vacation	**(b)** during Summer vacation	_____
5.	**(a)** a victorian home	**(b)** a Victorian home	_____
6.	**(a)** the 22d of June	**(b)** the twenty-second of June	_____
7.	**(a)** thirty dollars	**(b)** $30	_____
8.	**(a)** on 12th Street	**(b)** on Twelfth Street	_____
9.	**(a)** on June 9th	**(b)** on June 9	_____
10.	**(a)** in view of the fact that	**(b)** since	_____
11.	**(a)** now	**(b)** at the present time	_____
12.	**(a)** in the amount of	**(b)** for	_____
13.	**(a)** by your Mother and Father	**(b)** by your mother and father	_____
14.	**(a)** proceed west on Highway 5	**(b)** proceed West on Highway 5	_____
15.	**(a)** our vice president, Traci Moon	**(b)** our Vice President, Traci Moon	_____
16.	**(a)** their shipping department	**(b)** their Shipping Department	_____
17.	**(a)** a message from Linda Barneson, Marketing Manager	**(b)** a message from Linda Barneson, marketing manager	_____
18.	**(a)** a message from Marketing Manager Barneson	**(b)** a message from marketing manager Barneson	_____
19.	**(a)** for the next five years	**(b)** for the next 5 years	_____
20.	**(a)** 3 seventy-five page booklets	**(b)** three 75-page booklets	_____
21.	**(a)** two copiers serving 11 offices	**(b)** 2 copiers serving 11 offices	_____
22.	**(a)** our company president, Ms. Osterello	**(b)** our company President, Ms. Osterello	_____
23.	**(a)** U.S. President-Elect Mulder	**(b)** U.S. President-elect Mulder	_____
24.	**(a)** an envelope stamped "photographs"	**(b)** an envelope stamped "Photographs"	_____
25.	**(a)** our 40th anniversary	**(b)** our fortieth anniversary	_____
26.	**(a)** less than 0.5 percent	**(b)** less than .5 percent	_____
27.	**(a)** 2 quarts of motor oil	**(b)** two quarts of motor oil	_____
28.	**(a)** an 8% return	**(b)** an 8 percent return	_____

29. **(a)** on his 21st birthday **(b)** on his twenty-first birthday ____

30. **(a)** under the hot sun **(b)** under the hot Sun ____

31. **(a)** arab and asian cultures **(b)** Arab and Asian cultures ____

32. **(a)** a 3/4 interest **(b)** a three-fourths interest ____

Each of the following sentences illustrates one of these sentence faults:

a. faulty parallel construction (such as *eating*, *sleeping*, and *to read*)
b. faulty phrase placement (phrase is distant from the words it modifies)
c. faulty pronoun reference (pronoun such as *this*, *that*, or *it* lacking clear antecedent)

Write the letter that describes the sentence fault in each of the next three sentences.

33. Inadequate ventilation, poor lighting, and hazardous working conditions were cited in the complaint. It must be improved before regulators return. ____

34. Fabric divider panels were installed in the office to provide privacy, enhance concentration, and they should effect a reduction in sound. ____

35. We can make arrangements with the tax collector that you can live with. ____

Hotline Review

Write the letter of the word or phrase that correctly completes each sentence.

36. I heard that (a) most, (b) almost everyone arrived late to the meeting. ____

37. Analysts (a) implied, (b) inferred from the CEO's remarks that profits would fall. ____

38. Be careful not to (a) lose, (b) loose the key to the safety deposit box. ____

39. Everyone feels (a) bad, (b) badly about the proposed cutbacks. ____

40. Only the manager and (a) myself, (b) I, (c) me will be working this weekend. ____

1. b, 2. b, 3. b, 4. a, 5. b, 6. a, 7. b, 8. a, 9. b, 10. b, 11. a, 12. b, 13. b, 14. a, 15. a, 16. a, 17. b, 18. a, 19. a, 20. b, 21. a, 22. a, 23. b,
24. b, 25. b, 26. a, 27. a, 28. b, 29. b, 30. a, 31. b, 32. b, 33. c, 34. a, 35. b, 36. b, 37. b, 38. a, 39. a, 40. b.

APPENDIX

Developing Spelling Skills

WHY IS ENGLISH SPELLING SO DIFFICULT?

No one would dispute the complaint that many English words are difficult to spell. Why is spelling in our language so perplexing? For one thing, our language has borrowed many of its words from other languages. English has a Germanic base on which a superstructure of words borrowed from French, Latin, Greek, and other languages of the world has been erected. For this reason, its words are not always formed by regular patterns of letter combinations. In addition, spelling is made difficult because the pronunciation of English words is constantly changing. Today's spelling was standardized nearly 300 years ago, but many words are pronounced differently today than they were then. Therefore, pronunciation often provides little help in spelling. Consider, for example, the words *sew* and *dough*.

WHAT CAN BE DONE TO IMPROVE ONE'S SPELLING?

Spelling is a skill that can be developed, just as arithmetic, typing, and other skills can be developed. Because the ability to spell is a prerequisite for success in business and in most other activities, effort expended to acquire this skill is effort well spent.

Three traditional approaches to improving spelling have met with varying degrees of success.

1. Rules or Guidelines

The spelling of English words is consistent enough to justify the formulation of a few spelling rules, perhaps more appropriately called guidelines since the generalizations in question are not invariably applicable. Such guidelines are, in other words, helpful but not infallible.

2. Mnemonics

Another approach to improving one's ability to spell involves the use of mnemonics or memory devices. For example, the word *principle* might be associated with the word *rule*, to form in the mind of the speller a link between the meaning and the spelling of *principle*. To spell *capitol*, one might think of the *dome* of the capitol building and focus on the *o*'s in both words. The use of mnemonics can be an effective device for the improvement of spelling only if the speller makes a real effort to develop the necessary memory hooks.

3. Rote Learning

A third approach to the improvement of spelling centers on memorization. The word is studied by the speller until it can be readily reproduced in the mind's eye.

THE 1-2-3 SPELLING PLAN

Proficiency in spelling is not attained without concentrated effort. Here's a plan to follow in mastering the 400 commonly misspelled words included in this appendix. For each word, try this 1-2-3 approach.

1. Is a spelling guideline applicable? If so, select the appropriate guideline and study the word in relation to that guideline.
2. If no guideline applies, can a memory device be created to aid in the recall of the word?
3. If neither a guideline nor a memory device will work, the word must be memorized. Look at the word carefully. Pronounce it. Write it or repeat it until you can visualize all its letters in your mind's eye.

Before you try the 1-2-3 plan, become familiar with the six spelling guidelines that follow. These spelling guidelines are not intended to represent all the possible spelling rules appearing in the various available spelling books. These six guidelines are, however, among the most effective and helpful of the recognized spelling rules.

Guideline 1: Words Containing *ie* or *ei*

Although there are exceptions to it, the following familiar rhyme can be helpful.

(a) Write *i* before *e*
(b) Except after *c*,
(c) Or when sounded like *a*
As in *neighbor* and *weigh*.

Study these words illustrating the three parts of the rhyme.

(a) *I* Before *e*		(b) Except After *c*	(c) Or When Sounded Like *a*
achieve	grief	ceiling	beige
belief	ingredient	conceive	eight
believe	mischief	deceive	freight
brief	niece	perceive	heir
cashier	piece	receipt	neighbor
chief	shield	receive	reign
convenient	sufficient		their
field	view		vein
friend	yield		weight

Exceptions: These exceptional *ei* and *ie* words must be learned by rote or with the use of a mnemonic device.

caffeine	height	seize
either	leisure	sheik
financier	neither	sleight
foreigner	protein	weird

Guideline 2: Words Ending in *e*

For most words ending in an *e*, the final *e* is dropped when the word is joined to a suffix beginning with a vowel (such as *ing*, *able*, or *al*). The final *e* is retained when a suffix beginning with a consonant (such as *ment*, *less*, *ly*, or *ful*) is joined to such a word.

FINAL *e* DROPPED	FINAL *e* RETAINED
believe, believing	arrange, arrangement
care, caring	require, requirement
hope, hoping	hope, hopeless
receive, receiving	care, careless
desire, desirable	like, likely
cure, curable	approximate, approximately
move, movable	definite, definitely
value, valuable	sincere, sincerely
disperse, dispersal	use, useful
arrive, arrival	hope, hopeful

Exceptions: The few exceptions to this spelling guideline are among the most frequently misspelled words. As such, they deserve special attention. Notice that they all involve a dropped final *e*.

acknowledgment	ninth
argument	truly
judgment	wholly

Guideline 3: Words Ending in *ce* or *ge*

When *able* or *ous* is added to words ending in *ce* or *ge*, the final *e* is retained if the *c* or *g* is pronounced softly (as in *change* or *peace*).

advantage, advantageous	change, changeable
courage, courageous	service, serviceable
outrage, outrageous	manage, manageable

Guideline 4: Words Ending in *y*

Words ending in a *y* that is preceded by a consonant normally change the *y* to *i* before all suffixes except those beginning with an *i*.

CHANGE *y* TO *i* BECAUSE *y* IS PRECEDED BY A CONSONANT	DO NOT CHANGE *y* TO *i* BECAUSE *y* IS PRECEDED BY A VOWEL
accompany, accompaniment	employ, employer
study, studied, studious	annoy, annoying, annoyance
duty, dutiful	stay, staying, stayed
industry, industrious	attorney, attorneys
carry, carriage	valley, valleys
apply, appliance	**DO NOT CHANGE *y* TO *i* WHEN ADDING *ing***
try, tried	
empty, emptiness	
forty, fortieth	accompany, accompanying
secretary, secretaries	apply, applying
company, companies	study, studying
hurry, hurries	satisfy, satisfying
	try, trying

Exceptions: day, daily; dry, dried; mislay, mislaid; pay, paid; shy, shyly; gay, gaily.

Guideline 5: Doubling a Final Consonant

If one-syllable words or two-syllable words accented on the second syllable end in a single consonant preceded by a single vowel, the final consonant is doubled before the addition of a suffix beginning with a vowel.

Although complex, this spelling guideline is extremely useful and therefore well worth mastering. Many spelling errors can be avoided by applying this guideline.

One-Syllable Words	Two-Syllable Words
can, canned	acquit, acquitting, acquittal
drop, dropped	admit, admitted, admitting
fit, fitted	begin, beginner, beginning
get, getting	commit, committed, committing
man, manned	control, controller, controlling
plan, planned	defer, deferred (but deference*)
run, running	excel, excelled, excelling
shut, shutting	occur, occurrence, occurring
slip, slipped	prefer, preferring (but preference*)
swim, swimming	recur, recurred, recurrence
ton, tonnage	refer, referring (but reference*)

*Because the accent shifts to the first syllable, the final consonant is not doubled.

Here is a summary of conditions necessary for application of this guideline.

1. The word must end in a single consonant.
2. The final consonant must be preceded by a single vowel.
3. The word must be accented on the second syllable (if it has two syllables).

Words derived from *cancel, offer, differ, equal, suffer,* and *benefit* are not governed by this guideline because they are accented on the first syllable.

Guideline 6: Prefixes and Suffixes

For words in which the letter that ends the prefix is the same as the letter that begins the main word (such as in *dissimilar*), both letters must be included. For words in which a suffix begins with the same letter that ends the main word (such as in *coolly*), both letters must also be included.

Prefix	Main Word	Main Word	Suffix
dis	satisfied	accidental	ly
ir	responsible	incidental	ly
il	literate	clean	ness
mis	spell	cool	ly
mis	state	even	ness
un	necessary	mean	ness

On the other hand, do not supply additional letters when adding prefixes to main words.

Prefix	Main Word
dis	appoint (*not* di*ss*appoint)
dis	appearance
mis	take

Perhaps the most important guideline one can follow in spelling correctly is to use the dictionary whenever in doubt.

400 MOST FREQUENTLY MISSPELLED WORDS*
(DIVIDED INTO 20 LISTS OF 20 WORDS EACH)

List 1	List 2	List 3
1. absence	21. afraid	41. applying
2. acceptance	22. against	42. approaches
3. accessible	23. aggressive	43. appropriate
4. accidentally	24. all right	44. approximately
5. accommodate	25. almost	45. arguing
6. accompaniment	26. alphabetical	46. argument
7. accurately	27. already	47. arrangement
8. accustom	28. although	48. article
9. achievement	29. amateur	49. athlete
10. acknowledgment	30. among	50. attack
11. acquaintance	31. amount	51. attendance, attendants
12. acquire	32. analysis	52. attitude
13. across	33. analyze	53. attorneys
14. actually	34. angel, angle	54. auxiliary
15. adequately	35. annoyance	55. basically
16. admitted	36. annual	56. beautiful
17. adolescence	37. answer	57. before
18. advantageous	38. apologized	58. beginning
19. advertising	39. apparent	59. believing
20. advice, advise	40. appliance	60. benefited

List 4	List 5	List 6
61. biggest	81. companies	101. description
62. breath, breathe	82. competition	102. desirable
63. brief	83. completely	103. destroy
64. business	84. conceive	104. development
65. calendar	85. conscience	105. difference
66. capital, capitol	86. conscientious	106. dining
67. career	87. conscious	107. disappearance
68. careless	88. considerably	108. disappoint
69. carrying	89. consistent	109. disastrous
70. cashier	90. continuous	110. discipline
71. ceiling	91. controlling	111. discussion
72. certain	92. controversial	112. disease
73. challenge	93. convenience	113. dissatisfied
74. changeable	94. council, counsel	114. distinction
75. chief	95. cylinder	115. divide
76. choose, chose	96. daily	116. doesn't
77. cloths, clothes	97. deceive	117. dominant
78. column	98. decision	118. dropped
79. coming	99. define	119. due
80. committee	100. dependent	120. during

*Compiled from lists of words most frequently misspelled by students and businesspeople.

List 7	List 8	List 9
121. efficient	141. February	161. happiness
122. eligible	142. fictitious	162. hear, here
123. embarrass	143. field	163. height
124. encourage	144. finally	164. heroes
125. enough	145. financially	165. hopeless
126. environment	146. foreigner	166. hoping
127. equipped	147. fortieth	167. huge
128. especially	148. forty, fourth	168. humorous
129. exaggerate	149. forward, foreword	169. hungry
130. excellence	150. freight	170. ignorance
131. except	151. friend	171. imaginary
132. exercise	152. fulfill	172. imagine
133. existence	153. fundamentally	173. immediately
134. experience	154. further	174. immense
135. explanation	155. generally	175. importance
136. extremely	156. government	176. incidentally
137. familiar	157. govenor	177. independent
138. families	158. grammar	178. indispensable
139. fascinate	159. grateful	179. industrious
140. favorite	160. guard	180. inevitable

List 10	List 11	List 12
181. influential	201. leisurely	221. mechanics
182. ingredient	202. library	222. medicine
183. initiative	203. license	223. medieval
184. intelligence	204. likely	224. mere
185. interest	205. literature	225. miniature
186. interference	206. lives	226. minutes
187. interpretation	207. loneliness	227. mischief
188. interrupt	208. loose, lose	228. misspell
189. involve	209. losing	229. mistake
190. irrelevant	210. luxury	230. muscle
191. irresponsible	211. magazine	231. mysterious
192. island	212. magnificence	232. naturally
193. jealous	213. maintenance	233. necessary
194. judgment	214. manageable	234. neighbor
195. kindergarten	215. maneuver	235. neither
196. knowledge	216. manner	236. nervous
197. laboratory	217. manufacturer	237. nickel
198. laborer	218. marriage	238. niece
199. laid	219. mathematics	239. ninety
200. led, lead	220. meant	240. ninth

List 13

241. noticeable
242. numerous
243. obstacle
244. occasionally
245. occurrence
246. off
247. offered
248. official
249. omitted
250. operate
251. opinion
252. opportunity
253. opposite
254. organization
255. origin
256. original
257. paid
258. pamphlet
259. parallel
260. particular

List 14

261. passed, past
262. pastime
263. peaceable
264. peculiar
265. perceive
266. performance
267. permanent
268. permitted
269. persistent
270. personal, personnel
271. persuading
272. phase, faze
273. philosophy
274. physical
275. piece
276. planned
277. pleasant
278. poison
279. political
280. possession

List 15

281. possible
282. practical
283. precede
284. preferred
285. prejudice
286. preparation
287. prevalent
288. principal, principle
289. privilege
290. probably
291. proceed
292. professor
293. prominent
294. proving
295. psychology
296. pursuing
297. quantity
298. quiet, quite
299. really
300. receipt

List 16

301. receiving
302. recognize
303. recommend
304. reference
305. referring
306. regard
307. relative
308. relieving
309. religious
310. reminiscent
311. repetition
312. representative
313. requirement
314. resistance
315. responsible
316. restaurant
317. rhythm
318. ridiculous
319. sacrifice
320. safety

List 17

321. satisfying
322. scenery
323. schedule
324. science
325. secretaries
326. seize
327. sense, since
328. sentence
329. separation
330. sergeant
331. serviceable
332. several
333. shining
334. shoulder
335. significance
336. similar
337. simply
338. sincerely
339. site, cite
340. source

List 18

341. speak, speech
342. specimen
343. stationary, stationery
344. stopped
345. stories
346. straight, strait
347. strenuous
348. stretch
349. strict
350. studying
351. substantial
352. subtle
353. succeed
354. success
355. sufficient
356. summary
357. suppose
358. surprise
359. suspense
360. swimming

List 19	List 20
361. syllable	381. tremendous
362. symbol	382. tried
363. symmetrical	383. truly
364. synonymous	384. undoubtedly
365. technique	385. unnecessary
366. temperament	386. until
367. temperature	387. unusual
368. tendency	388. useful
369. than, then	389. using
370. their, there	390. vacuum
371. themselves	391. valuable
372. theories	392. varies
373. therefore	393. vegetable
374. thorough	394. view
375. though	395. weather, whether
376. through	396. weird
377. together	397. were, where
378. tomorrow	398. wholly, holy
379. tragedies	399. writing
380. transferred	400. yield

INDEX